I, of all People

SELECTED WORKS OF JAMES KIRKUP

The Submerged Village
A Correct Compassion
A Spring Journey
The Descent into the Cave
The Prodigal Son
Refusal to Conform
A Bewick Bestiary
Zen Gardens (photo-etchings by Birgit Skiöld)
Paper Windows: Poems from Japan
White Shadows, Black Shadows: Poems of Peace and War
The Body Servant: Poems of Exile
Scenes from Sesshu (photo-etchings by Birgit Skiöld)
To the Ancestral North: Poems for an Autobiography
Cold Mountain Poems
Scenes from Sutcliffe (portfolio of poems and photographs)
The Tao of Water (photo-etchings by Birgit Skiöld)
Miniature Masterpieces by Yasunari Kawabata
Insect Summer (children's novel)
The Magic Drum (children's novel)
The Love of Others
The Only Child: An Autobiography of Infancy
Sorrows, Passions & Alarms: An Autobiography of Childhood
These Horned Islands: A Journal of Japan
Tropic Temper: A Memoir of Malaya
Filipinescas
Streets of Asia
No More Hiroshimas: Poems & Translations
Selected Poems of Takagi Kyozo
Modern Japanese Poetry
Zen Contemplations
The Guitar Player of Zuiganji
Dengonban Messages: One-Line Poems
Ecce Homo – My Pasolini: Poems & Translations
Fellow Feelings
The Sense of the Visit: New Poems

JAMES KIRKUP

I, of all People

An Autobiography of Youth

WEIDENFELD AND NICOLSON

LONDON

This paperback edition published in 1990

First published in Great Britain in 1988
by George Weidenfeld & Nicolson Limited
91 Clapham High Street, London SW4 7TA

ISBN 0 297 79569 4

Printed and bound in Great Britain by
Butler & Tanner Ltd, Frome and London

In memory of
YAMAGUCHI TAKEYOSHI

O que nos vemos das cousas as cousas.
Por que veriamos nos uma cousa se houvesse outra?
Por que e que ver e ouvir seria iludirmo-nos
Se ver e ouvir sao ver e ouvir?

O essencial e saber ver.
Saber ver sem estar a pensar.
Saber ver quando se ve,
E nem pensar quando se ve
Nem ver quando se pensa. . . .

What we see of things are things themselves.
Why should we see a certain thing if something else were there?
Why should seeing and hearing be self-delusion
If seeing and hearing are seeing and hearing?

The essence is to know how to see.
To know how to see without thinking we see.
To know how to see when we are seeing,
And not to be thinking when we are seeing
Not to be seeing when we are thinking.

FERNANDO PESSOA
From *O Guardador de Rebanhos*/translated from the Portuguese by James Kirkup

Live all you can; it's a mistake not to. It doesn't so much matter what you do in particular, so long as you have your life. If you havn't had that what *have* you had?

HENRY JAMES
From *The Ambassadors*

Contents

Acknowledgements xi
Prologue xiii

PART ONE: PRE-WAR
A Grave of Academe 1936–8 3
First Steps Abroad 1938–9 15
Summer in the Alps 1939 36

PART TWO: WAR
A Poet at War 1940 45
One Day in the Middle of a War 1940–3 59
Strange Tenant 1943 69
A Labourer Unworthy of his Hire 1943 75
Forest and Farm 1943–5 88
A Day on the Thresher 1945 101
Towards Hiroshima and Nagasaki 1945–6 105

PART THREE: POST-WAR
Peacetime Fighter 1946–7 115
A Post-War Outsider 1947–8 134
'I, of all People' 1948 144
The Poets' Other Corner 1948 157
Hell is a City 1948 165
'I'll Turn it All to Poetry' 1948 174

PART FOUR: PRE-ORIENTATIONS
Dear Old Joe 1948–55 187
Unfellowly Fellowships 1950–6 208

Epilogue 241
Index 253

Acknowledgements

Parts of this book have appeared in *The London Magazine, Peace News, The South Shields Gazette and Shipping Telegraph, Eigokyoiku* (Tokyo), *The Listener, The Times Literary Supplement* and *The Britishness of the British* (Seibido Publishing Company, Ltd, Tokyo).

I am grateful to the editors and publishers for permission to reproduce material here.

The quotations preceding each part of the text are taken from W. H. Auden's poem No.11 in *Some Poems* (Faber and Faber).

Prologue in Retrospect

Tightrope and Seesaw: The Makings of a Poet

In those magic days of my childhood, in the twenties and the early thirties, large, boisterous families were common in working-class districts of Britain, especially among the Roman Catholics, whose religion commanded them to 'be fruitful and multiply', and in families of Irish, Arab, Indian and Chinese immigrants, most of whom had come to England as British citizens from the colonies we then still held in S.E. Asia, India and Africa.

By contrast, our own little family of mother, father and only son was therefore unique in our working-class street, and something of an anomaly, because though we were definitely working-class, socialists, 'the salt of the earth' and proud of it, having only one child was somehow construed as a sign of middle-class superiority, and my mother and father were the last persons in the world to put on airs of superiority, to pretend to be what they were not – as some working-class people with social ambitions did.

All the other families in our street had at least two children, often three, four or five, and sometimes even six or seven children had to share a three-room flat with their parents and grandparents. I can remember two families who had ten children, all living together in four small rooms: in summer, during fine nights, they used to sleep on mats in the back yard – to me a very romantic thing to do, but I was never allowed to do so. The gypsy in me wanted to get away from the care and comfort of the home and the parents I loved with undivided devotion.

So the neighbours often used to call the Kirkup family, with Geordie wit and affection, 'The Holy Family'. This is a good example of the inventive and sometimes caustic humour of Tynesiders, which has a touch of salty bitterness in it from the sands and the sea, but is always based on certain humble truths. It is a deflating but not damaging sense of the ridiculous, and is used with consummate skill to puncture any delusions of grandeur in fellow-Geordies, or to deride any mistaken notions we might have about our own importance. It is really a very healthy humour, that helps us to see one another – and ourselves – as we really are, in the unsparing but desirably welcome light of prosaic reality. I would call it a mordant sense of wholesome mockery and affectionate fun. But as a child, I was very shy and sensitive, and took everything people told me for the truth: so my fragile innocence was often shattered by Geordie down-to-earth witticisms and carefully chosen insults. For this reason, I think, I am still frightened of my fellow countrymen: their ironies are too painful to bear, especially after living so long in Japan. The British have lost some of their affectionate sense of fun, and have turned self-destructive, always complaining and back-biting and trying their best to pull other people down, to destroy whatever comforting illusions they have left after years of war and unemployment and racial strife. Writers and poets in Britain today are particularly vicious in their attacks on one another: one finds none of the fellowship and solidarity among all kinds of writers that I have enjoyed in Europe, America and Japan. Perhaps this is the reason why modern British poetry is now such a boring mess of domestic and academic conflicts, without a trace of originality or curiosity about other literatures: it is insular and pedantic and terribly provincial, and I despair of ever persuading my fellow British authors to try to see the world around us as I see it – with an open, internationalist mind.

Anyhow, I soon became aware of the fact that the Kirkups of Ada Street were known as 'The Holy Family'. It seemed to set us apart. My mother's name was Mary, and my aunt's name was Anna, and though my father was not called Joseph, the suggestion was inescapable – and quite acceptable to my child's mind – that I was the boy Jesus. And after all, had not Joseph been a carpenter, like my own father? 'The Holy Family' was not a bad nickname for the three of us. It did not at all surprise or alarm me to be thought of as Jesus Christ come back to earth in the form of a carpenter's son.

As a child, I suffered from anaemia, and my skin was so pale, almost translucently white, and my pallor would increase to dead white whenever I was up beyond my usual early bedtime, or when I was extremely tired. At such times, I would look as frail and insubstantial as a ghost, so I was also sometimes called 'The Holy Ghost' by the young, tough lads in our back lane. They were rosy-cheeked, vigorous and full of lusty life. No one would ever have thought of comparing them with Jesus. But I was not as they were. I was so quiet and pale, with hair ash-blond almost to the point of whiteness, and my big, dark blue eyes were deep, mysterious pools in thick, blond lashes.

In some ways, too, I was unnaturally wise: not for nothing had my Granny Johnson called me 'a wise bairn'. My father agreed with her, saying that my intelligence came from the Kirkup, Earl and Falconer side of the family, only to be contradicted by mother claiming that it was certainly inherited from the Scots and Irish side of the family, from her own Scots mother and her Irish father.

My mother's sister, Aunt Lyallie, with her delightful Scottish accent, was a very humorous, down-to-earth but warm-hearted woman whose three grown-up sons were my idols, though they obviously thought I was something of a joke because I could not play football or ride a bicycle or swim. Aunt Lyallie used to defend me against their often incomprehensible jokes – I always had difficulty in telling whether people were joking or serious – and, taking me lovingly in her arms, would call me her 'wingless angel'. When I look at the very few photographs of me at that period in my childhood, I can indeed see something angelic in my pale, dreamy face and rather bemused smile and look of a boy with manners too gentle, too refined for his own good.

As there was something girlish, diaphanous, almost androgynous in my boyhood appearance, a French master at school used to call me *sainte nitouche,* which I did not at first completely understand: I thought it must be simply the name of some famous French saint, and I felt obscurely flattered, though I was not sure if the master meant it as a joke or not. I got a nasty shock when I looked it up in my *Dictionnaire Larousse* – after our first year of French we were not allowed to use French-English dictionaries – and discovered that *sainte nitouche* meant 'a demure young miss pretending to be holy and saintly'.

Yet there was something of the truth in that French master's insight into my juvenile character. I knew I was no angel, and certainly was not as fatuous as to think of myself as the reincarnation of Jesus Christ, yet I had mystical, religious yearnings, a sense of the spiritual quality in the humblest objects, the commonest words and events of working-class daily life. And, deep in my soul – though I never consciously formulated the idea – I knew I was different from other children, a self-knowledge that was instinctive rather than reasoned, and was to become stronger and stronger to the point of absolute conviction as I grew into adolescence and felt myself inexplicably becoming more and more solitary, further and further apart from my contemporaries and their ordinary boyish interests and enthusiasms. My sorrows and passions were of another kind altogether, the sorrows and passions of a child when he first realizes that other people do not like him, and do not try to hide their dislike. In order to escape from that aching sense of lonely apartness from others, I became wrapped up more than ever passionately in my reading and writing.

But I liked, also, to play the fool with myself and others. From time to time I would feel compelled to do something preposterous, or say something idiotic, sing verses of inspired silliness, simply in order to make people laugh. I did not care that their laughter was mocking, even contemptuous. I did not mind their rejection of someone they took for an imbecile, a moron. All I wanted was to hear them laugh, laugh *at* me, if not *with* me. (It was not until I got to Japan that I found people who could laugh *with* me rather than *at* me.) Making others laugh was the only way I knew of feeling for a few precious and never-to-be-forgotten moments less lonely, less divided from others, in touch with people.

How did I make people laugh at me? I could waggle my ears, which were rather large and prominent. I could demonstrate the double-jointedness of my fingers and thumbs. I could lie on my back, kick up my legs, and grin inanely at people through my thighs. I was able to contort my body in all kinds of surprising ways, and do eccentric dances invented by myself that must have looked something like the 'breakdances' we often see young black adolescents performing in the streets today. I could make a face like a demented gargoyle or mythological monster: this was an old form of simple rustic entertainment in the North of England, called 'gurning', and there are still contests of gurners to see who can make the most hideous or most comical grotesque face. I was very good at that, and it entertained people and made them laugh. But my mother, wiping tears of laughter from her eyes, would warn me: 'Jim, your face will stay like that if the wind changes!' And when I told jokes against myself, my father would smile and say: 'There's many a truth told in jest'. Such remarks only temporarily dampened my high spirits: soon I would be back at my old tricks – standing on my head, walking on my hands, doing incompetent cartwheels that always ended with me falling on my bottom, to the delight of watchers. I would put out my tongue at cats and dogs: the cats used to back nervously away from such a spectacle, but it always made dogs bark and wag their tails and stick their own tongues out at me. 'Teaching dogs to talk, you'll only learn to bark', my Granny Kirkup, highly amused at my antics, used to tell me. When I was feeling really naughty, I would make 'Queen Anne's Fan' – that is, put the thumb of my right hand to my nose and waggle the fingers at someone, quite an insult, especially if I did it with two hands, adding the thumb of my left hand to the little finger of my right hand and spreading them and waving them derisively like fans of flesh and bone. Even worse, I would sometimes lower my breeches and show my bare bottom to people, in a gesture of supreme defiance that today has become a popular sport among American students, who call it 'mooning'. Once, when I was 'mooning' in front of my Uncle Bob, he took the wind out of my sails by remarking, with a delighted laugh: 'Well, Jim, your bottom's prettier than your face!' My mother taught me to dance all the popular steps, and even showed me how to do the can-can, kicking my legs above my head along with her, and doing those *ronds de jambes* at which she was so good. When I was alone in the house, I used to dress up in her clothes and do the can-can with all the sexual abandon of the dancers at the Moulin Rouge, whom we had seen in a movie. I also used to put on her make-up: but her style of make-up was too modest and ladylike for me. I wanted to look like a real tart, so on my upper lids I would stick some semicircles of blue paper from the paper twists of salt in Smith's Potato Crisp bags, press scarlet rose petals on my lips, hang cowslips from my ears as earrings, 'clag' huge, dark crimson peony petals on either cheek, scatter buttercup petals on my hair, and, putting a finger up the chimney, blacken my blond eyelashes and eyebrows with our rich coal soot. Thus adorned, I would start reading *Oliver Twist* or *Uncle Tom's Cabin* or *A Child's Garden of Verses,* completely entering into the spirit of my book, and so forgetting myself that when there was a knock at the door I would run to answer it, forgetting that I had made up my face in that fantastically ridiculous way, to the extreme surprise and even dumbfounded shock of the postman or the minister from The Gleve, our straight-laced local church. A short-sighted insurance salesman, gazing in astonishment at my get-up, hesitated before asking: 'Are you the lady of the house?' To which I replied: 'We're already fully insured, thank you. I'm the *daughter* of the house. The *lady* of the house is in bed with a severe chill.'

I also liked to sing sacred hymns to which improper words had been fitted. My father had brought back several of these from the war, where disillusioned soldiers composed horrifyingly obscene lyrics to the National Anthem, *Hymns Ancient and Modern* and the *Moody and Sankey Hymnal* tunes, with their swinging revivalist rhythms and juicy melodies. In the midst of a quiet teatime snack, I would convulse my parents and any guests who might have dropped in by, without warning, belting out one of these bawdy perversions of religious lyricism. Some of the things I sang were meaningless to me; I did not know how awful they were, except for the fact that they often brought a delicate blush to my mother's cheeks, and provoked explosions of mirth from my father, hastily suppressed with: 'Jim, how dare you sing such filthy songs at the tea table!' And my mother, half-proudly, would add: 'Jim, you're a proper character! You should go on the stage. You'd make a fortune in the music halls. But sing something nice for a change.'

So I would pacify her by singing 'Annie Laurie' or 'Danny Boy' or –

her favourite – 'Believe Me, If All Those Endearing Young Charms' and other traditional Irish melodies and Irish opera arias she had learnt from my Irish grandfather, who was himself a fine singer and reciter.

At times, I would pretend to sing popular songs in obscure foreign languages like Icelandic or Finnish or Africaans, and performed these so well that some of my classmates were astonished by my precocious knowledge of these remote tongues, that I improvised on the spur of the moment: so I would sing 'Tea for Two' or 'Tiptoe Through the Tulips' or 'Stars Fell on Alabama' with a newly invented, fluent Russian, Chinese or Japanese accent. 'That boy has the gift of tongues,' our minister once said, with reference to the tongues of fire that descended upon Christ's disciples at the Feast of Pentecost, enabling them to utter divine words in strange languages, as if they had been drinking 'new wine'. The technical term for such a gift is 'glossolalia' and it is much practised in the Pentecostal and revivalist missions of American black society. Without my realizing it, the gift of tongues had been conferred upon me, but for the moment I was using it, or rather abusing it, in a highly unspiritual manner.

Such outrageous exhibitionism and tomfoolery helped me overcome some of my feelings of sadness and solitude. But at times, my sense of being totally alone became so intense I was desperate to make some kind of contact with my fellow human beings, to take away the growing fear that I might not be human at all, but rather some sinister visitor from another world, from outer space, making only a temporary sojourn on this Planet Earth, until I was called back home to instellar infinity by my spaceman brothers.

If I was really an angel (as I sometimes truly believed myself to be), I wanted occasionally to be a fallen angel, an angel with wings singed by the fires of damnation, for the burden of being different, being angelic, was too painful, too frightening to bear. So I played the clown, the rustic oaf, the idiot of the village, the city-centre freak, to disguise my real nature. I respected only those who could see through my masks, and, apart from my parents, they could be numbered on the fingers of one hand. But clowning became a way of life for me, and often the masks seemed to be fixed permanently to a face that was secretly weeping underneath. Clowning was a by-product of feelings too intimate to be revealed, of loves too impossible to be even hoped for or dreamed of, and the fool I played was a brilliant shadow of my solitude, sadness, poetry and mysticism.

At times, for no reason at all, I would be overtaken by wild, maniac laughter. If my Granny Kirkup happened to be present, she would bring out one of her favourite Norfolk-Viking sayings: 'Have you found the giggle's nest?' In those days, the sight of a loaf of bread could make me laugh. This gift of laughter was something I did not discover again until I came to Japan, where there is laughter in the air everywhere one goes. But my particular kind of laughter in childhood was self-releasing, exactly like the laughter of the ancient Zen illuminaries, tickled by their realization of the absurdity of life's illusions – the laughter of Han Shan and Shih Teh. Irrational, spiritual, fantastic laughter still shakes me from time to time when I consider the stupidity of war and the senselessness of education.

As a first-year student in modern languages, I recognized the truth of my cruel French professor's sarcastic but acutely insightful remark: '*Monsieur Kirkup est un farceur.*' Yet he was deeply mistaken. I felt a quiet pride in having convinced a noted French intellectual that I was a silly ass, but at the same time his remark made me realize how wrong he was, how limited in his perception of my real self, which I felt to be almost indescribably remote from his.

This split in my character was something I had soon learnt to live with – the angel and the clown in me soon learned to live together as an integrated human being. There was nothing schizophrenic in my bifurcated being. The two aspects lived in harmony, in peaceful coexistence. One of the basic reasons why I am essentially a pacifist is that I know, from experience of my personal inner contradictions, how easy it is, and how satisfying it can be, to reconcile opposites, to mediate between warring but not necessarily destructive divisions in my psychological make-up, in human society, between nations, and in the world at large.

The only trouble was that my multiple personality would suddenly switch from one aspect to another, without warning: from fool to intellectual, from clown to poet, from angel to malicious wit, from mystic to monster, from saint to corrosive critic, from kind-hearted child to mischievous young devil, from frivolous adolescent to wise old man. These unpredictable switches never bothered me, but naturally they used to disconcert others, particularly strangers – and most of the people passing through my life were strangers.

My parents, and, to a certain extent, my relatives and the other kids in our street were accustomed to my rapid changes of feeling and self-expression. 'Here comes Dr Jekyll and Mr Hyde,' my father would say, to my great delight, for I admired Stevenson's fantastic novel as if it were a portrait of myself. My mother would sigh, and amiably inform her visitors that: 'He's a difficult child,' but with a note of fearful pride in her gentle voice; while my father merely laughed at my abrupt and clearcut switches of feeling and self-expression. After any abrupt change of mood in my speech or behaviour, he would call me 'temperamental, like the Irish – it's the Irish in him, Mary. He doesn't mean any harm. But I can tell you he doesn't get it from *our* side of the family. We never had anyone like Jim in our family before. He must be a changeling.' At that, my mother would pretend to sniff indignantly, as if *her* side of the family had been insulted by my father's insinuation.

My devoted parents sometimes reminded me of those deluded, bedevilled birds who dutifully hatch and rear the eggs and the young of the pushy cuckoo. Our expression 'a cuckoo in the nest' means a simpleton, and that word seemed to fit me, for I saw myself often as a kind of Simple Simon of nursery rhyme fame.

Indeed, my classmates often said I was 'cuckoo' or crazy, and I secretly revelled in that unjustified reputation, as if it were a kind of recommendation, an assurance that I was human after all. To this day, there is nothing I like so much as making people believe I am a simpleton 'pure and simple' and therefore being able to look down upon those who make that mistake because of their lack of perspicacity. This attitude might be construed as arrogance or egotism, but it is simply an example of how I prefer being myself, even though it confounds others and antagonizes them. I relish being misunderstood.

My classmates also used to criticize my unpredictable behaviour by saying: 'Oh, that Kirkup, he always has to be different from everyone else,' as if I were being 'different' deliberately, when most of the time I was simply being my own divided, restless, curious, ambiguous, androgynously split self. I was thankful to be different from my classmates, none of whom I liked, for children are terribly right-wing and conservative and conventional. I was not.

The gap in my front teeth was 'lucky' but it was also the image of the Viking, of the real man (or men) within me. I think it was this inborn split, the ability to be many persons within one body, that made me a writer intent on seeing into the lives and characters of others. I believe the art of poetry to be the perception of essences, of resemblances and differences, and also the continual desire to reconcile opposites in image and idea, form and style, substance and dream. It was no wonder writing, and particularly poetry and the translation of poetry taught me how to seek the essences of my heart, soul and mind, and to compose and reconcile the at first bewildering contradictions in my own split nature, my parallel lives that often made me feel, as I do today, that I am continually treading a tightrope, trying not to fall. Somehow I manage to make my parallel lives meet at infinity – the starting-point of artistic craft and poetic vision.

When I look back at that period of my growing-up from childhood into troubled and unhappy and frustrated adolescence, and compare it with my life today, I realize how little I have changed. I am still impulsive, dreamy, unpractical, romantic, longing for the ideal friend who never comes, full of impossible loves and intense enthusiasms, and still subject to bewildering switches of mood and behaviour. I am a walking contradiction. I still feel like that precocious, old-fashioned, absurd little boy, like one of the fantastic child characters from Salinger or Truman Capote or Carson MacCullers or James Purdy, authors I was to discover at the end of the war, and in whose novels and short stories about life in the Deep South I was to recognize, against all expectation and probability, something of my own entranced, legendary boyhood in the far North-East.

PART ONE

Pre-War

'Fear gave his watch no look. . . .'

A Grave of Academe

1936–8

I wanted to murder the Professor of French. He was Cuthbert M. Girdlestone, head of the Department of French at Armstrong College, a typically drab little red brick grove of academe in Newcastle upon Tyne. It was one of the colleges of Durham University, and is now called King's College, a much less plebeian appellation.

I had the misfortune to select this dump in order to obtain a degree in Modern Languages, because at the time it was the only place where I could take a Double Honours degree of Bachelor of Arts in French and German. It was also the cheapest place: by travelling by Northern bus to and from Newcastle each day, I spared my parents the expense (which they could not have afforded anyhow) of my living in a Hall of Residence – which, having had some experiences of such places in later life at Leeds, Sheffield and Cardiff, I realize I should certainly not have enjoyed.

I had wanted to read English Literature, but the excellent woman who taught me French and German at Westoe Secondary School (later High School) convinced me that it would be more to my advantage to continue my modern languages. 'Anyone can study English Literature on their own,' she told me. 'It's not worthwhile wasting your time on such a useless subject.' So I did not study English under Professor Renwick, the celebrated authority on Spenser, but French under Girdlestone, German under Professor Mennie, a great Scot from Aberdeen and a wonderful teacher, and Italian and Spanish informally with various lecturers. It was the best decision I ever made.

However, the syllabus for the French Literature course was dismal in the extreme. I was simply not interested in most of the works listed there: Descartes' *Traité des passions*, Fléchier's *Oraisons funèbres*, Sedaine's *Le Philosophe sans le savoir*, Condorcet's *Esquisse d'un tableau historique des progrès de l'esprit humain*, Rousseau's *Héloise* (*La Nouvelle*), Renan's *Marc-Aurèle et la fin du monde antique* etc. etc. – all to me as dry as dust and unreadable, so I did not bother to read them. The only modern author was Julien Benda, with his tedious *La Trahison des clercs*, which induced jaw-splitting yawns.

Fortunately, there were some authors I already knew and loved: Madame de La Fayette's *Zayde* (though I should have preferred *La Princesse de Clèves,* one of my favourite novels), Molière's *Le Misanthrope* (which suited me perfectly), Fromentin's *Dominique* and Vigny's *Chatterton,* both characters with whom I closely identified myself. However, I read these authors for pleasure, not for academic study, and the result was that my essays on their works were far from scholarly in the accepted sense of academic scholarship at that time. I got bored with Girdlestone's eccentric expositions of his favourite subjects, which included romanesque architecture and Mistral and the Félibrige, about which he later wrote a tedious opus that I had to review for *The Listener.* The literary editor, Joe Ackerley, would not allow me to demolish it as I thought fit. So it never got printed.

Benda's *La Trahison des clercs* was the start of my persecution by Girdlestone. We had to read the book chapter by chapter for each class, and then be interrogated on the contents. I had more interesting things to do than read Benda, so I skipped a number of Girdlestone's classes, and when at last I thought I had better put in an appearance I had not read the prescribed chapter for that week. When Girdlestone, enraged by my absences, called upon me to talk about it, I tried to waffle my way through, but of course he at once spotted that I had not read the text at all. Then, with his usual ferocious grin of triumph, he pronounced: '*Monsieur Kirkup, vous êtes un farceur!*' I remained silent, of course, but at once I was struck by the aptness of the remark: I was, indeed, a farceur, and nobody could take me seriously because I could not even take myself seriously – a failing that has dogged me all my life.

Girdlestone also took the honours students for French prose translation. He used to hand out dismayingly difficult passages from my most hated writers, Virginia Woolf, Conrad, Galsworthy, Charles Morgan among them. Whenever a student came up with a particularly good turn of phrase, the Professor would scribble it down in his notebook, using a red stylo. Only two or three times did I see my French flow in bright red ink among the versions Girdlestone had made himself. I found these classes interesting, and I admired the erudition and the knowledge of etymology he displayed, but each class was a *tour de force* on his part, leaving his students dumb and in my case scared out of my wits. He scented my fear, and that goaded him to heap insults and humiliations upon my head, while I sat silently, blushing, trying to outface him with a timid smile, which he once referred to as '*votre sourire ensorceleur et charmant*'. He must have thought I was trying to seduce him, for he was rabidly anti-homosexual. The rest of the department staff lived in terror of his whims.

His office, in which we met for prose translation, was right at the top of a pseudo-classical Victorian red brick tower. It was reached by an endless spiral stone staircase that first led to a landing with a circular, balustraded hole in the floor giving a dizzying, sickening view of the convoluted stairs and the hall far, far below. From there we had to climb a flight of narrow wooden steps to the professor's eyrie, of which he was immensely proud – he called it his ivory tower, of course.

I gave up reading the set texts, and enjoyed myself reading the whole of Gide, Proust, Cocteau, Colette, Montherlant, Eluard, Valéry, Supervielle and many other contemporary French writers neglected by the stuffy syllabus. This feverish and excited reading was of no benefit to me at all from an academic standpoint. I could not even write a thesis about one of them, because as I was reading for Double Honours I was exempted from the requirement to compose a thesis for my finals. Girdlestone had little use for modern writers, and his animosity towards me increased. It became so painful I felt the only escape would be to murder him.

How was I to do it? Poison? We had some of that virulently vermilion rat poison at home: we used it on the allotment to discourage rats from eating the freshly planted green peas. At one of our genteel monthly tea-parties of the French Society, I might be able to slip a small dose into Girdlestone's tea. Later, when the war started, I took to wearing a capsule of cyanide on a chain round my neck. I intended to swallow it, not to avoid being raped by a Nazi invader, but to resist arrest if the morals police caught me performing unauthorized sexual acts in the black-out or in some conveniently isolated air-raid shelter or public toilet. But the opportunity to do him in with rat poison or cyanide never presented itself. 'The Prof' was always too wary of me, and I could never get near his cup of tea, which was adoringly prepared for him by lickspittle female students anxious to get a first class degree.

He used to race up the spiral stairs in the French Tower, taking the steps two at a time, and sometimes challenged me to compete with him. I was in poor condition, for in those days I smoked about ten cigarettes a day at least, and took as little exercise as I do now, while Girdlestone was a fitness fanatic. I kept hoping he would have a heart attack as I raced him up the stairs, and actually managed to pass him near the top, where I allowed him to overtake me – to have made him lose would have been to incur his everlasting displeasure. As we leaned on the circular balustrade round the hole in the floor, I watched him panting, trying to catch his breath with that insidious smile of small, perfect teeth lit by one gold crown, and considered my chances of pushing him over the edge, but I could see that the balustrade was too high, and I would never be able to catch him off his guard. I had a nice little switchblade knife: I could stab him in the heart, but lacked the courage. So I went on carrying a few pellets of rat poison round with me, inserted into soft-centred chocolates, in a small Beecham's Pills tin. But he did not have a sweet tooth. The war came, and I made my pacifist stand before Judge Richardson, and the Prof told me, grinning sideways on his twisted neck: 'I don't think you are a physical coward, Kirkup,' insinuating that I was a moral coward. He'd got it all wrong: I was terribly frightened of physical pain, but morally I felt I was a hero. His stupid remark incensed me, and I made up my mind I would get him somehow, even if I had to wait for years and years. I waited, and after he retired I cased his house in Paris, at St Cloud, intending to shoot him as he came out, but just when I had everything ready – my pearl-handled revolver concealed in a Japanese *furoshiki*, I learned that he had died of natural causes. It was one of the biggest disappointments of my life.

After the war, when I wrote to ask him for a reference when applying for a job, he did not answer. He was the sort of academic tyrant, a crypto-fascist, who would never be tolerated by today's outspoken and committed generation of students. But in those days, students had no power whatsoever: they had to do as they were told, or be failed, or receive a third-class degree. Girdlestone was the bane of my university existence, and I still have not recovered from the psychic injuries he inflicted upon me. Much as I love France and French literature, they are always tainted for me by memories of his voice, his sneering laugh, his eccentricity and heartless sarcasms.

He liked being the centre of attention, and he was a passable flautist. He had a head perpetually on one side, as if he had torticolis, and this was explained by the fact that he played the flute every day. His light, dancing walk had something oriental or Arab in it. When he appeared in an amateur production of *Sakuntala*, he had obviously shaved his chest and oiled his body, tanning it very evenly to give it an Indian tone. But his little blondish bourgeois moustache over that sparkling smile filled me with revulsion. One or two female members of staff were hopelessly in love with him. I remember one of them sitting in an attitude of prayer as he played the solo flute part in some concerto. Unfortunately, on that occasion something went wrong with his instrument, and an irreverant friend with me said quite loudly: 'He's lost his pea!' as if he were performing on a cheap whistle, which is what his flute often sounded like. In later life, he wrote a devastatingly dull tome on Rameau, that most delightful of all French composers. In 1983 I enjoyed a performance of Rameau's 'Zoroastre', in the Queen Elizabeth Hall, and to prepare myself for this unfamiliar treat I looked it up in Girdlestone, who comments: 'Sacrilegious absurdity. . . . It seems almost blasphemous to depict a figure like Zarathustra in love.' But this was not Nietzsche's Zarathustra, but a semi-divine figure from another legend, as Rameau and his librettist certainly were aware. Rameau's hero from the Avesta is a deeply human and attractive man. *Also sprach* Girdlestone. But even Richard Strauss thought Zarathustra to be an invention of Nietzsche. . . .

The final ignominy inflicted upon the honours students by 'The Duchess of Gerolstein' (as I nicknamed the Prof) was the annual informal inquisition that took place just before the final exam results were posted. I remember that the year I sat my degree we were all gathered in the French Tower, not in Girdlestone's office, but beside the balustrade round the hole at the top of the spiral stairs. The Duchess descended from the ivory tower, grinning maliciously, his short-sighted eyes twinkling bitchily behind his gold-rimmed glasses – how weird those eyes looked in their globular greyness when he removed his spectacles!

I was gazing over the edge of the balustrade down at the marble floor far below, wondering if I should ever have the nerve to throw myself down. In those days, I foolishly believed that life was the most precious thing, and that to throw it away deliberately was the ultimate gesture. Now I know better: life is simply not worth dying for.

Girdlestone took up his favourite position, leaning back against the balustrade, supporting himself on his elbows, one tiny foot crossed over the other. I had been trying to undermine the strength of the stone by sawing at it secretly with a large nail file borrowed from a woman friend, but had made very little impression: it was not likely that the balustrade would suddenly give way and send the monster tumbling backwards through space to crash on the hall floor down there.

I imagined what it would be like to leap upon him without warning, going for the throat and, half-strangling him, thrusting him gradually over the rim, while his face, white with terror and glassy with perspiration, goggled back at me in final realization of my detestation. . . .

Perhaps he caught something of my feelings in a flash of thought-transference, and attributed them to an episode at the end of the final examination, when he was invigilating. It was a prose translation paper, in two sections, and one was supposed to write each section on a separate sheet. I, however, had dreamily ignored or forgotten this, and had written my answers on a single sheet. When I went up to the front to hand in my paper to Girdlestone, he was suddenly convulsed with rage, that beastly rage of an aggressive wild animal that lurks in all of us. In a loud voice, in front of all the other examinees and the other invigilator, who happened to be my tutor, D. H. Macgregor from the economics department, Girdlestone lashed out at me: 'It's all very well being a poet, Kirkup, but you should read the instructions properly!' With that, he tore up my paper. I made no reply, and walked calmly out of the hall: my reaction was quietist, just as when I was caned over my open palms at school – in fact, I refused to react in any way. I left him fuming in his own miserable rage.

But the Girdle Scone (another of our nicknames for him) seemed to have forgotten his horrible violence towards me as he began asking each one of us in turn what kind of degree we expected to receive. It was a cruel question for all of us, already feeling tension about the result. The goody-goody girls who always sucked up to him simpered and said diplomatically they hoped the result would be as good as possible. Others refused to answer. When it came to my turn, I looked at him defiantly and answered: 'A first, of course.' The sharp little teeth at the corners of his grin seemed to gleam more wetly than usual at my reply, and he made no comment. I never saw him again.

My favourite place at the university had always been the library, and I spent most of my time there. I remember how shocked I was to find that the works of D. H. Lawrence were not allowed on the shelves. So I inscribed a request for them, in bright purple ink, in the request book. In the late thirties, Lawrence was still forbidden in the polite circles of British academe. It was to the library I went during the congregation for the conferring of degrees: I had no money to hire a gown and the white fur-trimmed hood of the B.A. The library was empty: everyone else was at the ceremony. A few days later, I received a typed form from the university office in North Bailey, Durham City, informing me that my degree had been conferred upon me in my absence.

I was glad and proud that I was the only student to absent himself from the degree ceremony, which I considered a complete farce. I never entered the library or the university again. But many years later, I visited the hated place for the purposes of a BBC television documentary on my life, filmed on my return – my brief return – to Newcastle in the 1970s. I received the same impression of being entombed in an academic grave.

Fortunately, some of the other lecturers were more sympathetic than the Prof. In the French department, my favourite was dear old Jean Vallette, a genial Provençal with the soft accent of the Midi who gave charming talks to us on poetry. He was the only person in the university who expressed any interest in my pacifism, and who sympathized with my stand. Indeed, I was the only conscientious objector among the students. The Prof, as might be expected, gave this gentle soul a terrible time.

Another fine lecturer and scholar was Lilias Macgregor, with a doctorate from the University of Grenoble. She was an Italian enthusiast, and offered extra, free classes in Italian literature, in which we read Dante, Petrarch, Leopardi, Michelangelo and – wonder of wonders – Montale and Ungaretti, my first acquaintance with modern Italian poetry. She was also a victim of Girdle Scone's merciless tyranny.

Then there was the exuberant Madame Tomlinson, an elderly French widow who conducted classes in conversation with great brio. She claimed that I was the only student in my year with a sense of humour, and certainly the things I said always seemed to make her roar with laughter. She was a kind, warm, generous character, very bourgeois, but also very intimidating. She was the only one who stood up to the Prof.

The German department was then very small, and classes were held in what was known as 'the German Hut'. In the first year, I had a refugee scholar from Vienna, but he was soon succeeded by the admirable Dr Duncan Mennie, a man of marvellous zest and humour, and a great Germanistik scholar. With him I read most of Goethe, Lessing and Schiller, and some Otto Ludwig, Hebbel, Grillparzer, Heine, Hauptmann, Hans Sachs and Heinrich von Kleist, whose drama, *The Prince of Homburg*, I was to translate for Eric Bentley's *Classic German Theatre* (along with Schiller's *Don Carlos*) for the princely sum of $50.

I enjoyed reading German Literature with Mennie, but I also did a lot of reading on my own. I discovered Hermann Hesse long before the hippies of the 1960s (by which time I no longer cared for him). I struggled through Musil and Mann, and my poets were Rilke and Stefan George. I was amused to discover that the latter had translated into German 'The Boy Stood on the Burning Deck', as well as Shakespeare's sonnets. I had already studied Theodor Storm at school, and now I became utterly charmed by the beautiful prose style of Kafka, Fontane and Konrad Ferdinand Meyer. I only wish I had been introduced then to the works of the great modern Swiss writer Robert Walser, but at that time they were completely unknown in Britain. When I started to read and translate him, it was too late: the one writer I should have liked to have met had died in a madhouse just a few years before.

Another unusual German writer I came to admire through my own explorations was Dietrich Christian Grabbe, whose *Ein Brevier* impressed me deeply because I found extraordinary resemblances between his character and my own. He, too, was an only child, son of an inadequate father and a doting mother, whose sensibility influenced him strongly. He was gifted with a copious imagination that was nourished by endless reading. From an early age, he led a life of debauchery, much more than in my case: for example, at his high school or *Gymnasium* in Detmold there was smoking, drinking and card-playing – things I did not experience until my first year at university. (I still remember the first packet of cigarettes I bought at Harton – an oval tin of twenty Piccadillies – and my first drink, a tot of straight gin in the Union bar at a Christmas fancy-dress party at which I revealed my shapely legs in the close-fitting tights of a red velvet Elizabethan costume of doublet and hose hired for half a crown from a theatrical costumier's.)

Here is an extract from Grabbe's book that portrays me with startling accuracy; Grabbe's character is being analysed by his trusty friend Ziegler – a friend such as I never had:

> It's so sad that one cannot get anywhere with him; that he's always breaking away from one, everything escape, haste, of short duration; that he changes from minute to minute, and never is nor remains what he appears to be; that he does not keep his promises, and that while he willingly accepts the good advice you give him, out of embarrassment with you, the next morning he will show no further wish to follow it, or else deliberately set himself against you, out of sheer willfulness; that misfortune dogs his steps, and he awaits its coming with dull indifference – a Proteus with a hundred shapes, all unseizable. It is shocking that he can never be a man of honour, never speak the truth, and that it has become second nature to him to misrepresent himself and to speak the opposite of what he really thinks, that he never expresses himself frankly, cannot be faithful, and that he amuses himself by chaffing his friends, or leaving them in the lurch, for ever possessed by an inner disquiet, posing and firing off witty phrases. . . .

This self-destructive nature was something Girdlestone observed when he called me a *farceur*. I spent a year in France from 1938 to 1939, and when I did not turn up to deliver a talk in French to the assembled French Society about my experiences as a *répétiteur* at the Ecole Normale d'Instituteurs at Douai on my return, he stopped me in the street, head on one side, little blond moustache bristling, eyeglasses flashing on mad eyes, and – all the time moving past with his little dancing steps – pronounced: '*Monsieur Kirkup est un homme qui ne tient pas sa parole*' – 'Mister Kirkup is a man who does not keep his word.' It was true of that particular occasion, no doubt. Nevertheless, I am a man who does keep his word. It was just unfortunate that I should have annoyed the Prof on the only occasion I did not do so:

I just felt that it was utterly impossible for me to describe what I had gone through during that terrible year before the war in France. I should have excused myself in a formal manner, but even that I could not bring myself to do: it was all too painful, and, to my mind, trivial. In the end, I did give my talk to the Society, in which, like Grabbe's anti-hero, I consistently misrepresented myself, deliberately showing myself up in a bad light and adopting a devil-may-care manner that was far from what I was really feeling and thinking. I was doing my best to hide a broken heart, but of course Girdle Scone did not see it that way: he was enjoying my discomfiture and the mess I was making of my life.

I had no friends like Ziegler, who might have advised and helped me out of my mental and emotional confusions. But there were people I liked to be with, like David Paul, who introduced me to Ronald Firbank and Ivy Compton-Burnett, and made some miraculous translations of Valéry's poetry. He himself was a very good and unusual poet and short story writer, and one of the wittiest men I have ever met. We always found ourselves laughing at the same things – something I discovered I could do with no one else.

Then there were two Turkish poets studying economics, Feyyaz Fergar and Sadi Cherkeshi. The former saw me one day in the Union carrying a book entitled *De Baudelaire au surréalisme* which I had 'lifted' from the library of the Ecole Normale d'Instituteurs in Douai, and from that moment on we were firm friends, discussing and criticizing our own poems in French and English – I wrote a lot of French surrealist poetry in those days – and helping each other with translations of poets like Supervielle, Eluard and Soupault.

There were two or three girls with whom I fancied I was in love: dear, sweet Mary Chapiet from St Lô and Madeleine Bell among them. Mary was taking courses in English for a year, and during that time we were always together. Then I had to spend a year in Douai, while she went to the University of Bonn, and after the war broke out we never met again. Madeleine or Madie was small and slight as a boy, an asthmatic like myself, a self-destructive chain-smoker. She was highly intelligent, reading English literature with Renwick and linguistics with Harold Orton. We both developed emphysema during the war. I survived. She died of it.

She was my true romantic passion in my student days. When she died in the fifties, a common friend at the university, Harry Bradshaw, wrote to tell me about it, and I quote part of the letter I wrote in reply:

> What a nasty shock your letter with the sad news about Madie's death gave me! We had completely lost touch, but I shall never forget those large, deep

violet eyes, and her long, dripping, straight hair of her later university days. And the birdlike fragility of her body when I held her in my arms as she wheezed and coughed. Her choking smile, her breathless gasps of laughter, her touching attempts to appear hard-bitten and cynical and to use rude words. The way she used to hold my hand without saying anything when Girdle Scone had been beastly to me, or when I was upset for any other reason, which was often. She always stood by me: behind that fragility there was an iron will, and she was a girl I felt very close too, partly because we were both severely asthmatic. We used to laugh helplessly in each other's arms when we suddenly found ourselves panting, not with passion, but with asthmatic attacks and emphysematical agonies of breathing. To see her sitting there waiting for me when I entered the Union cafeteria, her hair hanging over her left eye and the eternal cigarette smouldering in her tiny paw was one of the few delights of those horrible student years. Like everyone else, she laughed at me, and indeed I encouraged that laughter out of a kind of contempt for the blindness of others, but there was nothing bad in her smiles and her wit.

There was a fine school of philosophy at Newcastle, and I sometimes wished I had attended it, in order to study with Louis Arnaud Reid and Dorothy Emmet, though I doubt if I should have made a good philosopher, however much I admired Bertrand Russell. In the teacher training course, I could never get through Bosanquet, and I was bored by Plato. I might have turned to music, because the head of the department was the lively and comical Sydney Newman, who once did me the honour of laughing heartily when I gave, at the end of my sorry university career, a recital of my surrealist poetry. It was my only triumph.

Happy memories of the time are scarce, but I remember summer evenings, after the library closed, walking with David past the red and white and pink flowering hawthorn bushes that grew outside the main building, all sooty brick and stone. Walking and talking with David in Exhibition Park or among the factories and wharves and quayside buildings on the quayside – scenes like images from early Chirico paintings. Taking tea with David in the strange little teashops and cafés we discovered, going to concerts together, listening to David playing Chopin, Liszt, Scarlatti, Debussy, Ravel. These, not my academic studies, were the best things in my life at that period. I had hoped to meet fellow spirits at Armstrong College, but it was a resort of barbarians and boors, both on the staff and in the student body. For me, its only saving grace was the company of those two or three friends, and the lectures of two or three outstanding human beings. Apart from that, I learned nothing that I did not teach myself, often with great struggles. One of my problems, I now see, is that

I was totally unaware of the impression I was making on others, most of whom did not like what they saw.

I was trying to write prose and poetry, and the theme that appeared most often was that of loneliness, Rilke's '*Es gibt nur eine Einsamkeit, und die ist schwer zu tragen . . .*'. Yet the emotionalism of this subject was tempered by a sense of humour seldom appreciated by others, and derived directly from the anarchical desperation of surrealist fun. Anarchy and surrealism became driving forces in my youth, and I admired the English surrealist writer David Gascoyne, whose *Opening Day,** for a while, provided me with almost the same exciting stimulus as the French surrealist poets – I just had to read a few lines of Soupault, Breton or Michaux to feel a surge of poetic response that was almost impossible to convey in English. Gascoyne's surrealism was much gentler, and did not excite me in the same way, but in *Opening Day* I found passages that I might almost have written myself, and which seemed to refer to that loneliness I was learning to accept as well as distrust:

> . . . he had taken his loneliness as a matter of course, but seeing more of other children made him wish for that companionship that because of his unusual nature he was seldom to have.

Another writer, George Santayana, whose *The Last Puritan* I was unable to get through, was to write, in *My Host the World,* something that I felt could be applied to my own case, both banal and bizarre:

> And as the feeling of being a stranger and an exile, by nature as well as by accident, grew upon me in time, it came to be almost a point of pride; some people may have thought it an affectation. It was not that. I have always admired the normal child of his age and country. My case was humanly unfortunate and involved many defects; yet it opened to me another vocation, not better (I admit no absolute standards) but more speculative, freer, juster, and for me happier.

'A stranger and an exile' – In time, my sense of alienation from life was to lead me to believe I had come from outer space, from interstellar darkness. George Darley's *Sylvia* was a work in which I found surrealist correspondences with my perverse, poetic loneliness:

> . . . Yet, it is strange!
> There is a melancholy in sun-bright fields

* Published by Cobden Sanderson in 1933.

Deeper to me than gloom; I am ne'er so sad
As when I sit amid bright scenes alone. . . .

This speech by Romanzo brought me another kind of comfort, for I am one of the few people who do not enjoy bright sunshine: high pressure weather plunges me into deep depression, for which shuttered rooms provide the only relief.

First Steps Abroad

1938–9

Spring, 1938. The rise of Hitler and Mussolini and Franco – the whole of Europe seemed to be becoming one huge dictatorship. The prospect filled me with repugnance, but on the other hand I was curiously indifferent to the growing sense of impending war. I was busy with my reading of non-syllabus authors, writing poems, translations and short stories and bits of impressionist-surrealist prose. I enjoyed the Saturday night hops in the Students' Union, for I loved dancing. There were new plays and ballets and operas at the Newcastle Theatre Royal, where I was an ardent gallery-goer. I even took part in a French Society production of *Tovaritch*, playing the part of a taxi driver. There was some talk of my appearing in a production of *Bérénice*, though not in the leading rôle. . . .

With the small means at my disposal, I was enjoying life. But I was feeling very keenly the constraints of living at home. I found my mother's chatter tedious, and I had grown away from my father. There was an impression they were somehow observing me from a distance, and wondering what sort of bird they had hatched in their humble nest. I could sense their silent reservations about my increasingly precious appearance, in which I was trying to imitate Ronald Firbank, and my mysterious behaviour. What was I doing with my time? It was something I could somehow never explain to them.

My father may have suspected my antisocial and growing pacifist tendencies, for he one day showed me with pride a dusty certificate he had received from Lieutenant-General Oliphant, Commander-in-Chief, Northern Command, decorated with the royal coat of arms with *Dieu et mon droit* and with the following inscription:

> Certificate of Service. This is to certify that Lance Corporal Harold Kirkup served in Tyne Division R. E. Volunteers from the Thirtieth day of July 1903 till the Thirty-First day of March 1908 having served continuously for Four years Two Hundred and Forty-Six days. Corps in which Service was given: Tyne Division Royal Engineers (Volunteer).

Under the section entitled 'Campaigns and Medals' there were no entries. The certificate had been printed very beautifully by Andrew Reid and Compy. Ltd., Grey Street, Newcastle upon Tyne. My father gave me to understand that this voluntary service had helped him spend a rather peaceful First World War with an anti-aircraft battery on Inch Mickery in the Firth of Forth, where he had risen to the rank of Sergeant Major.

About the same time, he unearthed a copy of Benjamin Franklin's *Autobiography*, a pocket edition in very small print 'Edited by Professor Henry Morley' for Cassell's National Library, 1886. Facing the title page was a neat inscription in sepia-coloured ink: 'To Harold Kirkup from his Sunday School Teacher A. Sinclair for repeating the Golden Text of the lesson each Sunday during 1897. January 2nd. 1898.'

I wondered if he had ever read the book, which I found had a certain charm of style, and some interesting contents regarding Benjamin's inventions and early education. As I was dipping into this work, I came across references to the Quakers and their general willingness to wage *defensive* war. I was very surprised and somewhat disillusioned by this, for I had understood the Friends to be absolute pacifists. Was this what my father had wanted to show me? He had seen me reading Norman Angell and Max Plowman, and he knew I had been receiving literature from the Peace Pledge Union and the War Resisters' International. I had also expressed my admiration for the Reverend Dick Sheppard* and the various international peace services of the Society of Friends.

I had no religious convictions whatsoever: casting off all the dogma and claptrap of Methodism had been a great weight off my mind. So I was pleased to read in Franklin his account of the Dunkers and their rejection of self-righteous dogma, so that they refused to put their principles in print, lest some of them be mistaken or susceptible to improvement. Franklin gives a wonderful image of the bigoted and hidebound religious zealot in sects less flexible and enlightened than the Dunkers:

> This modesty in a sect is perhaps a single instance in the history of mankind, every other sect supposing itself in possession of all truth, and that those who differ are so far in the wrong; like a man travelling in foggy weather, those at some distance before him on the road he sees wrapped up in the fog as well as those behind him, and also the people in the fields on each side, but near him all appears clear, though, in truth, he is as much in the fog as any of them. To avoid this kind of embarrassment, the Quakers have of late years been gradually declining the public service in the Assembly and in the magistracy, choosing rather to quit their power than their principle.

* One of the founders of the Peace Pledge Movement, and Vicar of St Martin-in-the-Fields.

I was encouraged by this return to pacifist principle as I saw it, and as I hoped all English Quakers did, and I felt American Friends could not be true pacifists, or even true Quakers if they disowned their principles. When I pointed out this passage to my father, he made no comment, though my mother declared that she thought it made a wonderful picture, and that she had always believed Quakers to be good people, otherwise why would there be a picture of a prosperous Quaker gentleman on our packets of Quaker porridge oats, which were so good for breakfast?

When my father saw me reading Max Plowman's *The Faith called Pacifism*, which I had obtained from our enlightened public library in Ocean Road, he expressed unusual scorn for the writer. I am still astonished that my mild-mannered father should have displayed such hatred for Plowman. I showed him a photograph of Max with his son Tim, then just a baby, taken in June 1917, presumably on the sands at Whitley Bay. Max is wearing the uniform of a 2nd Lieutenant 10th West Yorkshire Regiment.

'That man was a coward and a traitor to his country,' my father told me. 'He was court-martialled. Can you imagine – a conchie in the army!'

His tone was scornful and bitter.

'And an officer at that!' he added.

I pointed out that Max's brave defence of his convictions was by no means the attitude of a coward, and that he had endured the inhuman hell of the Battle of the Somme. Indeed, it had been his experiences in battle that had prompted his change, had given him a vision of death so terrible that he felt forced to declare his new principles at a time when pacifists were being hounded by the public and put in jail.

For a while, my father was silent, out of respect, perhaps, for a man who had experienced the horrors of trench warfare as had my Uncle Charlie (who had been killed at the Somme) and my Uncle Bob, who had been invalided out after falling a victim to German poison gas attacks. As a child, I had been struck by the grotesque appearance of Uncle Bob's pock-marked face, the result, so my mother told me, of being gassed. It was to me an early proof of the stupidity of war, that men should do such despicable things to one another.

Then my father said: 'He was a traitor to his country.

I realized it was no use arguing with him when he was in this obstinate mood. We were miles apart in spirit, but I could understand his point of view. The sad thing was, he could not understand mine, or Plowman's. My poor mother gave a sigh of relief when we ended our discussion, and made a fresh pot of tea. There were homemade hot buttered currant scones, and these always put him in a good mood. But I was silent and sick at heart to feel that I was in conflict with him on this point.

It was only at home that I had such serious discussions. At university, I posed as an effeminate butterfly without pride or principles. I took a perverse pleasure in being insincere. At a meeting of the Spanish Society, we had as guests the Spanish Consul and his tall, beautiful daughter. (The Spanish Consulate at that time was in Betty Surtees House on the quayside, where Sadi Cherkeshi, the young Turkish poet, had a flat I often visited). The Consul and his daughter were enthusiastic supporters of Generalissimo Franco, a dictator I regarded with the utmost detestation. The conversation came round to a discussion about the Civil War and the new Franco regime, and they expressed fulsome admiration for the Caudillo, 'our great and wise leader'. The mood of the meeting turned decidedly cool. The Consul's daughter turned to me, and, smiling brilliantly, asked me if I would not support Franco. With unblinking insincerity I assured her that I had the greatest respect and even love for the Generalissimo, whom I called 'a great man, a true Catholic'. Hardly daring to believe her ears, she clapped her hands in girlish delight and leaned across to her father, saying: 'Here is an English worshipper of our Caudillo.' The Consul beamed at me, and invited me to a reception at the Consulate, which I did not attend. My fellow students, now accustomed to my peculiar sense of humour, took my words with the greatest glee. I had discovered that this was one way to amuse them. But they really thought I was incapable of any serious thought, or of expressing any genuine opinion. They had adopted the notion, spread by Professor Girdlestone, that I was a *farceur*. To counter this tendency, I would quote Baudelaire's *Notes sur Edgar Poë: 'Poë fut toujours grand, non seulement dans ses conceptions nobles, mais encore comme farceur.'* (Poe was always great, not only in his noble concepts, but also as a farceur.) But the idea of a 'farceur noble' is one the British temperament cannot accept, as I have often found to my disadvantage.

My antisocial activities, my pacifism and my pretended flippancy were, I now understand, one way of protesting against life at home, in all its dull convention and respectability. I wanted to break loose from all that stifling love and domesticity. I took up smoking as an outward symbol of my independence, to my mother's horror. But my father, a pipe smoker, thought cigarettes were effeminate, and said so. I expected to be sick when I smoked my first mild Piccadillies, but I was not: it was the beginning of a very moderate smoking habit that I had little difficulty in kicking a few years later. I did not take it up again until I reached Japan in 1959, where

I was practically forced to smoke as a kind of social obligation, for everyone smoked in those days. Cigarettes in my youth helped to give me a little self-confidence, and helped to establish my early pose as a Gay Young thing. But I never enjoyed them.

I finally got a chance to make my escape from a home that had become too confined. Students of foreign languages were encouraged to intercalate a year of work and study in France, Germany or Spain. One was given some not very demanding post in the foreign school or college in exchange for accommodation and meals. All the other expenses had to be borne by oneself. I saw this as an ideal opportunity, not only to acquire fluency and perfection in my foreign languages, but also to shake off, if only for a year, the shackles of home and of Tyneside, which to me seemed little more than an industrial ghetto. I was determined to get out of it as soon as possible. So I applied for a post in either France or Germany. I was hoping that I would be sent to Strasburg, where there was a bilingual tradition, or to Biel in Switzerland, birthplace of someone who was to become my favourite writer of German prose, Robert Walser. Or I would have been happy in Vienna, birthplace of Karl Kraus, a Taurean like myself – he was born on 28 April 1874.

But when I put this proposition to my parents, there was immediate opposition, as I had expected. I had suggested that, as I would not be at home, they could send me ten shillings a week for my basic expenses: in those days, students were not allowed to take part-time jobs. They felt they could just manage this, but my travelling costs were another problem. My small post office savings account could be used. But they had other objections: a stay abroad would delay my graduation, and the possibility of getting a job, by one whole year. And my mother in particular was worried about the worsening political situation on the Continent.

But there was another, unspoken obstacle, one which I did not understand at the time, and that I have only recently come to realize the nature of: both my parents were aware (though I did not know it) of my sexual preferences, and that I had become, in my decadent aestheticism, the sort of young man who is regarded as very peculiar by 'normal', bourgeois standards. They secretly feared that I might be made to suffer for being different if they were not at hand to protect me. At the time, I blithely disregarded whatever animosity my careless preciousness aroused in others, because I had been accustomed to hostility since childhood, so persecution did not worry me at all. But my parents must have regarded me almost as a handicapped child, whom they were reluctant to let out of their sight in case I had an accident. So they did their utmost to try to dissuade me from leaving the comparative safety of home for unpredictable foreign parts.

I think the university authorities must have felt the same. I could sense that Girdle Scone was unwilling to let me leave for Europe – I was the perfect victim for his cruelty. But he could not stop me making a formal application for a post. At the interview with the representative of the Department of Intelligence and Public Relations of the Board of Education in Whitehall, I could see that he, too, had his reservations about sending abroad such a peculiar example of British degeneracy. But as we discussed the matter, I could see that he was coming round in my favour. Girdle Scone, in his report on me, had obviously been trying to put a spoke in my wheels. The interviewer finally promised me that he would try to find me a position either in Strasburg or in some other town not too far from Germany.

But when I received, on 24 June, a communication from the Office National des Universités et Ecoles Françaises on the Boulevard Raspail, Paris, I was dismayed to find that I had been appointed to Douai, a town about which I knew almost nothing apart from the 'Dowy' version of the Bible and its Belfry in a picture by Corot. My heart sank: it was not even very close to the German border, and too far from Paris. The nearest big city was Lille. However, I resigned myself to a year of boredom and stagnation, academically speaking, and resolved to enjoy myself to the utmost in non-academic ways. It was at least a chance to escape from Tyneside, Girdle Scone and home.

About a week after I had received the notification of my appointment from Paris, I received a letter from a doctor's family in Douai, inviting me to spend the summer with them in their villa at Wissant, near Cap Griz Nez. In exchange for a room and food, I was to tutor their two teenage sons in English for a couple of hours a day.

I accepted at once, though again my parents were doubtful – doubtful, I now see, of how such a conventional French family would accept someone they perhaps were assuming would be a 'typical English gentleman'. My only thought was to get away from home: I would spend the summer at Wissant, enjoying myself as much as possible, then travel on to Douai for the beginning of the college year. I had been appointed as *répétiteur* – a sort of conversation teacher – at the Ecole Normale d'Instituteurs, a teachers' training college for men.

With an enormous box full of books – quite unnecessary – I arrived at Boulogne to find the doctor and his sons – sixteen and seventeen years of age – waiting for me with their car. I shall never forget their startled looks as they got their first sight of their summer visitor. I was neatly but plainly attired, but my androgynous face and figure and my long blond hair – Rupert Brooke style – for a moment stunned them into silence. In the car, I tried to keep up an animated conversation in French, but I could see the doctor's mind was not on it. He was wondering how to protect his sons from the foreign menace. But he need not have worried: teenagers do not attract me at all – I prefer mature men, even very old ones. Besides, the boys were both physically and intellectually null. They did not interest me at all. I used them only in order to practise my French, and they soon observed that my fluency had greatly improved, while their deplorable English was making no progress whatsoever.

The rest of the family consisted of a charming mother, a *bien-pensant* grandmother whose compressed lips and frequent liver complaints haunt my memory, an eight-year-old daughter who kept accusing one or other of her brothers of being *bête à manger du foin* – an opinion I secretly agreed with – a dog and a local daily maid. It was a summer of utmost tedium, and I nearly expired of boredom. Fortunately there was a local bookstore where I bought a few paperbacks of modern authors including Montherlant, whose *Infante de Castille*, which has a few mild lesbian hints, was condemned by the good doctor when I left it lying open at what he considered to be a particularly *croustillant* page on the dining room table where we had our English lessons every morning. He took me aside and said he did not think it a suitable book to be introduced into a respectable household.

The Munich crisis was gathering on the horizon, but I was sublimely indifferent to it as I wandered round the countryside and cruised the waterfront at night, without success. The old granny was the only one who seemed worried about the possible outbreak of the Second World War.

Meanwhile, the boys took me to what must be a typical Pas de Calais festivity. It was a kind of peasant dinner washed down with gallons of beer. The locals who organized this treat for unsuspecting summer visitors encouraged them to drink their fill of beer, while they themselves drank very little. But when I got up to the lavatory, I found that the doors were locked. This is north eastern France's idea of a joke. The summer visitors – both men and women – were allowed to squirm uncomfortably amid gales of hearty laughter from the locals until at last the doors were opened and there was a concerted rush for the toilets. That was the only time I was taken out by the family. I think they preferred to keep me as quiet as possible.

The Munich crisis reached its peak. The grandmother became very agitated, the mother slightly hysterical, the doctor gloomier than ever. But I, always trying to be a little ray of sunshine, pointed on the fateful evening to a beautiful rainbow spanning the heavens, and proclaimed that it was a good omen – I prophesied that there would be no war. Next day, Chamberlain returned to London with his rolled umbrella and 'Peace in our time'. It was the end of the holidays, too. I was hoping that the family would drive me back with them to Douai. But they made various excuses, and I had to get there by train and taxi – an expense I could not afford. I arrived at the college with only two francs in my pocket.

Though I fancied I detected an uneasy look in their eyes, I was kindly welcomed by the *économe* and the *directeur*, and shown to my room. It was in a wing of the college where several of the lecturers lived during term time, and was quite comfortable, though there was no bedside lamp – an absolute necessity for me – and no facility for brewing an early-morning cup of tea – just as essential. It was forbidden to introduce electric gadgets, but I took no notice of that rule and as soon as I got some money from home I purchased a small electric heater, a pan, a teapot, a cup and a plate. These I had to hide in my book box every morning before the cleaners came in. I also had to hide the bedside lamp I found in a junk shop. There was a small grocery store near the college entrance, and my first purchase there was a packet of tea and a bottle of milk. I then began to feel at home.

Term had not yet begun, so I was able to explore the town of Douai, which has a certain faded charm but is not really very interesting. There was a dim, musty museum that was destroyed during the war, and is now much more appropriately housed in a sixteenth-century Carthusian convent, beautifully restored. There was the famous Belfry of the Hôtel de Ville, which I climbed on my first day. The parks – Jardin or Parc Charles Bertin – were delightful, as were the tree-lined banks of the Scarpe. I discovered the local poet, Marcelline Desbordes-Valmore, a rather insipid minor romantic, whose statue is reproduced on souvenir postcards.

I found a plaque on a wall behind the Hôtel de Ville giving the interesting information that on 21 August 1907 the world's first helicopter, 'Le Gyroplane', designed by Louis Breguet with the help of his brother Jacques and Professor Charles Richet, rose from the ground in Douai, flown by the pilot Volumard. It does not say how far it rose, or how it came down.... Near the station, in the vast, dusty Place Carnot with its provincial bandstand and regimented rows of trees, there were the Café de l'Horloge and the Brasserie Moderne, where I was to spend some happy hours. On a recent visit, I had lunch at the Brasserie, and found myself sitting again on the same green moquette leather benches, amid brown woodwork and palms. On those *banquettes* of the Brasserie Moderne I wrote many of my early poems, in English, French and German, including my first very long, autobiographical poem on my life at that period, 'The Sound of Fountains', still unpublished: the sound of fountains was the noise of water flushing in the stalls of public urinals.

Then hundreds of young men training to be *instituteurs* arrived, and the whole place was in an uproar while they got settled down into their dormitories and their lecture rooms. I had classes of about one hundred, so 'conversation' was next to impossible, especially when most of the students could not understand a word of English. So I had lots of opportunities to practise my French, but I also just talked to them about contemporary subjects like literature and politics, using an English that was less than basic – yet trying to make it stylish, amusing and interesting as well as easily comprehensible through gesture, intonation, little jokes, drawings on the blackboard, songs, extracts from Shakespeare and the English poets. I remember doing a ten-minute 'Macbeth' which went down very well, though my ten-minute 'Paradise Lost' and two-minute 'Paradise Regained' were not so popular.

We all ate together in the big refectory, the lecturers at a separate table, and the food was simple but plentiful and good, with wine at every meal. We were served by Jean, an amiable old soldier who used to linger at our table to crack jokes and exchange reminiscences of past students with the older teachers. After lunch and dinner, the students left the refectory to the lecturers, and we all smoked and chattered and drank *digestifs*. But I soon detected a strange ambiguity in their attitude towards me. The very macho physical training teacher remarked one evening, after I had been there for about a month: '*Il* fume *comme un homme*.' Everyone looked at me, smiling, as I fiddled with my cigarette. Of course, I realized that the remark referred to me, but I preferred, as always, to ignore provocation, and let it pass with only a brief flash of my 'evil eye'. The next day, the P. T. instructor was rushed to hospital with peritonitis, from which he made a difficult and miraculous recovery.

All the lecturers had spent some time as conscripts in the army or the navy, and were fond of singing mildly obscene songs in my presence, hoping to make me blush or protest, but in such circumstances I was always able to exert a chilly self-control, and I who blushed so easily remained as stone when I heard:

J'ai fait mon temps
Dans la Marine,
Où les obus
Sont si pointus.

Ils entreraient
Sans vaseline
Dans le trou de mon cul
Dans le trou de mon cul
Dans le trou de mon cul . . .

In fact, I secretly relished these absurdities. Was I not a kind of clown? So I would be a silent one, like my favourite Harpo Marx. And in various subtle ways, I actually provoked and encouraged these *boutades*. There was no harm in them, though at times the purpose may have been to take me down a peg, to *déniaiser*, perhaps to humiliate me – a process I was well accustomed to in Britain. I shrugged it all off unconcernedly. It was like water off a duck's back, I thought. But those incidents have nevertheless stuck in my memory, along with many more. In one incident I became a kind of Malvolio, when a new assistant master, a *gringalet* of unprepossessing appearance, was prevailed upon by the others to write me a passionate love letter, asking for a rendezvous in his room, I must have been still very innocent, or just silly, or desperately in need of love: for I wrote him a reply and granted his request. After lying together for a few minutes on his bed, the door burst open and all the staff rushed in. It all ended in laughter as well as in contempt (on my part) and we went off to the Café l'Univers to drink ourselves silly on *guignolet kirsch* (my 'lover's' rather ladylike tipple), absinthe and Bière Pélican – '*toute la famille en boit*'. Really? *All* the family? Looking back now on that time, I am faintly surprised that I should have been tolerated at all, but I imagine I must have been a unique experience, a rara avis in their dull provincial academic lives, and they may have welcomed the opportunities I provided for tittle-tattle and practical jokes. The *directeur* himself, a tall, Spanish-looking gentleman with a cynical smile, a pencil-thin moustache and an unusually large, flaccid sexual equipment clearly outlined by his tight-fitting trousers, made fun of me on the occasion of an annual student festival, when a student 'princess' was elected, with 'her' attendant 'female' court. The *directeur* insisted on my exchanging kisses with the delightful young man who was beautifully attired and made-up as the '*princesse*', and I was requested to open the ball by dancing the first waltz with him/her. I found the entire occasion absolutely delightful, and I danced also with all the 'maids in waiting'. After that, everyone wanted to take a turn with me, and it was all unexpectedly and entertainingly camp, as well as madly gay. There was champagne with little fan-shaped vanilla wafers, and the decorations in the usually rather grim *réfectoire* were terribly chic and pretty. It was an evening all enchantment.

In the evenings, after classes and dinner, the boys used to go and dance together in the (surely disaffected) chapel that was just across the courtyard opposite my top-floor window. They still wore the dingy grey laboratory coats worn during classes and at meals, and I could hear the scrape and shuffle of their shoes on the stone floor of the chapel as they clung together, dancing to their favourite tunes of the day: Tino Rossi, Jean Sablon, Django Reinhardt. Though the boys were all over eighteen, there was a decided atmosphere of Roger Peyrefitte's *Les Amitiés particulières*, which I read with much amusement after the war. Sometimes, I could not resist the call of the music and of those languorous young bodies swooning in one another's arms, and I would quickly tidy my hair and put on a dab of 'Mitsouko' and dash down to join them in a tango or a java, or a sexy 'slow' to Tino Rossi's

J'attendrai –
Le jour et la nuit j'attendrai toujours
Ton retour . . .
J'attendrai . . .

Or we would kick up our heels to the strains of 'Qui a peur du grand loup méchant?' played by the intoxicating jazz violin of Stéphane Grapelli, while the evening light slowly faded in the chapel windows and in the end would find ourselves dancing in darkness. . . . It was all the most wonderful innocent fun. I was only a year or two older than my charges: we were all *copains*. But one evening the *surveillant de service* happened to look into the chapel during a particularly steamy 'slow' to Duke Ellington's 'Caravane', and I received a strong reprimand from the *directeur*: it was just 'not done', he explained to me with gentle severity, for a member of staff to join the boys in their evening dances. It was all right to meet them outside the college, he hinted, winking, but on the premises I must conduct myself like a proper English gentleman. I refrained from pointing out that that was exactly what I had been doing, and that dancing with boys was part of the British public school system. But when I declared that I would leave at once and go to Paris, he gave way, and said I might continue to dance with the boys, 'but not *every* night', if I were discreet and did not make the other teachers feel discriminated against, for they were absolutely forbidden to join the dance, and, indeed, I think the idea of doing so had never entered their heads, for they were great sticklers for the *comme il faut*, and the *qu'en dira-t-on* – concepts totally foreign to my nature, and expressions that did not belong in my very personal and precious vocabulary. So I went on enjoying myself in a nightly 'cheek to cheek'. By the time I reached the end of my year in

Douai, in June 1939, we were passionately waltzing in one another's arms to the saccharine strains of 'Un jour mon prince viendra'. I once thought of calling this volume of my life story 'One Day my Prince Will Come'.... Or is it 'Some Day ...?' No matter.

The sinister undertones of song titles in those days did not altogether escape my attention, whose span I tried to keep as short as possible. There was a certain sensation of dancing on a burning deck, from which no one had fled but certain privileged, lucky ones like Auden, Isherwood and Britten. 'Who's Afraid of the Big Bad Wolf?' was a question I refused to take very seriously. Had not Chamberlain brought us 'peace with honour?' My parents occasionally sent me copies of the *Manchester Guardian* and *Picture Post*. I could not help noticing that many people in Britain looked upon Chamberlain's 'appeasement' as treason. I did not think it was all that bad: I felt grateful to him for having preserved peace at all costs, for using diplomacy for its rightful ends. But at the same time, I could see that something had to be done about the repulsive Nazi movement, without getting ourselves tarred with the same brush. We also had a duty to Czechoslovakia and the Sudeten Germans whom we had left in the lurch. I had always despised logic, and was baffled by politics. In short, I was in a state of mild confusion, wilfully self-induced, until I read a letter from Max Plowman in the *Manchester Guardian*:

> Every sane person in this country realizes that he owes an immense debt of gratitude to Mr Chamberlain for saving the world from the unimaginable horrors of war, unlimited at a moment when war on such a scale seemed inevitable. But do we all realize that our honour has been put in pawn unless this country accepts a full and practical responsibility for the terms of the settlement? Peace has been purchased at a price, but British honour can only be maintained if this country shows its readiness to pay its share of the purchase price and its unwillingness to allow the whole of the burden to fall upon Czechoslovakia....
>
> As matters stand, a State whose boundaries were determined by our act and deed in the Treaty of Versailles has suffered dismemberment under threat of force, with our consent and assistance.... The people who have purchased peace for us must not be allowed to suffer wantonly for want of British assistance....

Max went on to plead for the immediate opening of a Mansion House fund for the relief of refugees in Czechoslovakia. The letter was printed in October 1938, at a time when I was starting to dance the nights away with my students. I think I was greatly influenced by the general mood in France at that time, which was one of comparative insouciance except for the protests of members of the Front Populaire: an insouciance that would eventually prove to be weak-kneed degeneracy leading to the downfall of France, and the subsequent collaboration with the occupier (never the 'enemy') of large numbers of writers and artists and ordinary citizens. But under all the gaiety and irresponsibility there lurked at the back of my mind the shadow of the coming war, which I soon realized was inevitable. The prospect filled me with disgust for humanity, and I determined to have no part in it, an attitude both praised and mocked by the French people I explained it to. But within the next twelve months, several of my dancing partners were already dead or in concentration camps in Germany.

I made some half-hearted attempts to continue my studies, and registered for several courses at the University of Lille. To my surprise, I found myself greatly interested by the phonetics course for foreigners, for which I received a diploma at the end of the year: I still have the enthusiastic and extensive notes I made during this course, but I have forgotten everything about phonetics, which scandalizes some of my Japanese colleagues who are constantly asking me to write the phonetic equivalents of English words.

I also followed courses in literature, which, after the drudgery of Girdlestone, were electrifyingly brilliant. There were exciting lectures on modern, romantic and classical literature that opened up vistas denied to me in the intellectual morass of Newcastle. I remember in particular the fascinating expositions of the text of Musset's *Lorenzaccio* by Professor Pierre Gastinel. But there were also courses in Old French (not required for my Double Honours degree in Newcastle) by Professor Guerlin de Guer, who enchanted me with his talks on Villon, and Monsieur Audra's course of translation from English into French, a stimulating exercise, and one I thoroughly enjoyed: it was a far cry from Girdle Scone's pernickety pedantic approach.

I loved the easy-going student life of Lille. The men seemed so much more intellectual and mature than in Britain, and the girls were friendly and clever in a way that was rare among English girls at that time. There was a sense of intellectual ferment and a wealth of political discussion that constantly excited me. These French people, at least, were serious thinkers, and I often felt lost as I listened in fascination to their accomplished logic and insight as well as their lighthearted doggedness in argument – something I felt I should never master. I fell in love with one or two of the most brilliant exponents of literary and economic theories, a totally platonic love. They accepted me as one of themselves. It was a period when I, usually a silent person, became intoxicated by talk and dazzled by discussion.

We used to meet at the Brasserie Métropole in the main street leading from Lille station to the opera house, where we would talk about professors and classes and examinations, but also about the new films and plays. With one particular friend, with whom I was deeply in love, I used to sit in a booth downstairs, '*à l'abri de l'orchestre*' as he used to say, and talk about poetry. There was an enchantingly pretty young flower-seller who used to come round with a tray of dewy roses, and my friend used to laugh when she stopped beside us and suggested he buy one for me. But he never did ....

The magnificent Opéra in Lille with its imposing classical front adorned with extravagant romantic sculpture of the usual attributive kind, was a place that completed my musical education. There I saw great operatic productions, including my first experience of what was to become my favourite opera, Debussy's *Pelléas et Mélisande*. I attended a Chopin recital by Cortot, and drama performances by first-class touring companies as well as by the Comédie Française. Until then, the only French theatre I had seen had been in November 1935, when our French class, guided by Miss Robinson and Miss Craig, was transported to the Newcastle Empire to see two plays by Labiche, *La Grammaire* and *La Poudre aux yeux*, played by '*des comédiens de Paris*', sponsored by the Modern Languages Association: the *comédiens* were excellent players from the Odéon and the Théâtre Antoine, whose director, Pierre Gayan, a fine comic, played in both pieces and led the tour. A year later, we saw a marvellous production of Molière's *L'Avare*, in which the beautiful young ingénue seemed to me the most enchanting creature I had ever seen. At these performances, it was a great thrill to sing '*La Marseillaise*' before 'God Save the King': for some reason, I sang the former with all my heart, and remained silent for the latter. I have always refused to salute the Union Jack and to sing the National Anthem from my earliest years, despite punishments with the cane and the strap.

But in the charming little theatre in Douai, too, we had concerts and plays and lectures. There was one recital I remember with the actress Béatrix Dussane, 'La Dussane', then in old age, who had been one of the youngest comediennes at the Comédie Française, and in later life a great authority on the French theatre. She had known Sarah Bernhardt in decline, as she told us, and gave us some reminiscences of the actress, which she later included in her book, *Reines de Théâtre*. La Dussane gave us a selection of great scenes from Racine, Corneille, Musset and Victor Hugo, as well as poetry by Lamartine, Baudelaire, Verlaine, Mallarmé, Valéry and Rimbaud. For the first time, I realized the magnificence of Racine, who had always seemed to me stuffy and dry as dust.

The Opéra at Lille had other attractions: the basement public toilet in the street outside was one of the hottest spots in all France, and men used to travel from all parts of the 'Hexagon' to visit it. I am told it rose to even greater heights of sexual license during the Nazi Occupation, when the handsome young blond invaders were very popular in the blackout. Certainly it was very active still in the years after the war, but on my last trip to Lille I was disappointed to find it had been closed down. Another *lieu de rendezvous* was the Jardin Vaubam, an exquisite public park, still popular today, but very dangerous now.

I used to travel nearly every day from Douai to Lille by the 'Micheline', a kind of turbo-train which no longer exists. It was very fast and very sophisticated. I often caught the last train back and had to ring the bell of the concierge's lodge in order to gain admittance to the college. Those were wild days and nights, and I was completely contented. But at Christmas, the *directeur* invited me into his *salon* to take tea with him and his wife, and questioned me about my studies: he had to make a report to Girdlestone, to whom I was supposed to send an essay and a letter once a month. I had failed to do so. I think I wrote to him only once in that year, hypocritically beginning my letter with '*Cher maître*'. *The directeur* seemed to suggest that if I was not happy at Douai I might return home without any difficulties being made. I now see he was hoping I would agree: his British gentleman had grown too hot to handle. But I indignantly refused to return to Britain, and perforce he had to keep me on. I suspect that he wrote a shocked report on my behaviour and appearance to Girdle Scone and to the Department of Intelligence and Public Relations of the Board of Education in London.

So I stayed on at the college during the Christmas and New Year vacation, when everyone went home. I was the only person there apart from the concierge, and even he went away for a few days, leaving the key to the front gate with me. The heating had been cut off, and I froze in my room, where my illicit *réchaud* provided the only warmth. Post from England was delayed, and I ran out of money and had to ask for credit from the old lady in the little grocery shop. I lived mostly on tea and biscuits, but in the end I could not afford even these, so I was reduced to eating dates. My mother sent me a homemade Christmas cake, and I rationed myself to a small slice each day. I wondered how I would survive when that was finished. I had my monthly student rail pass Douai–Lille, and I used to take the train every day, simply in order to get warm, riding back and forth between the two cities.

There was an unexpected visit from a French teacher in one of the *lycées*, with whom I was hopelessly in love. He kindly took me to bed once or twice. When I was completely without resource he gave me dinner in town, and we got quite drunk. Then he took me to the local *bordel*, to me a place of unimaginable horrors: among the beauties on offer was a stocky little woman with a pug face and pendulous breasts wearing only a man's bathing trunks and ragged fur-trimmed slippers, who took me in charge. She was surprisingly sweet and gentle, and when I was in the money again I several times went back to enjoy her services. She used to call me 'Blanche Neige' after Disney's *Snow White and the Seven Dwarfs*, which had just come out in France.

But the visit gave me an idea. Why not sell my own body to the highest bidder? I felt no compunction at all about doing so, and I was ready to sell it to either men or women, provided they paid me well. After all, it was my own body, and I had a right to do with it as I pleased. I had often seen boys in Lille escorting elderly gentlemen to a certain small hotel in the vicinity of the Opéra. So I decided to take up the business myself, just to tide me over during the holiday season.

My first client was a squat, bald-headed, middle-aged man for whom I felt a thrilling repulsion. I got the impression that he was not French but either Egyptian or Lebanese. As it was the holiday period, 'trade' was rather slack, so I had to go with the first man who picked me up under the Opéra. I told him I was hungry, so he bought me a ham sandwich and a cup of coffee, and stood weighing me up as I ate and drank at the counter of the bistro. I suppose that being a foreigner I always had a certain curiosity value in France. Anyhow, he took me to a very *louche* little hotel and paid for a room. My knees were trembling as I followed him upstairs. We undressed, and then I saw that the region round his genitals and parts of his flabby, thick thighs were covered with a vivid red rash. This put me off completely. I told him I just could not do whatever he wanted me to do, which I suspected was something I did not like (I practically invented, single-handed, what was to become known many years later as 'safe-sex'.) He watched me open-mouthed as I hurriedly got into my clothes. Then, still stark naked, he sprang up from the bed and took me by the throat and shook me with unsuspected strength. He was in a rage at having paid for the room for nothing, and he shouted at me: 'If you were a woman, I'd kill you!' I backed out of the room, to find the proprietor of the hotel and one or two scantily-dressed young ladies on the landing outside the door.

As I was dashing down the stairs, I heard my client calling to one of the girls to come in and service him. But I had made fifty francs and got a free snack! I was over the moon! I made quite a few scores over the New Year, enough to see me through until the next letter from my parents, containing ten shillings, and another from my Aunt Anna, containing *two* ten shilling notes. I was well away.... For a few weeks, I lived an idle life of luxury, and I felt that prostitution could be an ideal way of life for a poet. Ever since then, I have had a soft spot for prostitutes of both sexes, and in later years regarded Mandy Rice Davies and darling Christine Keeler as typical heroines from a naturalist novel.

The political tensions were heightening all over Europe, and the dark shadow of war seemed to grow ever more menacing as I frittered away my final weeks at Douai. In the end, I was cutting all my classes and spending most of my time in Lille, with occasional excursions to Paris, where I saw glorious Barbette dancing on a tightrope to the music of Rimsky-Korsakov and Wagner. I had already read the delightful essay on this amazing transvestite performer by Jean Cocteau, in which he says:

> The poet 'de-classes' everything and thus becomes a classic. Barbette pantomimes poetry itself, and this is his fascination. For his acrobatics are not really dangerous. His affectations ought to be unbearable to us. The principle of his act embarrasses us. What is left then? That thing he has created, going through its contortions under the spotlight....

I felt when I first read these lines that they were a good description of my life as a poet-prostitute, living in the glare of danger and perilously negotiating a never-ending tightrope – so terribly un-British a poetic calling! I exchanged a few letters with Cocteau while he was writing *La fin du Potomac*, and, with my ill-gotten gains, made a quick journey down to the Bassin d'Arcachon, where Cocteau was staying at the Hôtel Chantecler in Le Piquey, where he had lived twenty years before with Raymond Radiguet. Cocteau looked dried-out, withered, bird-like, but with fine dark eyes that summed me up in a moment, for he asked me: 'Have you found your Dargelos?' Yes, I had found him in Douai, of all places, I told him. 'There is a Dargelos in every town,' he replied. We had lunch with Jean Marais* and Roger Lannes.† Then Cocteau retired to his room with them, and I was left alone to make my way back to Paris, then Douai, by night train.

I also had a brief correspondence with André Gide, who wrote me a

* The actor who appeared in many of Cocteau's plays and films, notably *L'Aigle à deux têtes* and *La Belle et la bête*.

† A writer and poet who wrote an excellent study of Cocteau's early poetry.

charming letter in green ink, its long lines slanting off the page. I gave it away to some worthless person in Paris after the war; I had carried it everywhere with me. I wish I had made a copy. All I have now is the draft of a letter in French which I sent to Gide in the spring of 1939 from Douai. I translate:

> Cher Maître (and I really meant it this time)
> You ask me about my experiences at this college. I should like to have an opportunity to tell you about them in an intimate *tête-à-tête*, as I do not feel I can write about the most interesting ones in this letter. The college is very modern, with a gymnasium, showers, music room, lecture theatres. There is also a magnificent park, and an orchard which at the moment is all in flower. My room, which is very comfortable, gives onto this orchard. One morning, just before the Easter holidays, I awoke with a start, with a kind of childish joy such as I feel whenever there is an overnight fall of snow. For my room was flooded by that liquid light, without shadows, that one sees in spring when the morning sun begins to shine in a cloudless sky and melts the snowfall. But there was no snow, for that divinely deliquescent radiance came from the sun shimmering on every petal of the cherry trees, apple trees, pear trees, whose impetuous buds had burst open overnight and covered the branches with the unexpected splendour of a fall of lightly-scented snow. But now the petals are falling in the wind – rough winds do shake the darling buds of May – and the trees seem covered with melting flakes.

That was written on 5 May, 1939. A few days earlier, I had written a 'duty letter' to Girdlestone, apologizing flippantly for my total silence. Here I translate the most interesting part of a very dull letter:

> . . . There are six *surveillants* in the college, but they are not at all interesting, since they talk shop all the time, or discuss sport, neither of which subjects interests me. The professors are not interesting either. As for the *directeur*, I make a point of seeing as little as possible of him, and when I do I rarely speak to him. He was in the First World War at the age of eighteen in 1917, and unfortunately he never lets us forget it, as he seizes every opportunity to boast about his regiment, cannon, artillery, battles, etc. etc. He is a bore of the first water. Moreover, he considers the British to be 'degenerate' – have I set a bad example? – and is an enthusiast of the Hitler regime. . . .
>
> I have been very disappointed in the character of most French people. Where on earth are all those witty, artistic and talented French we hear so much about in England? But perhaps I am wrong to judge the character of the French in general from those I have encountered in Douai, who are good, solid, bourgeois bon-vivants and not much else. . . .

I went on to say that I hoped to apply for a grant from the Carnegie Fund, to enable me to travel to the south of France, and to spend some weeks in

Germany in order to brush up my German, which had got a little rusty. But needless to say, Girdlestone did not add his recommendation to my application, as I had politely requested him to do, and I did not receive my much-needed grant which I was hoping would free me from casual prostitution and allow me to get on with my studies and my sexual experiments. You have to be serious, to be gay.

My time in Douai was coming to an end. I was sad to leave France for a Britain I dreaded. I knew it to be a place where, if I continued my homosexual adventures, I could be arrested by the police *agents provocateurs*. In such an event, I had my personal statement prepared for delivery to the court: 'I shall turn it all to poetry.' I wanted to take risks, both in my life and in my poetry, but, like Oscar Wilde, I realized how dangerous it would be in a land as sexually bigoted as Britain to prefer aesthetics to ethics. Wilde wrote:

> ... sin increases the experience of the race ... and is even ethical: in its rejection of the current notions of morality it is one with the highest ethics. ... The goal of man is the liberation of personality.

There was no doubt in my mind that the coming years would be painful ones. It did not make sense to me to fight a Second World War in order to save the Czechs, Poles and Jews. But however much I might personally suffer, those Czechs and Poles and Jews would suffer even more horrible fates. Even so I believe my pacifism was strictly moral, and that the world around me was immoral. In particular, I felt that arms manufacturers, inventors of bigger and better bombs, arms salesmen and their military consultants in governments and in warlike preparations were the embodiments of evil. I still believe that wars are created by sinister politicians, defence ministers and armaments manufacturers. Until they are abolished, there will always be wars.

My hatred of Hitler and Nazism existed alongside a belief that war was not the way to stop their rise. I believed in continual negotiation, until in the end the tyrants were overwhelmed by their own evil. That is how I saw the overthrow of Hitler, Mussolini, Franco: give them time and enough rope, and they will hang themselves. In my room at Douai, I had pinned up a large photograph from *Picture Post* of the handsome young Jew, Herschel Gryszpan, who had assassinated a German diplomat in Paris. He was my hero, and not just because he was good-looking. There was a prim young Nazi academic with impeccable French teaching at a *lycée* in Douai, and I sometimes met him for a coffee and an exchange of conversation in

German. I took him up to my room one day and let him see that photograph of Gryszpan on my wall. He made no comment at the time. But a few days later, when he had got all his propaganda arguments together and had recovered from the shock, he spoke to me severely about what he called my 'idealistic infatuation'. We all thought he was a spy and an informer, but I told him my true feelings about the appalling situation of the Jews in Europe, and particularly in Nazi Germany. He did not speak to me again. Later, through a secret source, I learned that among Hitler's preparations for an invasion of Britain there was a list of persons to be destroyed, and I was one of them.

There was a final farewell dinner, and a last passionate dance with my favourite students, unsupervised by the patrolling *surveillants*: by now they had given me up as incorrigible. I paid a last visit to the brothel, and said goodbye to the motherly madame and my pug-faced pleasurer whose real name, I had discovered, was Héloïse.

I spent my final evening in Lille, dragging the Opéra, the Métropole and the station. It was at Lille station, on New Year's Eve, that I had fallen in with a tramp who, after I had missed my last train to Douai, took me back to his filthy garret, where I shared his bed. It was snowing, and perishingly cold in his little room, which had no ceiling: I could see the roof-tiles from the bed. We had a bottle of cheap wine and a couple of sandwiches, and the tramp rubbed his hands with glee as well as with cold as he cried: '*Nous battrons la froidure, mon pote!*' I can still remember, with the quality of a bad dream, the sad smell of poverty and sickness in that freezing garret.

I used to pick up quite a few clients on the station before it closed. Eventually, I took the last train back to Douai and roused the concierge for the last time. I was taking a shower at 4 a.m., trying to wash away the evening's depravities, when I was surprised by a *surveillant*: 'It's the first time I ever heard of anyone taking a shower at 4 a.m!' he exclaimed. That, too, became part of my legend at l'Ecole Normale d'Instituteurs du Nord, Douai.

But despite all the dangers and distractions and disapprovals, my year in France had been a profitable one. I had studied and written much more than I realized, as is usually the case with me, though I have the impression that I am bone-lazy, and work only when I feel like it; some latent, inexhaustible energy impels me to be creative. So many times I have stopped writing poetry, and forced myself never to write another line of prose, and yet in spite of myself I find myself compelled, sooner or later, to return to the only thing I know how to do, and I start writing poetry and prose and translations again. In Douai, I had my first real rush of ideas and creative energy, released at last by the vivid strangeness of life that was not British, and that I felt at once strangely at home in.

I had the literary enthusiasms of countless young Frenchmen: the rich revelations of Gide's *Les Nourritures terrestres* and *Paludes* and *Les Faux Monnayeurs* and *Si le grain ne meurt*, that liberating autobiography. I was dazzled and fascinated by Cocteau, a writer whose hidden seriousness seemed to echo my own tightrope tread between irony and sensibility. I deepened my appreciation and understanding of Rimbaud, Verlaine, Huysmans and Proust, and was confronted by the immense monument of Flaubert, the fevered impressionism of Maupassant. I became familiar with all the *poètes damnés* from Villon to Baudelaire to René Crevel, and found in their intensities something of my own disturbances.

But I also discovered a new way of writing, when I picked up Sartre's *La Nausée* in 1938, and his book of short stories, *Le Mur*, in 1939. In them I recognized many of my own problems as a person, a pacifist and a poet, and found a confirmation by a contemporary of my *nostalgie de la boue* – an obsession that was never to leave me. I did not care for any other of Sartre's works, and it was sheer agony to have to translate Simone de Beauvoir's *Mémoires d'une jeune fille rangée* – that almost interminable, humourless menstrual flow that spread like a dull, sick stain over so many subsequent volumes, from the Englishing of which I was mercifully reprieved.

I had been an existentialist without knowing it long before Sartre and de Beauvoir and that lot gave it literary-philosophical airs. I soon saw through their little game and concentrated on the more truly existential works of Jean Genet and the psychological novels of Simenon, who easily surpasses Conrad and Maugham in his evocations of Africa and the South Seas.

I was an existentialist *malgré moi* all through the Second World War and right up to 1959, when I first set foot in Japan and found an existentialism of a totally different kind, far from the moralistic and philosophical clichés in black and white of the rigidly bipolar West.

So I was astonished, and not a little amused, to find Japanese writers aping the existentialists – until the *nouveau roman* came and went. And even in the seventies, Japanese authors like Oe Kenzaburo and Takeshi Kaiko were still clinging to the tenets of long-discredited French existentialism, with Oe Kenzaburo's endlessly boring re-hashes of atomic scenarios, and Takeshi Kaiko's barefaced imitation of *La Nausée* in his pseudo-novel, *Darkness in Summer*.

But that lies in the future, whose ground was being well prepared during that first year in *la belle France*.

Summer in the Alps

1939

During my stay in Douai, I had had my hair cut only once, so by the time I reached London it was a wild blond mane. Its length and brilliance would go unnoticed today, but in those days of 'short-back-and-sides' it appeared scandalous to one of my female cousins who came to meet me: I can still remember the look of shock on her face as she kissed me. I was going to stay with her in London for a couple of nights, and as she lived in a very respectable suburban neighbourhood she at once sent me to the station barber's shop at Victoria. I am amazed to think now that I submitted without protest to this demand: but perhaps I did feel I stood out more than usual in that grim London environment. The barber, as usual in those days, made some facetious remarks about 'haystacks' and 'wigs' and 'mops'. I paid him no heed, but as I paid him, without giving a tip, I let him have a good flash of my 'evil eye'. I wonder what happened to him.

I emerged from his hands all shaven and shorn. Nothing could have better symbolized the difference between my bohemian days in France and the stiff-upper-lip and no-nonsense atmosphere of boring Britain. I think that for most British people who live for any length of time abroad, particularly in the Far East, every return to Britain is a melancholy event, a sad let-down. There is a meanness and dinginess and provincial stuffiness, far removed from the freedoms and differences of foreign lands one loves. I determined that if ever I survived the coming conflict I would get out of the country as quickly as possible; but I had to wait until 1950 before my next trip to Paris.

During my days in London, I raced round art galleries and bookshops, and on my very first night I antagonized my hosts by dashing off after tea to Covent Garden to see Massine and the wonderful new ballet he had created to Brahms' Fourth symphony: the slow movement, with its long, sinuous line of dancers in long, dark red dresses, was unforgettable. I also recall the performances of a shy young pianist I later met in Leeds, Eric Harrison, who performed brilliantly the solo part in Rachmaninoff's *Pagan-*

ini Rhapsody, in a remarkable ballet version by Fokine. I was up in the gods: there were no seats left, and it was standing room only, all the way down to the 'slips'. But I felt I was not only in the gods – I was in very heaven that night.

The train journey back to South Shields was, as always, filled with painful associations: I was deeply moved by the sight of Durham with its castle, cathedral and prison, and by the River Tyne. I was even more moved when I got off the train at Tyne Dock and found my father waiting for me: he looked more than ever like the Danish composer Carl Nielsen, to whose music I had been introduced at Newcastle by Sydney Newman,* an enthusiast for his work. My mother broke into tears as we embraced on the doorstep of our house in West Avenue. It was the first time I had been away from home for so long a period.

But I was soon to be off again. As soon as I got back to the university, I went to see Girdlestone and Dr Mennie in the German Hut. The latter was very concerned about the standard of my German conversation, which had declined while I was in France. So he suggested that I should put an advertisement in a Swiss newspaper – I think it must have been the *Neue Züricher Zeitung* – with a demand for a summer vacation teaching post. He advised me not to go to Germany. I had no money to pay for the advertisement, as I told Dr Mennie. But he just gave me that big, cheerful grin and told me the German Society would pay for it. In fact, I think he paid for it out of his own pocket.

While we were waiting for a reply, I undertook the teaching of English to the many Spanish, Austrian and German refugees who had somehow made their way to Newcastle. Several of the students in the Modern Languages departments volunteered to give this kind of assistance to the poor, bewildered escapees from Hitler and Franco. We felt it was good for our language study, also, for most of the refugees could not speak a word of English. I remember in particular a pathetic middle-aged pair from Vienna, with the picturesque name of Vogelwasser, who hung on my lips, repeating carefully every new word, never taking their eyes off me. I was happy to be doing something, however small, for those unfortunate people.

Meanwhile, in the French Department, Girdlestone was planning to produce Racine's *Iphigénie*, with myself as Achille. . . . He had pronounced himself very satisfied with the progress my French accent had made. But when he asked me to prepare my speech for the French Society on my experiences, for late in the autumn term, I wondered if I should ever be able to do it.

* Professor of Music at King's College, Durham, and an authority on Nielsen.

I received several replies from Switzerland, and Dr Mennie decided I should accept the position of private English tutor to a young lady from a Viennese refugee family now living in Vaduz, in the Principality of Liechtenstein, which at that time was not part of Switzerland.

My journey by third-class slow trains seemed interminable, and when I reached Zürich it was late at night. I could not understand the Swiss telephone system so I decided to spend the night in Zürich, and through the station accommodation bureau got a bed in a private house in Seefeldstrasse. I was too exhausted to eat. I fell asleep at once, and did not wake until eleven o'clock next morning. Eventually I got on a train to Chur, where my young lady was waiting for me in a state of suppressed fury at the delay.

However, when she had calmed down and I had given my explanations, we took a taxi to Vaduz. Her father and mother had escaped to Spain, and were planning to settle in Portugal for the duration of hostilities which they considered inevitable. Meanwhile, the young lady was living in their very comfortable villa with their old cook and her grandmother.

It was a strange, tense period. My pupil was not very patient with my instruction, and she was utterly shocked by my extreme pallor when we sunbathed on the lawn before lunch. I was not very interested in taking mountain walks with her. After my two hours' instruction every morning I preferred to retire to my room and read, or to go off for solitary excursions on my own. A French girl who came to stay nearby became my friend, and I suspect this made the Viennese girl jealous, despite her unconcealed contempt for my 'degeneracy'. There was an excursion to Bad Ragaz, where the French girl and I danced to a local orchestra on an open-air dance floor surrounded by hundreds of drinkers and diners. But my Viennese young lady either could not or would not dance with me: perhaps she thought I looked too peculiar, because again I had begun to let my hair grow long. In the evenings, we played piano duets, sang folk songs and read Goethe's witty *Die Wahlverwandschaften*, bits of which we translated into English for performance as a play.

There was growing political tension, and when Hitler made his alliance with Russia, war became imminent as preparations were being made to invade Poland. It was obvious that Britain and France would soon be at war with Nazi Germany. I could have stayed in neutral Switzerland for the duration of the war, but I felt it was my duty to return home to be with my parents in that dark hour of their lives. They were all alone. I was their only child. I also felt I had to return to Britain in order to declare publicly my disapproval of war, and to register myself as a conscientious objector.

I got on the night express from Chur to Paris – Chur dep. 20.25, arr. Paris Gare de l'Est 7.26 – the times are still the same. It was a train with first class and second class compartments only, and I had a third-class return ticket, and no money to pay the difference. The only other person in my compartment (first class) was a wealthy German or Austrian who had got on at Vienna. We started chatting, and to my horror I discovered that he was an ardent Nazi and a keen supporter of the Berlin-Rome-Tokyo axis. He was obviously some high-ranking official in the Nazi Party. But he was a very charming, cultivated man. Perhaps he was a secret agent? An international spy? He said he was going only as far as Basel.

I began to feel very uncomfortable, talking to a person who by now was probably technically my enemy. I told him that I was a student, and that I had decided to hurry back to England for the outbreak of war. He laughed at this, and said I had made a big mistake. 'Our Herr Hitler will negotiate peace with Poland, France and Britain before the first shot is fired,' he informed me. I thought now that the man must be a complete fool.

But my enemy did something very nice for me. When the ticket-inspector came to our compartment to check our tickets, I felt very embarrassed, and rather frightened. What on earth would I do? Would the ticket-inspector make me get off at the next stop, Zürich? Would I be arrested for travelling first class on a third-class ticket?

While the puzzled Swiss ticket-collector was trying to decide what to do with me, my travelling companion spoke up: 'This young gentleman is a student who in the emergency of a possible outbreak of war has to hurry back to England. It is an exceptional situation, and I am sure the Swiss authorities would regard it as such. Please allow him to continue his journey to Paris.'

The Swiss are very efficient, but they are also very kind and sensible. They know when to be flexible, and not to abide strictly by the letter of the law. They are very civilized in that respect. So the ticket-collector, though he knew he was breaking the rules, allowed me to continue my journey as far as Basel, where I could change to a train for Paris with third-class seats.

I felt deeply grateful to that Swiss ticket-collector; and, of course, to my enemy, whose authoritative manner had allowed him to intervene for me so successfully. When we reached Basel, he tried to persuade me to stay with him for a while at his house there, and to remain in the safety of Switzerland. I could not accept his offer, which I declined politely. As we said goodbye, I felt humiliated as he raised his right arm in the Nazi salute and said: 'Heil Hitler!'

I responded with a rude gesture of the middle finger of my right hand – 'Up you!' – though I am not sure if he understood this example of British body language. Perhaps he did, for his parting words to me were: 'Whatever happens, never forget that the Germans want peace with Britain. Your own Royal Family is largely of German origin. Why should we want to fight with our friends, our relatives? It is Winston Churchill who is responsible! I heard his speech in Munich last year. At once I knew he was a warmonger. He is your British bulldog, yes. But bulldogs can be savage beasts! He is far worse than our good Herr Hitler. You will see!'

His face had turned red with fury, and he marched away without any further salutes in the Nazi style, to my great relief. All through that long night on the train, I pondered over what he had said, and found I partly agreed with him. As a pacifist, I had always loathed Churchill. As a socialist, I disliked his upper-class accent and arrogance. As a writer, I deplored his bombast, his pompous, windy style and cheap, melodramatic rhetoric. It was not much different from Hitler's, I thought. And of course I believed that the British Government would be utterly wrong to declare war. What are our diplomats for, if not to negotiate? Not to appease, as Chamberlain had done at Munich, but always to negotiate, negotiate, negotiate – anything rather than another bloody war! But the British Government, its diplomats and its politicians, were to my mind totally incompetent. They were failing in their first duty, which was to preserve peace. I felt as if I were at war, not with Germany, but with my own country. I could do nothing except to refuse to fight in their disgusting war. Such a small personal protest would be utterly meaningless. But I had to make it.

On the French railways, there was already chaos and panic. The train, after it passed the Swiss border, filled up with French troops who just sat anywhere and packed the corridors. All through that awful night, at every stop – Mulhouse, Metz, Belfort – soldiers and more soldiers joined the already-packed train. No ticket-inspector could pass along the overcrowded corridors. Fortunately, I had a seat. But I could not sleep.

The windows of the Gare de l'Est had been blacked-out with a sort of royal blue distemper. I spent my last francs on a taxi to the Gare St Lazare, and went without breakfast. On that journey across Paris, I was amazed to see crowds of people sitting in the morning sun outside cafés, sipping coffee and apéritifs as if they did not have a care in the world: it was the celebrated French *insouciance* again. The Gare de l'Est and the Gare St Lazare were both milling with troops called up to the colours. They, too, seemed cheerful and insouciant. That spirit was to last right through the *drôle de guerre*, as if they were all playing at being soldiers, until the unbelievable fall of France. The blue-painted peacock-tail windows of the Gare de l'Est and the colossal glass roofs of the Gare St Lazare's dark azure skies shed a subdued radiance, a mysterious, melancholy shade. But outside, the skies were really blue and hot with summer sunshine. I got on one of the last ferries from Dieppe to Newhaven. In London, I hung around Piccadilly, and made a few scores, making enough money to enable me to stay the night and return home with something over for my parents. I told them I had made the extra cash by doing translations, which was not altogether wrong, for prostitution is a kind of translation. Blacked-out London was an ideal place for illicit rendezvous. . . .

I reached home in time to hear the announcement of war over the radio, and to listen to the false alarm of the first air-raid warning siren.

PART TWO

War

'Where Poland draws her Eastern bow. . . .'

A Poet at War

1940

On the day the results of the final examinations came out, the 'phoney war' ended, and Tyneside received its first heavy air raid by German Nazi bombers. After going to the university in the late afternoon to find out what kind of a degree I had received (a second-class, division 2), I did not attend the final tea-party given by the students of my year. I felt I would not be able to hide my disappointment, and that I might burst into tears. So I took the bus back home to West Avenue, and had a late tea with my parents. My father came back from work at Binns Department Store in King Street, where he now had a regular job as the house joiner, looking tired and hot on that ominous summer's day. I waited until he had washed and had his tea, then I told him the result.

I shall never forget how he just smiled at me, and said: 'It doesn't matter, Jim.'

'Of course it doesn't,' my mother added, with a laugh. 'You did the best you could.'

I felt like crying then, because I knew only too well that, from the conventional academic point of view, I had not done my best at all. I had studied only to please myself, not to please Girdle Scone. I realized that at that university, first-class degrees were given only for good behaviour. My friend David, for all his brilliance and high intelligence, had only received a third-class degree the year before. If that was their standard, I was glad not to be judged by it. All the goody-goody girls in my year had got first-class degrees, and I regarded them as little better than idiots.

Of course, in those days, we used to think that a university degree was terribly important, and that a poor degree could end one's hopes of a successful career. How mistaken that was! Whatever successes I have had in later years were quite independent of my university degree. There was something almost pathetically comic in the solemnity with which students in those days used to regard the acquisition of a first-class honours degree.

I wanted to forget it all, to shove all my sad and bitter memories of my university days into the dark cupboard of the past and let them rot there for ever. So as darkness was falling I went out for a long walk to Marsden and along the clifftop paths to Frenchman's Bay and Trow Rocks. It was a beautiful moonlit night, and the sea, the bays and the beaches had a dreamlike emptiness. I encountered no one. At that period, the coastal area must still not have been off limits for civilians, because I remember that walk so well. It took me about three hours to reach the pier approaches, and now I am not quite sure whether I was able to walk along the pier. It was a calm night, but something I wrote about walking along the pier around that time seems to suggest that there were some heavy waves breaking over it:

> I walk the long, dark pier that bends out of the seaport's empty streets into the unlit centre of the northern sea. No moon shines there, so far out. But it shimmers on the waves that keep washing across the sands with plumes of phosphorescent spray. Slowly I leave the land's hard lights behind, and turn to the deadly power of the stars, the full moon's malignance racked in clouds.
>
> The sea runs on either side of me, banging the stone defences of an endless sleep with bitter tons of salt that fly in fits of foam. Only the lighthouse at the end is true. To touch its burning tip will give me life. I shall not reach it if the gates are shut against the storm that now is rising.

But though the gates are shut, the lighthouse reaches me. I walked along that pier so many times, usually at night, and often I was the only person walking there. My ghost will haunt that pier when I am dead. I remember my mother telling me how she loved to walk along it on stormy days, and would stand clinging to the iron railing fixed in the wall's massive blocks of stone, letting huge fountains of spray arch right over her. She did this even when she was pregnant with me. No wonder the sea is one of my passions.

As I was walking up Fowler Street, the air-raid sirens sounded. It was so unexpected. They had not been heard, except for practices, since that fateful morning the year before when war had been declared against Germany. The awful ululations had a sickening menace. It was very late, nearly midnight. There were no trams or buses running, and I was the only person on the streets. I started to run, my heart beating loudly with fear. As I ran up Westoe Lane, the sirens stopped, and there was an eerie silence, broken only by the sound of my running feet and by my panting breath. Somewhere around Westoe Village I heard an air raid warden shouting to me to take cover, but I took no notice of him and went on running towards Caldwell, where the park lay still under the moon.

I had to stop for a moment to get my breath. Then for the first time I heard the sound of German bombers overhead, dozens of them, flying in from across the North Sea: they had a distinctive sound, a rhythm of the engines that we were to become very familiar with during the next five years. It was an almost obscene pulsing sound, quite different from the sound of our own planes.

'Take cover!' another air-raid warden shouted at me as I started running again, but his next words were lost in the sudden barrage of anti-aircraft shells from the ground defences, situated some distance away, I think, at Whitburn Colliery, but sounding as if they were right beside me. The impact of those massive bursts of anti-aircraft fire half-stunned me, but I kept on running. I knew I had to get home as soon as possible, otherwise my mother and father would begin to worry. They would by now be in the Anderson shelter we had dug in our garden.

The evil throbbing of the engines of the German planes could be heard quite plainly now above the anti-aircraft firing. Then bombs started falling, fortunately some distance away from me. I began to panic. I did not know which way to run. Then I remembered some advice to civilians that had been issued in the event of one's being caught on the streets in the middle of an air-raid: it said that we were to seek shelter in the nearest house. I stopped running, hardly knowing where I was, and knocked on the first door I saw. No answer. The bombs and anti-aircraft fire were deafening, and I was shaking with terror. I knocked again on the door. And again, harder.

Finally it was opened. In front of me I saw a little old man in his pyjamas, holding a black-out torch which he shone suspiciously on my face.

He asked an unnecessary question. 'What do you want?' Strong Geordie accent.

Shrapnel was falling in the street. I answered, panting: 'Can you let me take shelter here for a while?'

'Shelter?' he muttered. 'What for?'

'There's an air raid on,' I answered.

'What's your name? Let me see your National Identity Card.'

'I don't have it on me.'

'What do you want to come waking me up for in the middle of the night? I had just got to sleep. Go on, young man, get yourself off home or I'll call the police. I'm in the Home Guard, I'd like you to know.'

He slammed the door in my face just as a particularly bad blast struck me, nearly lifting me off my feet.

Despite the danger and the seriousness of my situation, I was suddenly convulsed with laughter as I remembered the sight of that little old man in his droopy pyjamas claiming to belong to the Home Guard and refusing to give me shelter.

I waited by his gate for a moment and the noise seemed to be abating a little, so I started off jogging again towards home. On and on I ran, alone in the wartime streets, with the air battles between German planes and Spitfires going on overhead, the bombs falling, the shrapnel rattling the roofs of houses, the anti-aircraft guns booming and barking. From time to time I took shelter in someone's doorway. It was very odd: everything was blacked-out, of course, and only a thin, dim ray of light came from each street lamp. But everyone seemed to be sleeping – everyone except me. With all my experience of loneliness, I had never felt so lonely, or so vulnerable, as at that time.

Finally I reached home and dashed into our air-raid shelter, where my mother and father were sitting patiently, drinking cups of tea from a flask. Our next-door neighbours were sharing the shelter with us. My mother silently poured me a cup of hot tea, as I told them of my nightmare run back home. After a while, the bombers left, and we went to bed. It had all been like a surrealist dream.

It was the end of the 'phoney war' – what Edward Blishen, in a fascinating semi-fictionalized memoir, called 'A Cackhanded War'. With all my academic problems and miseries, I had hardly noticed the fall of France. If anything, I looked upon it as a just revenge on the sort of French civilization the Girdle Scone stood for, and I welcomed it as a kick in the teeth for him.

My own private war against war, and against life itself, had started a year before, when I received, to my utter horror, my call-up papers. I was exempted from military service until I had taken my degree, but I had no intention whatsoever of being conscripted against my will to satisfy the demands of an incompetent beurocracy, and of a Government whose leaders I regarded as imbeciles and upper-class thugs. So I knew I was going to register some kind of protest: the best way to do it was to declare myself a conscientious objector to war, and to conscription.

Some of the books I had been reading confirmed me in this resolve. Among them were *Le Feu* by Henri Barbusse and Céline's *Voyage au bout de la nuit*. I had been deeply impressed by Norman Angell's *The Great Illusion*, and by the works of Max Plowman, whose early book of verse, *The Golden Heresy** I had discovered in a second-hand bookstore in Newcastle

* Published in 1914.

market in 1938. I had been attracted by the final item in the book, a dramatic dialogue between Mary and Martha awaiting the arrival of Jesus with Lazarus, and by a neat quatrain that seemed to speak to my own need at the time when I was feeling caged and almost oppressed by my parents' unrelenting love; the poem is called 'Mandatum Novum':

> Wean your love, O wean your love!
> Teach him to run alone;
> Or you will find your sucking dove
> Into a vulture grown.

I had read some of his essays in various pacifist left-wing magazines like John Middleton Murray's *The Adelphi*, and in *The Aryan Path*. These essays were later collected in *The Right to Live** with introductions by Murray and by Plowman's wife. I was interested to learn from her that it was being stationed at Whitley Bay during the First World War which had revealed to Max the necessity of pacifism. He was court-martialled for resigning his commission, declaring at his trial:

> If governments in the past have acted upon the belief that they could, when they thought fit, call upon men to destroy one another, the only way to prevent them from doing this again is to refuse to make good the Government's unwarrantable assumption. If it is said that the middle of a war is no fit time to come to such a conclusion, I reply that every moment is opportune in which to cease to do evil and learn to do well. We have no right to continue in an evil course because our behaviour in the past has led others to expect this of us.... Killing men is killing God.... Murder done in the heat of passion: rape committed through uncontrollable lust: treachery due to moral weakness, are venial sins compared with the crime of calmly resolving to destroy the lives of unknown persons.†

But the work by Plowman that influenced me most of all was *The Faith Called Pacifism*‡, which I read at the end of my schooldays. What attracted me to this work, the first I encountered by Plowman, was its epigraph from Milton's 'Samson Agonistes':

* In 1942.

† This magnificent statement of personal belief by a soldier who discovered the meaning of death in the Battle of the Somme is printed in full in the Appendix at the end of *Bridge into the Future: Letters of Max Plowman* (Andrew Dakers, 1944).

‡ Published by Dent in 1936.

Oh how comely it is and how reviving
To the Spirits of just men long opprest!
When God into the hands of thir deliverer
Puts invincible might
To quell the mighty of the Earth, th'oppressor,
The brute and boist'rous force of violent men
Hardy and industrious to support
Tyrannic power, but raging to pursue
The righteous and all such as honour Truth;
He all thir Ammunition
And feats of War defeats
With plain Heroic magnitude of mind
And celestial vigour arm'd,
Thir Armories and Magazins contemns,
Renders them useless, while
With winged expedition
Swift as the lightning glance he executes
His errand on the wicked, who surpris'd
Lose thir defence distracted and amaz'd.
  But patience is more oft the exercise
  Of Saints, the trial of thir fortitude,
  Making them each his own Deliverer,
  And Victor over all
  That tyrannie or fortune can inflict. . . .

My pacifism began when I was a child. I remember sitting on my father's knee, around the age of three, and listening to his stories of the Great War. They filled me with horror. It made an indelible impression upon me when he told me that all able-bodied men had to fight in the war, and that some of them had to kill their fellow men. The question I then asked my father is one of the earliest memories I have: 'Did *all* men have to fight in the war?' At that, he gave a laugh, and said the only ones who did not fight were the 'conchies', and he explained the term 'conscientious objector' to me. At once I replied that I would be a 'conchie' if ever there were another war.

'Don't worry, son,' he replied. 'That was a war to end all wars. There will never be another.'

I believed him, and I remember the rush of relief that I felt when he said those words: they were as memorable as the words 'conscientious objector'. I remembered those words when I read, in *The Faith Called Pacifism*, these sentences:

> In the year 1914, many inducements were offered and many promises made for the purpose of persuading the civil population of these islands to resist what then appeared to be the supreme threat against democratic liberty. Among these, none was more potent in drawing men to the colours than the promise contained in the slogan, 'Never Again'. Many thousands of pacifically minded citizens made what has since been called the great sacrifice on the strength of this promise.... They volunteered 'for the duration', and died to fulfil their part in the promise 'Never Again'....
>
> Promises, however rash, given to men in exchange for their lives, are sacred; and if we, as members of the nation which made that promise, are not prepared to fulfil it, then the blood of the men slain in the war is upon our heads.
>
> We can only avert the vengeance of Fate on behalf of the slain by dedicating our lives to the fulfilment of that promise, which means in effect by a corresponding offering of 'all we have and are' to the promotion of peace and concord in the world that began on 11th November 1918....
>
> The Cenotaph and every war memorial in the country and on the battlefields ... mock the unhappy dead.... Fascism, both in Italy and Germany, is now recognized as one of the direct consequences of the Treaty of Versailles.

I have another early memory, though not as early as that first one. It belongs to the period when Italy invaded Abyssinia. We had a truly remarkable and wonderful woman teacher of French and German, Miss Robinson, a person I deeply admired and indeed loved. She more than anyone at that time of emotional and intellectual confusion in my adolescent life showed me understanding, encouragement and sympathy. It was she who casually asked the class to translate into French Wordsworth's sonnet 'On Sleep', and, because I alone in all the class made a verse translation, showed me the way towards making creative versions of poetry and prose.

However, she was an ardent admirer of Adolf Hitler, and in that she was like many people of the period, including some of our own politicians. During the summer holidays, she used to travel to Germany, and would come back in September with stories about how she had attended Nazi rallies, and been thrilled by the sight of 'der Führer'. She truly believed him to be a great man. Incredible as it may sound today, she taught her classes to sing the 'Horst Wessel Lied', whose melody I thought was very fine, and I can still remember the words:

Die Fahnen hoch! Die Reihen fest geschlossen!
S.A. marschiert, mit ruhig-festem Schritt.
Kamaraden, die Rotfront und Reaktion erschossen,
Marschiern im Geist in unseren Reihen mit!

I still possess copies of the magazine *Unser Lager: Our Camp*, published in German and English by the Deutsch-Englischer Kreis in Germany and the Anglo-German Circle in England. These groups promoted visits to Germany and England by young people, and provided information on books, contacts and meetings. These were illustrated reports of mutual visits by English boy scouts and German Jungvolk. Mervyn Thompson, in the second issue, writes about English public schools and in particular Bryanston, illustrating it with a photograph of the serried ranks of Bryanston Pioneers. Someone signing himself 'Rudi' gives an account of meetings between German youths and boy scouts in Dorchester, while another illustrated article shows a model airplane competition and a military training parade of boys at the 'Nationalpolitische Erziehungsanstalt' or 'National-political Training Institute', a kind of Cadet Corps school. Girls were not neglected either, and Rose Kerr describes the visits of English groups to the Bund Deutscher Mädel (Union of German Girls – though the German title is much more emotive than that) in Cologne and in towns and villages along the Rhine:

> ... At every place to which we came there sprang up to greet us with unfailing regularity, two maidens, in the simple and attractive dress ('uniform' is too military a word for it) of the BDM – a dark blue skirt, with short-sleeved blouse and black neckerchief.... There cannot be a spirit of hate and revenge in the Germany of the future if these girls are to be the wives and mothers of the race....

This was written in 1935. There is also a page of photographs showing Hitler-Jugend groups and British boy scouts, together with pictures of their respective badges: that of the Hitler Youth is a lozenge with a swastika at the centre.

And at the end of the magazine there are two camp-fire songs, one of them 'Loch Lomond', the other, '*Auf, hebt unsre Fahnen in den frischen Morgenwind*' ('Raise our flags on high in the fresh morning wind'), and the first verse cries at the end: '*Sie weichen alle unserm Siegeslauf!*' (They all fall back before our victory surge.) Ambassador v. Ribbentrop contributes a speech that begins, with ominous nationalism, 'We in Germany.... We believe in a strong Europe and a strong British Empire.'

I feel that much of this flapdoodle was springing from a genuine desire for peace and international understanding, and that some, at least, of the contributors were making honourable efforts to bridge the gaps between the two countries. There was an innocent enthusiasm for a new way of life that seemed to be putting Germany, the fallen enemy, on her feet again. It was this kind of idealistic fervour I imagine inspired Miss Robinson's paeans of praise for Herr Hitler, and the whole class was swept away by her obvious sincerity, so that we wholeheartedly practised the Nazi salute, shouting at the tops of our voices 'Heil Hitler!' without any sense of incongruity.

However, when Mussolini invaded Abyssinia, I remember she asked the boys in our class if they would fight to defend their country as the Abyssinians were fighting to defend theirs, and all the boys answered 'Yes'. Excepting me: I said 'No.' And when the teacher asked me why, I replied that I believed it was wrong to fight. At that age, I could not put my feelings into better words. She seemed pleased by my answer, and defended me against the hostility and contempt it aroused among my classmates. For a long time after that, I was called a traitor and subjected to systematic bullying or being 'sent to Coventry'. I did not care. I had no friends in any case, so the animosity of my classmates meant nothing to me. I kept it all secret from my parents. Now I realize that Miss Robinson must have admired Mussolini, too. After all, he was her idol Hitler's ally, and there were many British people who shared her views. So my resounding 'No' in answer to her question must have seemed to her support for her beliefs. After all, Baden-Powell, the founder of the boy scout movement (which I adamantly refused to join) said in 1937: 'I think the time has come when we, in the British movement at any rate, ought to do something to be friendly with the Hitler Youth.'* The chief scout had apparently not heard of *Unser Lager: Our Camp*, despite all the emotional links it tried to create between the two youth movements.

All these memories were in my mind when I became eligible to be conscripted for National Service. It was a dreadful shock to my parents when I informed them that I had no intention of taking any part whatsoever in the war effort and that I was going to register as a conscientious objector. I felt that I had been betrayed, that a solemn promise, 'Never Again', had been broken, a promise that had been given me by my own father.

I think my mother minded less than he did. She knew I would never make a soldier. It was one of the rare occasions when I saw my father angry: his face turned white and he addressed me in a contemptuous way that distressed me all the more in that I knew he was not being true to his own gentle character. As is my custom when arguments start, I remained silent. 'There's no arguing with him,' my father told my mother, who was also sitting silently, letting the horror of this moment pass by with as little

* This is reported, along with many other Fascist remarks, in *The Character Factory: Baden-Powell and the Origins of the Boy Scout Movement* by Michael Rosenthal (Collins, 1986).

interference as possible. I feel she must have been secretly thankful that her only child would not have to fight, even if he had to go to prison for his beliefs, which I assured my parents I was fully prepared to do.

That silenced my father for a while. Then he said something to me that shocked me more than my anti-war protests could ever have shocked him. He said: 'You'll find plenty of "friends" in the army or the navy.' The look he gave me when he said 'friends' and the contemptuous tone he put into the word struck me to the heart and are seared into my memory. His words made it plain that though he disapproved of homosexuality he was prepared to allow it in me if only I would spare him the embarrassment, shame and humiliation of what to him was an even greater disaster, my refusal to join the forces.

Since about the age of ten, I had grown away from my father because I had seen him get rather drunk with my Uncle Bob at my cousin Lyallie's wedding in the Felling. I had been brought up to regard 'drink' as a dreadful sin. As we staggered home with my drunken father, my mother on one side and me on the other, trying to support him without attracting the attention of passers-by and the neighbours, I felt for the first time a deep revulsion for my poor father, and I was pitiless as only a child can be towards his failing. For years, we who had loved one another so much remained cold and distant. I could hardly bear to look at him or speak to him. Yet he continued drinking in the local pubs, though he was never a heavy drinker – he could not afford to be, and a pint of bitter was about as much as he took after dinner. I now think the reason he went to the pub was for male companionship and friendly talk about masculine things, in which I was not at all interested. He must have been deeply disappointed in his son's growing effeminacy, because he never took me out walking with him, never took me to a football match at Horsley Hill – and I was curious to see what a professional game was like, though the sport bored me.

Another hurtful moment was when, one evening after supper, in the presence of my cousin Lyallie and my mother, he attacked me with brutal words: 'You're growing into a proper nancy-boy, with your long hair and all this book-reading.' There was more in the same vein, but as was my wont I remained silent, refusing to react in any way until the storm had passed over.

I felt I would never be able to forgive him for those remarks, for being drunk, and for what he said to me when I told him I was a conscientious objector. But in the end, I found I could forgive him, though I could never forget. And he began to accept my pacifist position long before the war ended with the disgusting slaughters of Hiroshima, Nagasaki, Hamburg and Dresden. In the end, he told me: 'You were right, Jim.' At those words, I felt my heart fill again with the love and admiration I had felt for him as a little boy, before the deep trauma created in me by his drunkenness and his attacks on my appearance, my girlish ways and my romantic affection for other boys. In the end, he accepted my homosexuality, and when, at Corsham, where I was lecturing at Bath Academy of Art, the villagers and even some of the so-called artists and intellectuals on the staff denounced my sexual preferences – in fact, I was bisexual but they interpreted it in an ignorant way – he felt sympathy for me, and I remember him saying: 'It's all a lot of nonsense, Jim, take no notice of them. They're beneath contempt.' I am still not sure why my behaviour caused such an uproar in that poky, prejudiced little village community of gossips and scandal-mongers. As I have said before, I was completely unaware of the effect I had on other people. I was just being myself. What was wrong with that?

For me, one good thing emerged from the war: my mother and father learned to accept my pacifism and my sexuality. The war, when it came at last, seemed to be a fatal resolution of our deep family conflicts, but as it proceeded towards its horrifying end, we had reached an understanding of one another deeper than we had ever known before. That was the only victory I could celebrate, and I celebrated it by drinking with my father and mother a bottle of Algerian wine – cheap Sidi Brahmin, that to us tasted like the nectar of the gods.

But I had to register my conscientious objection, and in due course I made my first appearance before a magistrate, the gruesomely patriotic old Tory, Judge Richardson, in Newcastle upon Tyne. The date was 7 December 1939. I was told that I did not have the remotest chance of obtaining exemption from military service, because Judge Richardson had only the day before received word that his son had been killed in action. For my part, I was hoping that this personal tragedy would have made him less tolerant of modern warfare. But it was not to be so.

In fear and trembling, I entered the witness-box. There were some pacifist sympathizers in court to hear my first appeal. I carried with me a copy of Rilke's poems, one of the volumes in the brown-bound collected edition from the university library. I was sorry to learn that Judge Richardson had thought I was carrying a copy of the New Testament, and that he had expected a defence on the grounds of religion. But I had decided that I could only object to military service on ethical and – this was the very original twist I brought into the case – aesthetic grounds. Indeed, I felt that modern warfare was the height of ugliness, both spiritual and physical, and that the claptrap of patriotic jargon spouted by politicians as well as the windy oratory of Churchill were defilements of the English language. And I said so. The judge turned purple with fury. I can still remember his puffy, fat old face growing red with indignation as I expressed my contempt for the Government, and for Winston Churchill in particular. I called him a 'war-monger'.

In my 'Application to Local Tribunal by a Person Provisionally Registered in the Register of Conscientious Objectors', issued by the Office of the Ministry of Labour and National Service, there was a section headed: 'Any statement you wish to submit in support of your application should be made below.' The first part of my statement was taken from Max Plowman's *The Faith Called Pacifism*; after making the brief personal statement that 'my conscientious objection is based on ethical and aesthetic grounds,' I proceeded to quote Max thus:

> In all wars the ends do not justify the means. The evil means of war have always brought evils ends, and will always do so. Killing is no cure for wickedness. The existence of this moral principle is unaffected by the causes and aims of any war, and is a reasonable imperative to those who know that, however plausible the occasions of war and however outrageous the actions of those who precipitate it, existent evil cannot but be increased by the barbarity and personal injustice of war.

I remember I delivered this half-turned to the court, a very tactless stance that must have infuriated the judge even more than my quotation from Plowman, which he naturally failed to recognize. Then I went on, in my own words:

> I object as a poet, as a thinking artist, to methods of violence which are patently unaesthetic and degrading, and which constitute a negation of all beauty as men through the ages have known it, a negation of cultural progress, a negation of all aesthetic appreciation, a negation of the living soul. I therefore renounce this war, refuse to take part in or be even indirectly responsible for the mass slaughter of innocent men, women and children by the ignoble methods of modern warfare.
>
> I need hardly add that I have held these views from the age when I was first able to think sanely and humanely and without fear.

Judge Richardson countered this by growling: 'Kipling did his bit.' To which I audaciously replied: 'The best critics do not think very highly of Rudyard Kipling.' This was a remark widely publicized in the newspapers, and one which I am told inspired T. S. Eliot to publish his sycophantic essay and selection of Kipling's poems for Faber and Faber.

My defence of my opinions had been deliberately provocative, and, to say the least of it, pompous and hot-headed. But in those days I was not ashamed to arrogate to myself the name of poet. I knew I was a poet. But there was no need to trumpet it abroad in a way that made it seem self-serving. That is the only thing I dislike about my statement. Naturally, my application was rejected out of hand by Judge Richardson, as I had expected it to be. I left the court still clutching my copy of Rilke and glad that I had made a stand, however wrong-headed and unsuccessful.

A few months later, I was again before a tribunal, in London this time, in Westminster, at Church House, of all places. By that time I had moderated my views, and felt I was prepared to join the Friends' Ambulance Unit or to do work on the land. The chairman of the Appeals Tribunal was the distinguished historian H. A. L. Fisher, whose books I had read with pleasure. I pleaded my case as briefly as possible, avoiding the emotional rhetoric of my first hearing in Newcastle. Fisher was urbane and sarcastic, and made several demeaning remarks about my rather-too-precious personal appearance, and made cruel fun of my poetry. But he granted my request to do alternative service in ambulance work or on the land. It was not without a certain satisfaction that I read next day that he had been knocked down and killed by a bus on coming out of my tribunal.

Fisher's final spiteful remark before he dismissed me from the court was: 'If you take up land work, you will be able to see plenty of beautiful poetic sunrises on the farm.' I gave him my usual faint but withering smile, and a flash of the evil eye, but otherwise admitted no reaction. I remember he looked at me a moment in astonishment and perhaps with a touch of alarm. An hour or so later, he was dead. But his prediction came true. I saw many sunrises – six years of them – on the land.

A fellow conscientious objector invited me to have dinner at a Chinese restaurant in Piccadilly Circus, to celebrate the granting of our appeals.

On the way home from King's Cross, I read 'A Declaration from the Harmless and Innocent People of God, called Quakers, 1660':

> We utterly deny all outward wars and strife, and fightings with weapons for any end, or under any pretence whatever: this is our testimony to the whole world. The Spirit of Christ by which we are guided is not changeable, so as once to command turning from a thing as evil and again to move unto it; and we certainly know and testify to the world, that the Spirit of Christ, which leads us into all truth, will never move us to fight any war against any man with outward weapons, neither for the kingdom of Christ nor for the kingdoms of this world.

I had already been attracted towards the Society of Friends, and in these grave and noble words the implications of the words 'outward weapons' interested me. I took them to mean that one could fight wars with the inward weapons of the mind and the spirit, with human reason and intelligence. This I was certainly prepared to do.

Is this what is meant by 'heaping coals of fire' upon one's enemy's head? If so, it appealed to an aggressiveness within me that, as a pacifist, I was reluctant to admit. It was part of the un-moral anarchist in me. But in my heart of hearts, I knew I wanted peace – for the world, and for myself.

One Day in the Middle of a War

1940–3

There was a kind of peace in the midst of war when I was sent to my first job as a conscientious objector. It was as a labourer in a vast, impersonal tree-planting project by the Forestry Commission among the wilds of the North Tyne that were being rendered grim and faceless by gigantic oblongs of Sitka spruce and Norwegian pine divided by dead-straight rides: all the wild beauty of the region had been severely brought to heel by these repressive and depressing afforestation programmes. There was day after day of back-breaking work in rain and snow. But it was here that I began to write prose, for which the writing of poetry was the best possible training. I wrote many stories about my daily life on those bleak moors and hillsides. One of them was called 'One Day in the Middle of a War', and can hardly be called fiction, for every detail is true, even to the 'met a bomber' heard every morning on the BBC News in Norwegian: I now know it was the Norwegian for 'meter band' I was hearing as I struggled into my army surplus greatcoat just before 7 a.m.

'Aye, it'll be a skitterin' sort of a day', Auld Andra remarked. We didn't look at the sky, but trudged up the ride behind the old Scotsman in a sleepy, silent single file.

The sun was rising in the late November mists, and trying to pierce through thick wads of rain cloud driven by a keening wind. It had just gone seven. We had left the labour camp at the end of the news in Norwegian, while the Norwegian announcer was rattling off the now-familiar phrases of the weather forecast, that sounded something like 'met a bomber, met a bomber'.

It was cold and damp. We shivered in our ancient clothes and our feet squelched already in worn-out wellingtons. The ride was a broad band of mud running due east across the bare Northumberland moors. It went on unswervingly like a Roman military road, hesitating at nothing, not even the steepest glensides or the darkest clump of pines.

We struggled along, hands in pockets, battling against the rain-pricked wind. We plodded higher and higher, leaving behind the drenched windrows of former afforestations, until we reached the topmost crest of the moors. Here there were no more trees or coverts. We were alone and tiny under a low dome of grey sky that descended all around us to a bleak, featureless horizon.

Once, with a metallic clatter of wings and a strange, hysterical cackle of frightened complaint, a grouse rose up almost from under our feet, followed in a few seconds by another, the hen bird.

'I wish I'd had me gun,' Auld Andra grumbled. 'Gey fat birds they be.'

We trudged on in silence, our old rags flapping, our feet treading up spouts of muddy water. It had rained all week. The beck somewhere in the hidden brae below us was thundering over its granite boulders. Andra broke our silence now and then with a remark about the weather or the day's work. It was always like this in the early mornings, having to leave the Nissen hut, the snug stove, the tin mugs of tea and the news just coming on over the antiquated wireless.

Not that we were particularly interested in the news. We heard it at night sometimes, listening as if to matters that did not concern us, that could have no bearing at all on our way of life. In that isolated part of Northumberland, on the North Tyne, miles away from anywhere, living by candlelight and lamplight in the midst of dreary desolation, we might have been in Siberia, and all war news had a quality of remoteness and unreality. During the long, tedious hours we spent on the fells each day, sometimes we would wonder where the German bombs had fallen the night before, or if the planes we had heard thrumming northwards over our camp had again struck at Glasgow or Belfast. Occasionally a Nazi plane would jettison its cargo of bombs on the moors before crashing, and I once found a dying German airman who had parachuted into a deserted glen. I was able to talk to him in German before he died in my arms. That was the nearest we ever came to war.

Rain began to fall sharply. 'Ah, to hell,' said Ralphie, the Tees-sider, a middle-aged ex-coalminer with the whole air and tradition of the pits about him, even here. He and Andra left the ride and we stumbled after them towards a small glen, at the bottom of which was a group of stunted pines surrounded by a dry-stone wall on whose loose limestone rocks grew delicate pale green brains of lichen.

Young Tom at the end of the line suddenly broke into a run, and Charlie, his mate, followed him, both whooping with joy at the steady downpour. (For regulations said that if it rained hard enough and long enough to wet us through to the skin we were allowed to go back to the camp to do inside jobs. However wet we got, we were rarely sent back. But we always hoped silently for a thorough soaking, though we older ones never showed such open gladness as Tom and Charlie did when the rain began to pour down.)

When we had reached a good sheltering tree in the middle of the covert, we were all thoroughly awake and more cheerful.

'I hope she pisses down,' Tom fervently prayed, lighting with a grimace the herbal cigarette that was supposed to be good for his asthma, but seemed to make him wheeze all the more, and made us all cough with its stink. Charlie lit up some filthy wartime Turkish fag, a 'Pasha' probably. Andra, Ralphie and I drew out pipes and scratched up a few scraps of shag from the corners of our pouches. We'd had no tobacco rations for weeks. Andra cut a thin slice of pigtail-like twist and began to chew it, neglecting his pipe. From time to time he would spit out a stream of rich brown tobacco juice with a kind of disgusted pleasure.

'Ah, it'll no be lang afore it's ower,' Andra growled, as a pale blue break appeared momentarily in the clouds. He was a local, a native of Hawick, a hard and steady worker, by far the oldest of us. The rest of us had once belonged to the unemployed of Tyneside, Wearside and Tees-side. In conversation, the old familiar names would come out nostalgically – Ferryhill, Blaydon, Consett, Cullercoats, Birtley, Chester-le-Street, Pity Me, Jarrow, Sedgefield, Durham. We had all been sent from the distressed areas of north-east England ('depressed' areas we called them) on some government scheme. We had come in the hope of finding a new life and a decent wage in the forests. I was the only conscientious objector; afforestation was part of my wartime service.

We had been here two years. Many of the men who had come from the pit towns and villages could not endure the solitude and the wildness, and had gone back to the dole queue, the unpaid rent and, now, the bombings. In those two years the work had been laborious and unchanging, the money small and eaten away by illness. We had expected to find standing timber to fell and log at good prices. Instead we had been given these endless acres and shires of bog and moor and steep-sided, stony glens to drain and sod-plant with young trees.

Day after day passed in work that was heavy and heartbreakingly monotonous in the vast sweep of silence and rain-lashed desolation. The one sign of life, which we looked for eagerly at midday, was the small plume of white steam pushing slowly along the distant fellside – the train from Hexham moving up the valley through Plashetts, Kielder, Deadwater, under Peel Fell and Slaughtree to Riccarton in Liddisdale. When we saw the steam from the train we would stop and eat our scanty rations. We were supposed to stop at 12.30, but mostly we stopped a quarter of an hour, or more, before time. We had a decent ganger, a young Ministry of Afforestation trainee from the Forest of Dean, who turned a blind eye if he happened to arrive and found us sitting down a few minutes before or after the official snack times.

'Clearing,' pronounced Ralphie, tightening his white silk muffler, always the sign of a coalminer, and straightening his limp-peaked cloth cap.

'Aye, it'll be on and off like this a' day, men,' Andra said. 'Niver enow tae get us sappin'-wet, but we'll be gaein' hame like drooned rats a' the same.' He spat, and moved out from under the dripping pines. Ralphie followed, and the rest of us joined them one by one, reluctantly. We began trudging on again, back up the glenside to the top of the windswept moorland; but we were not as glum as before.

'It still looks promising,' said Young Tom, and pointed towards the black clouds gathered below the sodden sun.

We got to the place where we had left off work the night before. It was certainly looking like rain again. We could see Joey, the young ganger, coming over the rise in the ride, walking fast in his kilt and swinging cape, but still a good way off. Charlie, big and raw-boned, wearing khaki mittens over his chapped schoolboy hands and a big red tam-o'-shanter on his rough ginger hair, threw off his coat, laid it over his army surplus canvas knapsack and with a bold, brief display of energy began to dig furiously. After two or three minutes he stopped and lit a half-smoked cigarette. We all took off our topcoats and each man laid his coat over his bag.

'We'd best be started when he comes,' said Andra, and he began to dig into the soggy turf steadily, cutting it in two parallel lines about a foot apart, then chopping it up into foot-square sods which I dragged out with a hook and laid out in neat rows for the planters. In all the two years we had been there, we had seen no sign of planters, though we had covered whole glensides and acres of flat moorland plateau with our regularly laid-out hummocks of sod. The landscape had the look of a checkerboard, on which we were the humble pawns.

The others took up their spades, filed their edges sharp then started digging and dragging the heavy, rain-sodden turfs into position: they had to be placed in dead-straight rows a yard apart. Our labours had made the moors like a landscape on the moon, with the bigger squares formed by the drains resembling lunar seas. The Sea of Tranquillity for us was often the Slough of Despond.

But Tom and Charlie soon stopped. Charlie had been to the market town on our last free half-day, about three weeks ago, and had scrounged everywhere for cigarettes, finding mostly 'Pashas' and some faded ladies' scented cigarettes in delicate pastel shades with gilt tips. He started smoking one of these perfumed fags, holding it with affected daintiness, his little finger genteelly crooked, and blowing out curiously dense clouds of smoke from rounded lips. Tom went over to him and started to waltz him around, singing 'Little Sir Echo' in a loud, amorous voice. The waltz developed into a giggling wrestling match that was also playfully sexual, and they were both rolling on the wet ground groping inside each other's trousers when young Joey the ganger suddenly appeared beside them, gazing down with a grim smile of appreciation on their sexual frolics.

'Git up off yer arses,' he grunted.

'It's that man again,' whispered Tom in mock fright. He and Charlie, buttoning up their trousers, ran off to their spades and draggers and started to dig and drag with artificial vigour.

We all kept hard at work, each one stopping to chat a moment with Joey as he walked around. We all liked him. He was quiet and no slave-driver, and gave orders as if absent-mindedly; his good-looking young face was unnaturally thoughtful, almost brooding, and we never knew what he was thinking. Certainly, however, he was not thinking of us or of his job. I sometimes suspected he was as fed-up with the war effort as we all were.

When Joey got to Andra, we all stopped to listen to what he would say. We always stopped to listen to what Joey would say to Auld Andra, because being our best workman, and, in a way, our leader, Andra was generally told matters of importance, such as a message from the forester, a rise in pay, piece-work rates, and so on. And what Joey said to Andra that morning interested us very much indeed.

'What fettle, Andra?'

'Aye, no sae bad, Joey. But it's a puir sort of a day.'

'Keep yer eyes skinned, Andra. The big bugs is comin' today.'

'Is that so, now?' Andra leaned on his spade. 'An' aboot what o'clock might they be comin'?'

'Mebbe they'll no come oot i' the mire,' Charlie shouted mockingly.

'They'll be here roond aboot ten,' said Joey, prodding a turf with his blackthorn.

'Hell, jist when we're hevvin' oor snack,' moaned Ralphie.

'Ach they'll no bother us lang, dinna fash yersels,' Andra said, starting to dig again to set us an example. (We all started to dig again.) 'We can hae oor snack when they're awa doon the glen.'

'Watch ye dinna sit ower lang, lads,' Joey warned us.

'Aye, aye, Joey.'

He wandered off to inspect the work we'd done the day before, and, seeming satisfied as always, strode swiftly along the ride and out of sight down the glen. A line from Burns (was it?) came into my mind as I watched him striding away with swinging kilt – '... and Colin's darkening plaid'. I tried to recall the poem, but in vain. My mind seemed numb and empty.

As soon as he was gone, work eased up a bit. We talked at intervals about the 'big bugs' – the contemptuous name we all used for higher officials of the Forestry Commission with their big cars and cushy jobs – and speculated on the reason for this sudden visitation.

'I'd no care to be in auld Deadwood's boots,' said Andra with a chuckle. Deadwood was the nickname we had given to Mr Harman, the forester-in-charge, a sour little bureaucrat with a bitter, sarcastic tongue who was always, like every other official of the Government Commission, issuing absurd and contradictory orders about the work to be done, until we didn't know where we were. Now we no longer took any notice of contradictory orders, but just went on according to our original instructions or as the fancy took us. It was much less confusing, and the work got done just the same.

' 'E'll be shittin' 'is britches if owt's wrang the day,' laughed Ralphie.

'Watch they dinna land ower the top o' the ridge an' ketch ye's set on yer arses, lads, or playin' wi' yersels,' Andra advised Young Tom and Charlie, with his warm little laugh and twinkling eyes.

'Hell,' cried Tom, 'it'd take mair'n that lot o' stinkin' windbags tae get me on ma feet if I felt like a spell.'

'Them?' snorted Charlie scornfully, 'a bunch o' soft-bellies i' their mackintoshes from Burberry's and galoshes and rubber trousies, wi' their setters an' their shootin'-sticks an' their *Well-now-and-how-is-the-work-proceeding-today-my-good-man?* Bloody fatbottoms! I'm naebody's "good man" either.'

'And why wouldn't they be fightin', I'd like to know?' Ralphie asked. 'Why are they not in the Army wi' the rest o' the lads, a-stead o' traipsin' aboot the bogs an' the moors in their motorcars and their fur-lined gloves to preserve their lily-white hands, daein' nowt but stare at ye breakin' yer back ower a damn drain, an' niver as much as pass the time o' day wi' ye, an' me auld enough tae be their father?'

'Not that I'd demean meself, fatherin' such lazy bastards,' he added.

'Aye, Ralphie,' said Andra with a chuckle, 'that's eddication, lookin' busy when ye're daein' nowt.'

We all burst out laughing at that. Then it began to rain again.

Towards ten o'clock it was still raining, a fine drizzle only, but it clung to our clothes. We were all for stopping work and sheltering in an old lambing hut down the other glen, but Andra was doubtful. He scratched his grey stubble.

'We'd be in a bonny pickle if the bugs come up on us an' we doon i' the barn.'

'Aye, but we're gettin' wet through,' grumbled Charlie, 'an' me biuts is full o' watter.'

'Ah canna help that,' replied Andra flatly. 'An' we'll no melt.'

'I'd like ter see them walkin' oot ower the fells in a' this clart, onnyways,' stated Ralphie grimly. 'An' if ye ask me, Andra, I say we could get oot o' the wet till it clears a bit.'

In the end we decided to take our things down to the lambing barn and have our snack there.

'Sit ye doon by the door, lads, an' keep an eye on the ride,' Andra said.

'Ah, hell,' said Young Tom. 'I'm no sittin' i' the wind an' rain be onny door, open or shut, bugs or nae bugs. Ye hae tae eat some time.'

'Aye,' commented Andra sagely. 'But it luiks awfu' bad tae a boss, specifically the likes o' they wi' their pates all a-muzzle wi' books an' papers an' clerkin' that if they happen see a mon set doon gettin' his strength back wi' a slice o' bread and drippin' instead o' workin' his guts oot they think 'e does that a' the day lang, gettin' his shillings fer nowt.'

'Better fifty shillings than fifty pun' or whativver it is they get a week fer keepin' their hands clean. Ah'd be ashamed ter look mesel in the face in the mornin',' said Ralphie bitterly.

A discussion began on wages, and we started guessing at the salaries the big bugs drew, and the extra rations they got – a favourite pastime. Extra petrol coupons, extra clothing coupons, extra food coupons, extra chocolate rations, extra cigarette rations ... the big bugs had it all.

By the time we'd finished our snack, the rain was coming down heavily. The two young lads lay on some old sacks listening to the raindrops drumming on the corrugated iron roof, rolling their eyes at each other happily and smoking old fag-ends.

Auld Andra puffed at his broken clay pipe. The stem had snapped leaving only an inch or two and the bowl: we called it his nose-warmer. He kept going to the door and looking out at the rain.

'It's not easin' up, is it?' the others would ask him worriedly.

At last he said: 'Aye, I think it's clearin' a spot.'

We all rushed to the doorway and looked out. It was certainly not raining so heavily now.

'Look ye at the game-cover yonder,' Young Tom protested. 'Ye can see the rain peltin' doon aginst it.'

We looked out at the clump of fir trees above us on the left, and in front of its darkness thin white spears of rain could still be seen falling. But suddenly they stopped. The sky was grey, and unbroken cloud still covered it, but for some reason it had stopped raining.

Andra stepped outside, and raised his grizzled head. 'If there's a breeze gits up,' he said, 'it'll drive oot the rain.'

We all groaned at his elderly optimism.

'Come on, lads, there's a war on, ye knaw,' said Ralphie.

'Oot ye come,' Andra chuckled. The boys took up their tools reluctantly and we all prepared to leave the barn.

Again we toiled up the glenside to the crest of the moors. It was bitterly cold up there now, with a feeling of snow in the air. Those clouds were surely getting as heavy as snow clouds.

But we had only been working about half an hour when it began to rain again. We worked on for ten minutes or so, and then it began to pour down, and there was a sudden unhesitating rush for the barn. We arrived breathless and dripping, faces wet with rain, hair drenched.

'This friggin' wet,' grumbled Charlie, his face beaming with contentment. He pulled a slimy pack of cards out of his pocket, and we settled down to a game of rummy. Andra lit a fire in an old bucket. Just before lunch time, when we could hear the little steam locomotive puffing away up the valley, Joey came in.

'Ain't come yet, the sods,' he muttered to Andra. 'Auld Deadwood's got the flippin' jitters, waitin' for 'em like this.'

'So hae we,' said Ralphie. 'But man, what can ye dae for the best?'

Joey decided that we could stay in the barn while the rain kept on, but if we saw Deadwood and the big bugs coming we were to slip out and start digging somewhere.

'It disna matter where,' said Joey. 'As lang as ye're movin' aboot. They can't say nowt then, an' it looks better.'

'Have no fear, Joey,' said Andra, 'we'll keep joggin' on if they come.'

Joey left us, because he always ate his snack separately from us, though his was no better than ours. We ate our unbuttered pilchard or meat paste sandwiches and drank our unsugared tea, warming our cans on the fire. On a normal day we would have gone back to the camp if it was still raining after one o'clock, to clean out the latrines or scrub the floors or put fresh dried bracken in the mattresses. But today was no normal day. Today was the day the big bugs were coming.

All afternoon it rained cats and dogs. Joey came in once or twice. When we finally asked him why the big bugs were coming, he said it was to help the war effort. Laughter loud and long greeted that reply, and Joey joined in it. 'There's a war on' was one of our favourite jokes.

The fire went out because no one would venture out in the downpour for fresh kindling. It would have been wet, anyhow. We were all glum and cold and shivering.

'I'm gettin' the rheumatics,' Charlie announced.

'A young buck like you!' Ralphie taunted him.

'Ah've had the ague and the gout and the dropsy and the lord knows what else but I'm still as sound as a drum,' declared Auld Andra. 'Ah'll ootlive the lot of ye's.'

We got bored with cards and feats of strength and wrestling and dirty stories about land-girls and sailors. The boys started singing Vera Lynn songs – 'We'll meet again, don't know where, don't know when, But I know we'll meet again some sunny day....'

Sunny days ... would we ever see a sunny day again?

We kept a lookout for Deadwood and the big bugs, but now only very halfheartedly. Almost we wished that they would come – anything to create a diversion, and to get it over with.

'There's a war on,' we kept telling ourselves morosely.

'Keep up the war effort!' we growled, imitating Churchill at his most pompous.

'Ye can't get the fats,' said Andra, chewing with toothless gums on the dry, stale wartime bread. 'You can't get the fats' was the perpetual refrain of housewives when their families complained about their poor cooking of wartime rations.

'Ye can't get the fats,' we all chorused in glum tones.

Towards five o'clock there was still no sign of the high-ups, and we began to gather our things together, ready to go 'home'. The atmosphere at once became livelier. The boys started fooling around again. Tom shamelessly exhibited his cock in a giant erection, shouting: 'Target for tonight! Any offers?'

But Charlie for the moment had other thoughts on his mind.

'I wonder what's for supper tonight?' he mused. 'Spam or whalemeat or black pudding?'

We all set off, again in single file, heads bent low under the driving rain. Through reeds and marshes and bogs and stretches of treacherous mud we plodded, hands deep in pockets, not speaking. We trudged through long, soaking grass and heather and under leaking trees, up one ride and down another, uphill and downhill, steadily, wearily. From time to time one of us stopped to piss: the cold was affecting our bladders.

Just as we were approaching the hollow in which the camp lay, an estate car appeared over the top of the hill, where the distant road dipped away down into the village. We saw five tiny figures get out, one of them recognizably Deadwood. They put up umbrellas – 'Umbrellas! The cissies!' muttered Tom – and walked a few steps while Deadwood gesticulated. They were all wearing expensive Burberries and tweed hats. One of them brought out a pair of binoculars and trained them on us but only for a moment, while we silently seethed with rage at being thus spied upon by some ignorant official.

After a few minutes they all got into the car again. It turned round and disappeared down the road leading to the village on the far side of the fell.

As we turned into the camp, Andra looked at me, winked and chuckled. 'Aye, lad,' he said. 'That's the big bugs, that was.'

Strange Tenant

1943

From childhood's hour I have not been
As others were; I have not seen
As others saw; I could not bring
My passions from a common spring.
From the same source I have not taken
My sorrow: I could not awaken
My heart to joy at the same tone;
And all I loved, I loved alone. . . .*

This is one of the many poems encountered in my reading that seems to echo my own life and nature. The poet sees things that others do not see, and shows them to a world that may not accept his way of seeing life. My passionate and emotional life could not be satisfied with ordinary domestic existence, socially acceptable feelings and the humdrum conventions of marriage and family. The truth is that 'all I loved, I loved alone . . .'. But utter solitude is a condition common to most writers. For it is only in solitude that a poet can write his deepest and most intimate thoughts. He learns to live with his solitude, however painful it may be, and in the end comes to love and cherish it, seeking to preserve it against all intrusions from the outside world. Loneliness becomes a way of life.

For even thus the man that roams
  On heedless hearts his feeling spends;
Strange tenant of a thousand homes,
  And friendless, with ten thousand friends.†

My life for the past fifty years has been one of continual changes of address, changes of home, changes of country, changes of loves and friends. I feel I am indeed a 'strange tenant' of this earth – a tenant who may take up his roots and carry them across the sea to plant them for a while in some unknown land, where they grow and flourish until the time comes for me to take them up again and proceed to another place. I have been a traveller

* 'From Childhood's Hour' by Edgar Allan Poe.
† Lines by Washington Irving, written in 1822.

all my adult life. My mother, before her death, often reminded me of the fact that when I was just a little boy in the confining environment of South Shields, I would repeatedly tell her, like a prophecy: 'I am going to travel over the whole world.' My parents used to laugh at what they thought was just a childish fancy, but in the end they saw that I had been deeply serious, for my prophecy came true: I have abandoned for ever my old home town and my native land.

My intense loneliness, and the feeling of utter stillness it brought to my being, sometimes seemed to make me invisible to certain people. I have described, in *The Only Child*,* how I would enter the corner shop so silently and, as it were, absently, the shopkeeper would not immediately realize I was there. I might have been a disembodied spirit, and when I materialized in her consciousness, it was so startling, she would jump with fright.

Something similar happened during the war, when I went to see Kay Dick† at a firm called Staples: she wanted to publish my long poem called 'Adolescences'. She kept me waiting a long time in an outer office, and I could feel myself slowly melting away into invisibility and absent stillness, so that I was not surprised when she entered and asked the receptionist where I was, though I was standing right in front of her. Perhaps my lack of 'presence' – of which she had an amazing amount – was the real reason she finally decided not to publish my poem. I think it was too daring for the times – and it has still not been published. But the other day I came across a letter from Kay Dick saying that Staples could not do it, because of paper rationing. So many of my books have been unborn, aborted in that way, have become as invisible as myself.

Around 1954, the BBC ran a short course for writers who hoped to work for television. I attended one of these courses, and at the reception, where twenty or so writers were gathered, I was standing right by the door when C. P. Snow oozed vigorously like some noisy octopus into the room and at once called out: 'Where's Kirkup?' When he found himself standing right next to me, he was dumbfounded. I was so withdrawn, he was suddenly deflated. A year or so later, when I was approached by the Massachusetts Institute of Technology to accept the post of Poet in Residence, Snow got the invitation cancelled: a 'gay' person could not possibly bridge the two cultures, was his opinion. . . .

Much later, when I got to Japan, I discovered a modern poet called Hagiwara Sakutaro, eccentric son of a well-to-do family. As far as I know, he was not homosexual, though he was deeply neurotic and may have been

* Published by Collins in 1957.
† The writer and journalist.

bisexual; at any rate, he was the antithesis of the average Japanese family salaryman. He wrote one poem, 'Loneliness Persona' that touched me, and still touches me deeply, like Robert Desnos' 'Today I Went Walking with a Friend'. In it, Hagiwara speaks of the kind of relationship, a loving friendship, that few gays ever succeed in establishing. I wish I could have shown this poem, which I have translated, to Joe Ackerley and James Pope-Hennessey, and to so many more –

Loneliness, my lone persona, cries out for a friend.
My unknown friend, come quickly, quickly.
Come sit down in this old armchair
And let us talk quietly together.

No sorrow shall ever cloud
The tranquil, happy days we pass together;
Listening to the lullabies of faraway fountains,
Tenderly – and so gently – we shall embrace.

Mother, father, brothers long since gone away,
We shall be bound to one another like lost orphans
Who never knew their missing parents.
We two, from the hub, the heart of humankind.

Shall talk together only of our life with one another,
Seek shelter from the world in secret plans we make.
– These words, they seem to me like autumn leaves
Falling in premature cold across my empty knees.

That sense of utter personal loneliness has never left me since early childhood. Even in Japan, where I finally found the friend I needed, it remains always with me, in all those vast, nameless crowds. But I have learned to see in loneliness an inexhaustible spiritual treasure. Without it, I should never have become a poet.

Another poem that expressed my wandering, lonely nature is 'The Wanderer to the Moon' by a minor German poet, which Schubert used as the text of one of his most beautiful songs.

In heaven thou, I on the ground
We both go wand'ring, wand'ring round:
I moody, sad; thou, radiant, pure,
Why we're so diff'rent, I'm not sure.

A stranger, I from start to end
Go rootless, homeless, without friend;
Through alleys and through woods I roam,
Yet nowhere can I feel at home.

But you sail on beyond the wave
To western cradle, orient grave,
Through every nation's night you roam
And everywhere you are at home.

The heavens, endlessly unfurl'd,
Are your beloved, starry world:
O happy he, where'er he lands
Who ever on his own earth stands!

O happy he, where'er he lands
Who ever on his own earth stands,

Who ever on his own earth stands!*

To this I must add some lines from St Augustine – who was born on the northern verges of the Sahara: 'Do not plan long journeys, because whatever you believe in you have already seen. When a thing is everywhere, then the way to find it is not to travel but to love....'

Advice which I have finally begun to take seriously.

My pacifism is partly the result of my sense of difference from others: my temperament could not allow me to be conscripted against my will by a government I utterly despised. Wilfred Owen's poetry speaks for me here. I encountered many types of 'Insensitivity' during the Second World War, even more than Owen describes in his great anti-war poem of the same name.

I remember talking to another famous war poet, Siegfried Sassoon, about Owen. I was staying with J. R. Ackerley at Sassoon's home, Heytesbury House, in Wiltshire, not long before Sassoon died. Sassoon, who was himself bisexual, gave us to understand that Owen was either homosexual or bisexual. In fact, I gathered from Sassoon that they had had a brief affair, though whether it was of a sexual nature or purely romantic friendship I do not know. He told us he had visited the wounded Owen in hospital in Scotland, and mentioned how surprised he was to find Owen so small, so gentle and quiet. 'His smile', said Sassoon, 'was the sweetest and purest I have seen on any man's face. It was a smile filled with pure pity – not for himself, but for his suffering fellow men.' Pity is what I feel most strongly when reading 'Insensibility' – pity for the waste of young lives, for the cruelty and indifference of war, that usually brings out the worst in men.

All through the Second World War, I carried Owen's poems with me from labour camp to labour camp. I admired particularly this last verse of 'Insensibility':

* My translation of this poem originally appeared in my translation of Friedrich Dürrenmatt's *Portrait of a Planet*, performed by the BBC and by the Prospect Theatre Company in Britain.

But cursed are dullards whom no cannon stuns,
That they should be as stones;
Wretched are they, and mean
With paucity that never was simplicity.
By choice they made themselves immune
To pity and whatever moans in man
Before the last sea and the hapless stars;
Whatever mourns when many leave these shores;
Whatever shares
The eternal reciprocity of tears.

This became very relevant to the Second World War, in which both sides were led by 'dullards' – men whose stupidity is the quality I most associate with war, for war is madness, murder, mass destruction, and all unnecessary. The best word I can find for war is a French one: *bêtise*.

In the early 1960s, I was to study this poem with my students in the Modern Poetry Course at Japan Women's University in Tokyo. At such a distance from the First World War, and indeed from the Second – most of my students had no memory of war – it was a difficult poem to explain. But then I was able to bring it into the present by relating the 'dullards' who 'made themselves immune to pity' to those brutal American soldiers who had massacred innocent men, women and children and committed other terrible atrocities all over South Vietnam. There was a clear connection between the poem and the murders at My Lai and Song My.

As I spoke about these things, the bitterness of my past life flooded my heart, and I could hardly continue speaking as I tried to control my rising tears: tears of pity for man's inhumanity to man, tears of pity for all atrocities committed in the disgusting misery of the Vietnam war, tears of pity, too, for our human helplessness, the paltriness of our resistance to force.

I asked my students never to forget Owen's words. We need his compassionate vision, and his fierce indignation. The younger generation today is proud of being 'cool'. But it seems to me that this 'coolness' is just another word for 'insensibility'. No one today, in a world of nuclear terrorism, has the right to remain cool or insensible to pity. If we want to survive as human beings, and not turn ourselves into machines for killing, we must determine never to be cool and insensible to the sufferings of humanity, to 'whatever moans in man'. Let us be warned by Owen's words:

And some cease feeling
Even themselves or for themselves.
Dullness best solves

WAR

The tease and doubt of shelling ...
Having seen all things red,
Their eyes are rid
Of the hurt of the colour of blood for ever.
And terror's first constriction over,
Their hearts remain small-drawn,
Their senses in some scorching cautery of battle
Now long since ironed,
Can laugh among the dying, unconcerned ...

A Labourer Unworthy of his Hire

1943

From the North Tyne, I moved back to Tyneside and the air raids. I waited for the Ministry of Labour to send me to another camp. It was a grim time for all of us. My father now had to do fire-watching at Binns' department store twice a week. The incendiary bombs were doing as much damage as the explosive ones. My mother was worn out, queueing every day for what to us seemed very inadequate rations. Tyneside, as usual, was badly served in that respect. But whatever food she obtained from the butcher's or the fishmonger's after hours of queueing she cooked for us in the most tasty and attractive way. My father and mother had more or less come round to my pacifist point of view. After my first tribunal in Newcastle, which was fully reported in the press, my father came home with a drawn face, but his original aggressive attitude had melted away in sympathy for me. He told us that his fellow workers, on learning of my trial, had comforted him by saying: 'What a damned shame.' That also helped to reconcile him with me.

Meanwhile, I spent hours wandering around the bombed streets. The seashore, the cliffs and the pier were banned. Those were the parts of my home town I loved best. The only way I could get a breath of the sea was to ride the ferry between South and North Shields. Night after night I would make the crossing from the ferry landing just below the Market Place to the blacked-out pubs on the northern side, where I sometimes took a bus to Tynemouth and to Whitley Bay. Sometimes in the middle of the ferry crossing the air-raid sirens would sound their warning. But the ferry carried on across the river. The air raids still frightened me: it was the hellish noise rather than the danger of being killed that distressed me. But I was no longer panic-stricken as I had been on that first night of Nazi bomber raids.

I spent a lot of time in Newcastle. There was a feverishly gay nightlife in the pubs, parks and back streets. The Central Station, too, was a rendezvous for all kinds of homeless and loveless people, for soldiers with an all-night pass, for sailors on leave, for factory workers having an evening out. The station buffet with its vaguely Egyptian tiled pillars and enormous mirrors was a favourite refuge during air raids. The Turk's Head, the Eldon and a small, intimate pub near the station called the Queens – well-named – were also popular gathering spots for homosexuals. The gallery of the Theatre Royal was crowded with civilians and servicemen, many of them standing behind the wooden barrier at the back, which was more comfortable than the hard wood covering the cement benches without backs where, for very popular shows, we were squeezed in tight by the young male attendants trying to pack in as many people as possible.

It was there that I had my first sight of classical ballet – the Sadler's Wells company with Margot Fonteyn and Robert Helpmann. I shall never forget the endless delight of those ballets. The very first one I saw was *Les Rendezvous* by Frederick Ashton. Then came *The Gods go A-Begging*, also by Ashton. I still remember the plump calves of our English girls in the *corps de ballet* as they kicked up their heels under their knee-length dresses. I soon had my favourites in the company, besides Margot and Bobby. One girl in particular attracted me Annabel Farjeon. When I found a poem by her in an issue of *Life and Letters*, I wrote to her, and sent her some of my ideas for ballet scenarios. She replied kindly, but, alas, we never met. Another dancer I liked was Celia Franca, who danced in Helpmann's *Hamlet*, *Miracle in the Gorbals* and Andrée Howard's *The Spider's Banquet*, in which the Butterfly was another adored one, Moira Shearer, with the lovely legs and red-gold hair. Once, unexpectedly, she danced the polka in *Façade*: what a wonderful surprise it was to find her dancing so wittily in that part! I loved the way she dropped her skirt so daintily, flicked it aside with her toe, and started dancing in her frilly Victorian knickers.

I always wanted to be a dancer. Even when I was just a little boy, I would start dancing whenever I heard music. Dancing was in my blood. But my parents were too poor to afford expensive ballet lessons, and besides, my father, who would not even let me practise the piano while he was in the house, would have absolutely forbidden my taking up ballet. My mother was more sympathetic, but she was overruled by my puritanical father, who adamantly refused to allow me to attempt anything 'artistic' or 'cissy' – the two words were synonymous in his considerable vocabulary. So I became a poet, because writing poetry costs nothing, in material terms at least. All I needed were pencil and paper. And I could do it under my father's nose.

But I never lost my love of the dance. During the war, I took some secret tap-dancing lessons, with a view to joining the chorus of musical shows, like a boy I met from Gateshead, Jack Hewitt, who was a friend of the notorious Guy Burgess. Jack had met him while he was in the chorus of a touring show of *No, No, Nanette*.

When I first saw Fonteyn, she was only eighteen, fresh, exquisite, brilliant. I remember seeing her dance for the first time in *Les Sylphides*. Then she danced in Frederick Ashton's *Apparitions*, partnered by Robert Helpmann, who was later to become a star in the ballet film *The Red Shoes*, with Moira Shearer.

After matinée performances, the dancers used to go to a teashop next to the Theatre Royal to drink tea and eat scones and buns. I also used to go there while waiting for the evening performance to begin – I went to every performance, for I was a real balletomane in those days. (Now, alas, ballet no longer interests me.)

One afternoon I was sitting there at a little table, sipping my tea, and gazing discreetly but with adoration at the lovely face and bright auburn hair of Moira Shearer sitting at a table across the room. I was very shy. I never had the courage to speak to her, and now I regret my cowardice. Moira began to recognize my face. Sometimes she would give me a bewitching half-smile, but I was just too shy to smile back at her. I just blushed. Once, when she seemed about to speak to me on her way out, I was so startled I dropped my cup of tea on the floor.

No other leading dancer – not even Fonteyn or Markova – demonstrated such intelligence in her dancing, and such profound musicality as did Moira Shearer, at least among British dancers. One of her most superb roles was in Balanchine's *Ballet Imperial* in which I saw her dance time and time again at Covent Garden and in the provinces. In her book about Balanchine, *Balletmaster: A Dancer's View of George Balanchine*, she writes: '. . . had I not just been married and with my life about to take a new turn, I think I would have followed George Balanchine back across the Atlantic in the hope of joining his New York City Ballet.' In her physique and her presence on stage, and above all in her feeling for true expressiveness in her musical responses to all kinds of scores, she was a real Balanchine-type, before that generation of long-legged American dancers was thus described. Balanchine could have written immortal parts for her. So why did she marry? Why did she follow Ludovic Kennedy and not the Master? I think that decision was typical of something intensely warm and human in her dancing. She was an absolute professional – a great performer in the style of the classic *ballerina assoluta* – yet she remained, at least for me, not a sacred monster but a delightful woman, and so I could understand her choosing love instead of fame – which she had already, anyhow. Her four rehearsals with Balanchine for *Ballet Imperial* added some indefinable quality to her onstage presence, for apparently she was lacking in self-confidence, even though she had become an internationally celebrated movie star in *The Red Shoes*, a film that begins so brilliantly then degenerates into kitsch and sentimentality. If only Balanchine could have directed her in that!

I cut a picture of her marriage from a newspaper, and have carried it with me all my life, through all my moves and all my travels. At the 1954 English Festival of Spoken Poetry, I adjudicated: Ludovic Kennedy was a brilliant – the best contestant. He later did a programme using some of my poems on the BBC Third Programme. But I never told him of my love for his wife.

Once, Margot Fonteyn came in to the teashop, and as there were no vacant seats except at my table – I was always the last person anyone ever sat beside – she asked if she might sit next to me. She was very pale and thin, and seemed very hungry. She had a pot of tea, buttered toast and teacake and two cream cakes which I offered her from my own plate. I told her, in a voice breathless with panic, that she had danced Odette perfectly that afternoon.

'Did I really?' she replied, looking very serious. 'I thought I was terrible. I'm never satisfied with my performances. I made several silly mistakes. You must have noticed.'

'Oh, no, no!' I stammered. 'You were exquisite. Really.'

Once more she gave me her beautiful, slightly mischievous smile, and laughed: 'Are you coming tonight?'

'Of course. I'm at every performance.'

'I'll be better tonight,' she smiled. 'I always seem to dance better in the evenings.'

I have never forgotten her saying: 'I'm never satisfied with my performances.' Indeed, she has always been a perfectionist. In her *Autobiography*, written in her fifties, she says: 'The one important thing I have learnt over the years is the difference between taking one's work seriously and taking oneself seriously. The first is imperative and the second disastrous.' I, too, could never take myself seriously, but I took my poetry very seriously indeed – it was my whole life, and it was the one thing that helped me get through the war. That, and music. I was just discovering Vaughan Williams, Bliss, Tippett, Delius, Walton, Moeran, Schönberg, Bartok, Webern and Alban Berg. I once saw Constant Lambert standing at the stage door of the Theatre Royal, as was his wont on fine summer evenings before the performance. He was leaning on a stick, because while conducting the ballet orchestra he had fallen off the podium and hurt his leg. He gave me such a look as I passed by that I turned back and started talking to him. He apologized for having stared at me, saying: 'For a moment, I thought you were the ghost of Alban Berg!' I told him how much I enjoyed his book, *Music Ho!* He was the first serious musician to discuss jazz.

There were other great ballet companies at the Theatre Royal, including the thrilling modern dance company, the Ballet Joos, with its anti-war ballet *The Green Table*. Kurt Joos came to talk to students at the university. Today, he would have an audience of hundreds. But in those days, ballet, especially modern dance, was far from being as popular as it is now, so he spoke to only about a dozen people. I think I loved ballet then because it was really something very special, and a minority cult. Today, when almost everyone goes to ballet, and there are so many companies, I have lost interest. Joos was a very solid, not to say stolid, middle-aged man who had danced the important role of Death in *The Green Table*. I did not see him in this part, though I saw all the other fine male dancers of his company perform it – Sigurd Leeder, Rolf Alexander and my favourite, Hans Zullig. I was later to see the part danced by a fine Chilean performer, Maximiliano Zomosa, with the City Center Joffrey Ballet in New York. Zomosa committed suicide when he was only thirty-one.

After the invasion of Poland by Hitler, many Poles took refuge in Britain; some served in the armed forces, while others formed the Polish Ballet, a wonderfully virile company. There was also Mona Inglesby's International Ballet, in which, after the war, a young dancer called Maurice Béjart gave his first public performances.

There was Russian ballet and opera, too, in which the great soprano Oda Slobodskaya gave some truly startling performances. She was more of a variety turn than an opera singer, but her voice was still wonderful and her eccentric mannerisms, her rather clownish face and her big smile were fascinating to behold. I heard her give a recital of Russian songs, and she was electrifying. Desmond Shawe-Taylor called her 'the outstanding interpreter of Russian song in this country – perhaps in the world'. Even in a concert performance, her impressive figure, baleful white face and extravagant gestures were completely mesmerizing, and her voice, past its best when I first heard her, was unique. She, and her voice, were always larger than life. But she did remind me a little of Hermione Gingold or Beatrice Lillie.

I was very lucky to discover, recently, a cassette tape (Concert Artist/Fidelio TC-FED-036) of dear Oda Slobodskaya singing Russian songs, some of them very unusual ones, by Dargomizhky, Balakirev, Borodin and Liadov. She was accompanied at the piano by Frederick Stone. These amazing recordings must date from around 1960, when Slobodskaya was in her seventies, but that soprano voice is still rich and supple, full of that characteristic attack and dramatic panache I so well remember from those performances in Newcastle upon Tyne, when she appeared on stage in a long black gown and shawl to sing her arias after a spirited performance of 'Night on a Bare Mountain'.

Opera has always been my least favourite form of music. It was the inane libretti that exasperated me, much as the convoluted texts of the *kabuki* theatre were to infuriate me when I got to Japan. But I was entirely captivated by the music, and even more so by performers like Slobodskaya. The art of Schwarzkopf and Sutherland entranced me. But it was not until November 1952, when I first heard Callas singing in *Norma* at Covent Garden – from the gallery slips again – that I felt the force of that deep fascination La Slobodskaya had exerted upon me. After that, I heard Callas in most of her great roles in nineteenth-century *bel canto*, and I was present when she gave her farewell performance as Tosca at Covent Garden in 1965. I was not to hear her again in person until the seventies, on her worldwide concert tours with the only tenor for whom I have felt the same kind of attraction, Giuseppe di Stefano. They appeared in a joint recital in Tokyo in 1974, and, freed from the often ignoble trappings of conventional opera, Callas seemed even more wonderful than before, radiating a kind of monumental grace, yet remaining both impulsive and refined. Di Stefano was a fitting partner for such a spectacular temperament, such an unforgettable stage presence. In later years, when Pasolini had become for me a literary and cinematic revelation, her portrayal of his Medea seemed to me one of the greatest achievements in sheer acting ever seen in the cinema.

We were very well served by the various touring opera companies at the Theatre Royal. I spent all my spare cash on gallery seats to attend every performance of the Carl Rosa Opera Company, which gave me a solid grounding in Italian and German opera. Their scenery was weird and wonderful, often delightfully archaic, as were the costumes and the general style of production. There was no naturalism. Opera from the Carl Rosa was full-blooded melodrama.

I had had a passion for the music of Verdi since childhood, when my mother, unbeknown to my anti-musical father, taught me arias and choruses from *Il trovatore* and *La traviata*. I believe we had some early opera recordings which we played (when my father was out) on our wind-up gramophone with steel needles, the green trumpet horn and the very heavy old soundbox. But the Carl Rosa extended my experience of opera with Puccini – heavenly *Madame Butterfly!* – and with the delightful works of the Irish composer

Balfe ('I dreamt that I dwelt in Marble Halls' was one of my mother's party pieces, learnt from her Irish father).

Then there was the enchanting D'Oyly Carte Gilbert and Sullivan season for two whole weeks every year: I knew most of *The Gondoliers* and *The Mikado* by heart.

Our Theatre Royal was also, of course, one of the provincial theatres that received first-class touring productions of successful London plays, and of new productions on a trial run before engagements in the West End.

The very first time I sat on those hard benches in the gallery was to see a delightful performance by the Hollywood actress Ruth Chatterton, in Somerset Maugham's *The Constant Wife*. It was a sparkling revival of a play first performed in 1927. I listened spellbound to some of the wittiest dialogue in the modern English theatre. It had an echo of Oscar Wilde's famous paradoxical style. Today that wit seems faded and mechanical. But then, to a provincial young man, it seemed the height of sophistication.

Besides lighthearted comedies like *George and Margaret* and *French Without Tears*, we had regular serious drama, usually in the persons of Donald Wolfit and 'my lady wife' Rosalind Iden doing popular Shakespearean plays. Wolfit's curtain calls at the end of the play were as much a part of the drama as Shakespeare's characters. We would see a large hand covered with stage rings grasp the edge of the curtain – 'Let them know you're coming,' was his advice – and into the subservient spotlight would step the actor whose Lear was the best I ever saw, not forgetting Wilson Knight's at Leeds University in 1951. Wilson Knight's acting was very much in the same style as Wolfit's, whom he much admired.

During the war, whenever there was an air raid, the leading actor or actress in the company would come to the front of the stage and announce: 'Ladies and gentlemen, the air-raid warning has just sounded. Those wishing to take shelter are requested to do so now. Our play will resume in a few moments.' I never saw anyone leave the theatre, even when bombs were falling in the vicinity and rattling the scenery. Wolfit's delivery of this warning was given in the tones of Mrs Siddons ordering a pint of porter, with an air of noble authority and of contempt for the enemy. How could anyone leave the theatre after that?

During the summer months, there were repertory companies doing popular successes like *Night Must Fall* and *Charley's Aunt*, and among the outstanding actors I remember in such summer stock companies was the tall, saturnine and fascinating Valentine Dyall, whose father, Franklin Dyall, made a special appearance with his son in that throbbing melodrama,

White Cargo. I went every week, usually on a Saturday night, to see these plays in the gallery. Often I was more interested in the audience than in the play: the gallery regulars were a vociferous tribe, and I was reminded of them when I saw the film *Les Enfants du paradis*. But they were good critics of a play, and would hoot and boo anything they thought second-rate. In those days, before the advent of television, the theatre was a truly popular art form.

For several years, ever since around 1935, I had been sending poems and essays and stories to various magazines. They were all returned with printed rejection slips. During my final year at university, Feyyaz Fergar, Sadi Cherkeshi and I produced two short-lived poetry magazines, *Dint* and *Fulcrum*. Both titles were suggested by me. In those days, the flash of what seemed, at the moment, an irresistible title was sufficient reason for starting a new magazine. Some of my early surrealist poems appeared in those magazines, and were reprinted in a rather tatty cyclostyled rag from Oriel College, Oxford, edited by one 'Tancred Paul', sub-editor David Wright. It was called *Platitude*, which was a good description of most of the contents. However, there were occasional good poems by Keith Douglas and David Wright himself. The price was threepence. Among my poems was the somewhat precious 'Croquis', which I never had the nerve to reprint, so here it is:

Among these hills,
a road

I have found the wind in my arms
and can do nothing

Being a tree alone
I dream standing.

Others, reprinted in my first book, *The Drowned Sailor*, were 'Legend' and 'Hornpipe'.

After my schoolday diet of the Sitwells, I had at last found merciful release from their whimsy in the poems of Auden and MacNeice. I did not care much for Spender or Day-Lewis, but Roy Campbell was another poet I liked at that time. Another was Dunstan Thompson, who got printed by John Lehmann, and whom I was to meet briefly in a progressive school community in Yorkshire. But the poets I really admired were Ezra Pound and all the modern Europeans. This preference for European and American poetry over British poetry marked my own work very deeply, and has remained with me to this day, with now the addition of Chinese and

Japanese poetry. Preferences like these set me apart for ever from the usual band of provincial-academic-domestic poets infesting modern British literature.

I had collected a big box of rejection slips, enough to paper the lavatory at West Avenue. But gradually my work began to appear in small magazines with big reputations. Someone who always encouraged me was Robert Herring, editor of *Life and Letters Today* who printed one or two of my early wartime poems. But the only really helpful advice I ever received came from the editor of *Twentieth Century Verse*, Julian Symons, who wrote me a regretful note in purple ink on his rejection slip, one of the few I preserved from that dark period:

> Dear Mr Kirkup – I'm sorry, *Twentieth Century Verse* has ceased publication. You might try *Life and Letters Today* with these – the 'Ballade' is I think the best – though they're all a bit *jammy*, sticky to touch, with too many [indecipherable word, but it may be 'irrelevancies'] in them. They glisten a bit too much. Or that's what I think.
>
> Sincerely, Julian Symons

It was what I thought, too, as soon as it was pointed out to me, and I set about trying to deglister my poems. It was the one occasion when an editor gave me some useful advice, and I was forever grateful for it. But it also made me aware for the first time of an unbridgeable gulf between my own experiments and what was considered acceptable verse in Britain. They have always been poles apart.

John Middleton Murry's *Adelphi* and Wrey Gardiner's *Poetry Quarterly* began printing my poems and reviews. The latter's Grey Walls Press published the anthology *Lyra*, edited by Alex Comfort and Robert Graecen, in which my poem 'Moorland', written while I was working as a forester on the North Tyne, was reprinted. It had first appeared in Tambimuttu's *Poetry London*, and this was really my first breakthrough, for Tambimuttu also printed my poem 'Variations on a Theme' and my reviews* of Eliot's *Four Quartets*, which prompted the poet to write me a letter of appreciation. In fact, Eliot was a poet I did not care for except in some of his early verse. I disliked all the 'stage Cockney' and false music-hall joviality in *The Waste Land*, and his use of Indian legend to justify the war. He seemed to me to be a typical American trying desperately to show how British he was.

But the poems in *Poetry London* had attracted the attention of William Plomer, who recommended my work to the editor of *The Listener*, J. R. Ackerley – a somewhat forbidding name that suggested to me a peppery

* Reprinted in *T. S. Eliot: The Critical Heritage*, ed. Michael Grant (Routledge & Kegan Paul, 1982).

colonel. Later I was to discover that Ackerley often used Plomer and a handful of other intimate friends as 'scouts' for new poets, because he himself did not trust his own judgment of poetry, though in fact he had a very sensitive and eclectic taste in verse. I had a brief note from Ackerley – on a rejection slip – asking me to send him some poems, which surprised me, because I already had a pile of rejection slips without words of advice or encouragement from *The Listener*, then just about the most interesting literary weekly in Britain.

Much heartened, I sent Mr Ackerley a poem which he returned with depressing haste, adding the comment: 'Not, I fear, for *The Listener*. Something not quite so steamy might suit. Do try me again.' The next poems I sent were all returned with notes like: 'Still too hot for us,' or 'A bit warm, don't you think – though I liked it,' or 'Great fun – but not, alas, for Auntie.' This was maddening, and I began to feel Mr Ackerley had no wish to do me any favours. But I kept on 'trying' him, and always the poems came back, week after week, with occasionally very curt remarks like 'Sorry – J. R. A.' scribbled in his inimitable, casually elegant hand on yet another rejection slip.

One letter from him is dated 14/7/41 when I sent him a group of very experimental poems in the French surrealist style:

> Dear Mr Kirkup
>
> Yes, I see that you are experimenting in form, and of course one always loses something in the process, but as with the artists, you may well emerge at the other end with valuable knowledge to fortify your poetry when it returns, as I hope it may, to subjectivity. So do not be discouraged (there is evidence of discouragement in carelessness of typing) if these experiments seem unsatisfactory to you; these transitional stages are always disappointing and limited. You are not free at the moment, but 'Persecution' in this bunch seems to me to show that you are not wasting your time, and you might do worse than work at it a bit more. Things improve amazingly the more one tries. It is an interesting surrealist nightmare poem, but very uneven. Verse 3 has gone typographically wrong somewhere. V.5 is excellent, V.9 incomprehensible (is it necessary to the poem?) and the remainder rather feeble. I think you might do something with it with a little more thought and invention: I should be interested to see it again.
>
> Yours sincerely
> J.R. Ackerley

I took his advice to heart. I re-worked the poem but it did not appear in print until more than twenty years later, in 1963, as 'They've Got Me' in *Refusal to Conform: Last & First Poems* (OUP).

Then one day in the dark winter of 1943, in a dreadful Forestry Commission labour camp in East Witton, the commandant handed me one of my self-addressed envelopes – a sight that always made my heart sink, though I was by now immune to the pain of rejection. It contained a galley proof from Mr Ackerley with the words: 'I like this – though I don't know why I should. J. R. A.' The poem was 'Mortally', and it puzzled my dear father and mother even more than it did Joe.

I remember my mother reading the printed poem with bewilderment, then saying: 'You shouldn't use words like "bifurcate", Jim' – as if she thought it was a dirty word. But my father, consulting our household dictionary, defended my usage, saying, 'It's in our dictionary, Mary, so it must be all right.' I was hoping for a flood of admiring fan letters after the poem appeared, but it sank without a trace until Wrey Gardiner reprinted it in *The Drowned Sailor*, some years later in 1946.

Around 1943, Wrey Gardiner's Grey Walls Press published another anthology, *Indications*, which contained the work of three poets: John Ormond Thomas, John Bayliss and myself. The selection of my early work contained most of the poems that would appear in *The Drowned Sailor*, also published by Grey Walls Press, and filled with hilarious misprints. I got a good review of my work in *Indications* from Hugh Ianson Fausset in *The Times Literary Supplement* and from William Plomer in *The Listener*. (I knew Ianson Fausset, and I found out later from Joe Ackerley that Plomer had reviewed me; in those days, reviews were unsigned in both periodicals.) There was a rather sniffy signed review in *Tribune* from Francis King. In the issue of 3 September 1943, reviewing me with Kathleen Raine's *Stone and Flower* (a very beautiful collection with Barbara Hepworth illustrations that I myself reviewed for *Poetry Quarterly*), King found me 'a highly ambitious writer' (chiefly, I think, because in 'The Drowned Sailor' I had attempted a very long poem in an unusual surrealistic style, and long poems were uncommon and considered 'Eliotic').* He was quite right to remark

* This poem first appeared in *Indications* (for which I provided the title). But I had been working on it all through my sojourns in France and Liechtenstein, and during the first three years of the war. My poem was directly inspired by T. S. Eliot's 'Burial of the Dead' section in *The Waste Land*, in which I had sensed that 'the drowned Phoenician Sailor' or Phlebas the Phoenician of Part IV were poetic symbols of a lost homoerotic passion of the poet's youth. When I had finished my poem, (some time in 1943), I sent it to Eliot at Faber's. But when he read it and saw the homosexual interpretation I had derived from *The Waste Land*, he was most upset, and sent the poem back with the comment 'This is completely absurd'.

It was not until the mid-seventies that I came across James E. Miller, Jr's extraordinarily insightful critical study, *T. S. Eliot's Personal Waste Land: Exorcism of the Demons* (The Pennsylvania State University Press, 1977), and learnt of Eliot's threatened libel suit against a Canadian professor, John Peter, for his 'A New Interpretation of *The Waste Land*' in *Essay in Criticism* which had to be suppressed by the editors. Then I began to realize the truth of my own insights into Eliot's life and poetry and its that 'he seems continually to be forcing his range.' I was indeed: I wanted to master my craft. He went on: 'At the moment, much is attempted and less achieved. But one does have a feeling that at any moment the elements will all coalesce, and when that happens the result should be something unique.'

This encouraged me to send some poems to *Tribune*. George Orwell was the literary editor. I did not like his novels very much, but admired his essays. One of them, I seem to remember, attacks the influence of French literature on English writers. So I sent him a poem with a French title, '*Nature Morte*', as a gentle provocation. It worked. He accepted the poem if I would change the title to 'Still Life'. I agreed. but the poem took ages, if not years, to appear – it did not, I think, until T. R. Fyvel had taken over the editorship. For him I wrote an essay about immediate post-war Tyneside, 'For Amusement Only', which he thought was 'not quite right for us'. He made some suggestions about how I might rewrite it, but I could not see it his way, so I gave up trying to fit my concepts to his social ideas. Slightly rewritten, the essay appears later in this book.*

All this literary activity was going on under the bombs, and under the agonies of my ever-worsening asthma. I was still smoking about ten cigarettes a day, and still leading a very promiscuous sexual life in the encircling gloom of the blackout in Newcastle and South Shields. I was hoping and praying for an invasion and occupation of Britain by the Nazis. If that happened, I had plans to join a resistance movement, though I would insist on using non-violent methods of resistance, which included infecting the whole of the Gestapo with venereal disease. But however hard I tried to catch syphilis, I never succeeded. I also collected bags full of the fibres from a certain plant well known to me from my schooldays, which made the most potent itching powder imaginable. I carried these stocks everywhere with me, intending to drop them down the necks of Nazi troops from upper windows as they marched by in triumph, thus incapacitating the entire German army. Because of my knowledge of foreign languages, I hoped I could become a double agent, working for both sides (and getting paid by both). By working dispassionately for both sides, I thought I would be able to, as it were, neutralize all their war efforts until the conflict came to an inexplicable grinding halt. But these fond dreams were never to come true, for Hitler never did invade Britain.

Instead, I was convoked to our local Labour Exchange in Wawn Street –

homosexual undertones which profoundly related to the secret passion of Eliot for a young French doctor, Jean Verdenal, who was killed in the Dardanelles.

* See pp. 138–43.

which I naturally referred to as 'Yawn Street' – in order to answer accusations from anonymous informants that I was not 'doing my bit' and that I was not carrying out the official instructions by the C.O. tribunal to take up work on the land.

I went to the office in Wawn Street, a depressingly drab and functional thirties' structure, and was received by someone with a very ugly expression on his face. Was this a British version of the Gestapo? I forget who the man was – possibly the manager of the Labour Exchange. He was sitting behind his desk to interrogate me. As a gesture of pacifist defiance, I had lit a cigarette before entering his office. I still remember that it was a cork-tipped Craven-A. Was I going to be handed over to the military authorities, or to the police? In any case, I had my answer all ready. As I was led away in handcuffs, smoothing back my long, fair hair, I intended to inform the press: 'I shall turn it all to poetry.'

But I never got the opportunity to deliver this terrific curtain line. The manager – if it were he – at once commanded me to put out my cigarette. Taking a final drag, I crushed it out on an ashtray; as I had only just lit it, there was quite a lot of it left, and in those days of tobacco rationing one did not throw away a just-lit fag. I crossed my long legs elegantly and gazed with lowered lids at my investigator. I could feel my 'evil eye' coming on, but he did not seem to notice as he harangued me about my duty to my country in its darkest hour and all that rot. Then he issued orders for me to be sent under escort to my next place of detention, the labour camp at East Witton in the West Riding of Yorkshire.

As I was leaving his office, the 'evil eye' that I had felt accumulating its mysterious powers within my mind came to a head, and I kept it under control so that it could attain its full potency whenever I wished to unleash it.

'Take your cigarette with you,' the manager shouted after me. At that, I turned in the doorway of the Labour Exchange, and merely looked at him. 'Take it yourself,' I calmly replied, and let loose the full force of my *malocchio*, accompanied by the middle-finger gesture of 'Up you!' Then I just swept out, quoting Virgil's line from the *Bucolics*:

> *Nescio quis teneros oculus mihi fascinat agnos . . .*
> I know not what evil eye casts a spell on my tender lambs . . .

A few days later, I read in the *Shields Gazette* that the man's house had been damaged by a bomb. I am not sure, but I rather believe he himself was killed by the blast.

Forest and Farm

1943–5

East Witton, near Leyburn, is a small, unremarkable village. That was where I was sent by the Labour Exchange. I took my bike with me. There was a camp of Nissen huts at the bottom of the fell on which I was to work. The first thing I had to do was to stuff my mattress cover with dry hay and bracken and pack it into my bunk. The bunks were arranged in tiers round the hut, with a wood-burning stove in the centre. There were no baths, and washing facilities were primitive. The lavatory was even more so – a deep pit with a wooden bar laid across it on which one had to squat. I was reminded of the place in later years when I read Solzhenitsyn's descriptions of a gulag. One of my few fellow C.O.s was a tall, red-headed, rather reserved lad who later became Willie Hamilton, MP, scourge of the Royal Family. Most of the other conscientious objectors were those with deep religious convictions. I liked their gentleness. One of them, pale and thin and abstracted, with a shy smile and the manners of a Victorian maiden aunt, was known as 'Creeping Jesus'. I need hardly add that I did not call him that: I called him Our Lady of Labour.

The rest of the workers at the camp were mostly social dropouts like myself – the dregs of the reformatories, war orphans no one knew what to do with, handicapped persons, alcoholics, out-of-work miners and one or two professional male hustlers who had been exempted from military service and who were there on probation. They soon recognized me as one of them. We were a right lot. On my first evening at that dire camp, I took the boys out drinking at the local pub, the Blue Lion. We got absolutely pickled and were sternly reprimanded next morning by the camp overseer, a county type in check cap, shooting jacket with leather patches and cavalry twill trousers. We took an instant dislike to one another.

He was a tough, aggressive Scotsman with a permanent sneer and a flow of bitter sarcasm for the rag-tag-and-bobtail under his command. There were some local village men who were his aides, accomplices and spies. Naturally, I was soon in Jock's bad books. He picked on me at every opportunity, having been instructed to do so by Wawn Street. I remember his intensely pale blue eyes in their fringes of black lashes – a combination that at first made me wonder if he, too, did not possess the evil eye. But I soon found out that his eyes were no match for mine.

Work started at eight o'clock and went on until seven. There were two short official breaks for tea in the morning and afternoon, and an hour at lunchtime. Most of us just sat or lay around as much as possible when Jock was not watching. We had a complicated series of signals for giving warning of his approach. We worked seven days a week.

My first job was to chop at stumps of trees with an axe that I was temperamentally quite incapable of sharpening, or of using. Again and again I would try to chip a bit off the stumps; I was supposed to make them all level with the ground, so that the tractors could proceed smoothly. Jock would stand over me watching my paltry efforts with a sneer on his lips, bared on cruel false teeth, his pale eyes fizzing with indignation at my obvious incompetence.

'You bloody nancy boy!' he would shout. 'Are you a man or a mouse?'

I paused and looked at him. I could feel the evil eye rising.

'A mouse,' I replied sweetly, giving him a false smile, and keeping my eyes on him.

'Give us it here!'

He seized the axe and started chopping expertly at the stump I had been doing my delicate embroidery on: 'It luiks as if the rats hae been nibblin' it!' Jock had commented.

After his demonstration of how it should be done, he handed back the axe to me with the order: 'Noo get on wi' it. Put yer back into it, man.'

(He called me 'man'! I thought to myself. Get that, you nancy boy.) I tried to swing the axe high over my shoulder as Jock did, but it did seem frightfully heavy. Jock stood watching with rising fury. I tried again, halfheartedly, and brought the axe down on the stump, a glancing blow which I could not control. It sprang off and hit Jock square on the right shin, quite a nasty, deep cut. He had to be taken to the infirmary. After that, he never stood over me again.

Indeed, he began to have what I sensed was a kind of respect for me. He started to give me 'cushy' jobs. Then I was put on piece-work sawing up pit props and stacking them. My stacks of pit props were the most artistic on the fell; I used to decorate them with wild flowers.

I asked Jock if he would approach the camp commandant with a request that I should be allowed to live outside the camp, though not in the village, where, to my dismay, I had discovered an old head mistress of mine was lodging. On my bike, I had discovered the romantic ruins of Jervaulx

Abbey, where there was a lodge at one of the gates. The family was still in residence at the Abbey. But I had made inquiries, and found that I could rent a room at the lodge, with full board, for only ten shillings a week, washing included. To my surprise, permission was granted for me to make the change, and I moved into the lodge at once. The mistress of the house was one of the dearest, sweetest souls I have ever met. She was an elderly countrywoman who looked after her husband and grown-up son as well as her fowls and beasts. Her name was Patty. Her warm heart and sympathy for my plight was to make my stay in that region a little easier. It was about half an hour's bicycle ride to work, and I made this journey in all weathers, fortified always by Patty's good breakfast of porridge, ham and eggs and homemade sausages with home-baked bread. Her husband was a big, good-natured chap who helped on the estate. He had been in the First World War; when she knew me better, Patty confided that he had 'never been the same' after his return from the front. 'He used to be that gentle – but he lost it all in the trenches. . . .' Patty was my best friend for the two years I spent in East Witton.

I had a few other friends as well. One of them was a C.O. from Tyneside who was trying to become an artist. He came to stay with me in my room at the Lodge. But he soon gave up his conscientious objection and became a paratrooper. We remained friends, and it was he who introduced me to the little group of artists at Castle Bolton near Redmire, not far from Leyburn. One could get to Redmire by bus from Leyburn, then walk up the steep road to Castle Bolton, named after the ruined castle where Mary Queen of Scots had been imprisoned for some years. After joining the paratroopers, my friend acquired a motorbike, and when he was on leave I would ride on his pillion up to Castle Bolton for the weekends I had free from work. Later, when I ran away from East Witton, I spent some weeks in hiding at George Jackson's cottage in Castle Bolton. George was a good artist, also a playwright. His cottage was very small, one room downstairs and one up, on the right-hand side of the road just before one enters the village of Castle Bolton. It was primitive, but surprisingly comfortable. When I was hiding out there from the Ministry of Labour, I wrote a number of poems, and a strange group of sonnets I called 'Ten Pure Sonnets', which were finally printed in my collection *Refusal to Conform* by the Oxford University Press in 1963. George did a water-colour portrait of me reading from *The Drowned Sailor*.

Why hadn't I become a painter? Then I might have been a war artist like Henry Moore, whose drawings and sculpture I found repulsive; or Paul Nash or Edward Wadsworth or Cecil Collins or Edward Burra? I worshipped these artists, and wrote poems about them – I even wrote a poem about Henry Moore and one of his ineffable reclining figures. I also liked the work of minor decorative artists like Rex Whistler and John Banting. The latter had designed for Constant Lambert and the Carmargo Society at Sadler's Wells a ballet décor inspired by Bassett's Liquorice Allsorts, my favourite food in wartime, even though rationed. Banting designed the extraordinary swirling settings for Robert Helpmann's ballet 'Hamlet', which I saw many times. The backcloth often floated through my siren-haunted dreams.

I was to meet two other artists in Yorkshire who were well-known locally, and very good in their very different ways. They were not great artists, but they gave me insights into art and painting that were invaluable. I even started painting myself, with the feeling that I could easily become an artist if only I put my mind to it, the sort of feeling many people have about writing.

Fred Lawson and his wife, Muriel Metcalfe, were both artists and illustrators of books. Fred was a real countryman, bluff and hearty and cheerful, always stuffing his pipe, and with a flow of humorous stories about the local people and his early life in Leeds. He gave me some excellent tuition in painting, and under his guidance I began to draw and do water-colours. Fred was out in all weathers, painting the landscapes of Wensleydale with a sure yet delicate, feeling touch and a subtle sense of colour and composition. I learned more than art from Fred, that good-natured, kindly, very wise soul. His rough humour helped me to see the comical side of all my predicaments, and he was one of the very few people who have accepted me without question, 'just as I am, without one plea ...' one might say. Nothing I ever said or did surprised him: he found it all completely natural and comprehensible. His warmth of heart and purity of spirit were equalled by his practical generosity; he was never well-off, but I was even worse-off than he. He and Muriel would bring me tea and sugar and milk and bread fresh-baked, as well as what had become on Tyneside unobtainable luxuries like butter and eggs and home-cured ham. The first time I tasted the home-cured slice of ham they brought me at the cottage, I was so overwhelmed by the taste and the aroma, I felt drunk. They also sent packets of tea – where they got them from I do not know – to my parents in South Shields, where constant cups of tea were the only things that helped my mother face daily life. Making the ration 'pan out' each week was more of a worry to her than the sirens and the bombs.

Muriel was an artist of a kind completely different from Fred, but she loved his work and was proud of his skills. She did very tender, wistful, delicate drawings and water-colours of children, usually local village kids, who, while remaining recognizably real, were somehow transformed into ideal beings by her unusual vision. She also painted allegorical and imaginary figures, or characters from poetry; her sensitive works adorn the covers of two of my books – *The Cosmic Shape* and *The Creation*, both very long poems that only she appreciated fully and responded to. When I first knew Muriel she had a beautiful, meditative face, fine-boned, with large, lustrous eyes. Yet she was full of fun, and could tell as many tales as Fred, so that often we spent whole evenings telling stories, reciting poems and talking about life. We ignored the war as much as possible, though I think both Fred and Muriel were on the conservative side. But Muriel, too, accepted me completely.

She knew many poems by heart, and in the many letters we exchanged over more than twenty years she would fill her pages with quotations and adorn the margins with little drawings and sketches of children and imaginary beings. It was Muriel who gave me the Longfellow translation from which I took the title of my second volume of autobiography, *Sorrows, Passions and Alarms*. And she had a passion for Dostoevsky, an author I have never been able to stomach. I preferred Tolstoy, Chekhov, Turgenev, writers she too admired. She tried to make me read *Crime and Punishment*, but I found it an awful bore.

One of the visitors to Castle Bolton was the major artist Jakob Kramer, whom I was to get to know very intimately in the fifties in Leeds. Epstein's head of Jakob is one of the sculptor's finest and most characteristic works.

One day, when I was in Leyburn, I met Hermann, one of the Dutch sailors who had got caught up in the outbreak of war and had to remain in Britain. Ignorant people called him 'Hermann the German'. He was very stolid, silent and humorous. We often drank together, with other members of the Dutch crew, in the Blue Lion in East Witton. Hermann told me that the police had been making inquiries about me, and that Jock and the camp commandant wanted me back. He advised me to stay low.

But I incautiously made trips to Richmond, a town I liked well, packed to overflowing with soldiers, some of whom became my friends. I remember one soldier, a conscript, who was so puzzled by my civilian status. Then he realized what I was, and said: 'Ah, so you are one of *them* – good for you.' I think he was referring not to my obvious homosexuality but to my pacifism. I only met him once. The bus services between Leyburn and Richmond were very irregular, and allowed me to spend only about one hour in the evening in that town, with its delightful old theatre.

On another occasion, I met Sam, an epileptic whom I had made friends with on my first day in the camp at East Witton. One morning I saw Sam lying on the ground, throwing himself about and foaming at the mouth. I had had a previous experience of helping an epileptic, in London in Camden Town, in a shop doorway during an air raid. A policeman had started to speak to the epileptic, who by then was recovering from his seizure, in a most unfriendly and unhelpful way, saying: 'You know you should not be out at night. You should not let yourself go like this. You are making trouble for people,' and so on. I asked the bobby to leave him to me, and I would see him home. At the time, I did not know what to do to help an epileptic, but just held him in my arms and talked quietly to him. When he was able to give me his address, which was not far away, I took him home to his family. I then found out what one should do in such circumstances, and I was able to help Sam several times, and protect him from himself. He was middle-aged, and his face always had a hopeless expression on it. I never saw him laugh, and he spoke very little. When I met him in Leyburn, he was going home; he had finally been recognized as unfit to work with saws and axes. As he said goodbye to me at the station, he told me they were looking for me.

I had no desire to return to East Witton, so I went home. After about a week with my parents, I was again called to the Labour Exchange, and sent to a hostel run by the War Agricultural Executive Committee in Thirsk. This was slightly better than East Witton. There was a Friends' Meeting House in Thirsk, and there were adult education classes at which I was able to study English poetry with a very sympathetic tutor who I believe was a C.O.

It was there that I met a secret supporter of Hitler and the Nazis, a certain James Gidley, who claimed he was a poet. He lived in a converted railway carriage near Kirkby Moorside, full of fascist literature and photos of Hitler, Goebbels, Goering and Nazi soldiers. We were working mostly on the big gentlemen's farms around Thirsk, ditching and draining and breaking open potato clamps in weather so icy the earth was like cement. At one farm where there was a problem with the drains from the gentleman-farmer's big house, we had to dig up the drains until we found the cause of the blockage: the farmer had been thowing his condoms down the flush toilet, and they had formed a dense mass at a bend in the pipes. We had to clean that up. Our foreman on the farm commented: 'What a daft way to go on! I throw mine on t'back o' t'fire!'

I escaped again, from Thirsk to the Lake District, where I found myself in Appleby, a delightful town. But I had no job and very little money. As I tried to catch my breath, and recover my shattered nerves – Thirsk was a region of airfields and concomitant enemy attacks – I got a bed at a small hotel on the main street in Appleby that rises to the castle. It was very cheap, and was in a kind of dormitory, where some nights I had to share my bed with a lorry driver on a long-distance run.

Then I moved on to the Y.M.C.A. hostel in Cliburn, near Penrith, where I did the cleaning and bed-making and various dirty odd jobs. I was quite happy being a maid-of-all-work, as the hostel was full of Irish labourers who had come to work on the farms: many the Irish flea I caught! There were also three young Finnish merchant navy sailors, who, like my Dutch friends in East Witton, had been caught in Britain at the outbreak of war and were not allowed to return home. They were jovial, muscular, enormous men, and loved getting drunk at the local pub with me. Then we would stagger back arm-in-arm to the hostel. They were wonderful singers and dancers. I taught them all the latest dance steps. Later they found girlfriends in Penrith, and I was not so popular, though we remained close friends.

At the Cliburn hostel, we had a gay old cook, who had formerly been in the chorus of many West End shows. He used to try to remember routines from 'The Scarlet Pimpernel' or 'The Maid of the Mountains'. He was a vicious tittle-tattle, and so very entertaining, and from him I heard lots of backstage gossip about figures like Ivor Novello and John Gielgud. He used to make me an early cup of tea each morning, before the labourers rose for their daily toil, leaving their beds in a total mess, which I had to clean up. The director of the hostel was an ex-army major, a real old fusspot, and when I told him I wanted some Keatings' Powder to delouse the Irish beds, he refused to believe that such vermin could exist in *his* hostel. I had to capture several prize specimens in matchboxes before he would order the powder. The Irish, and then the Finns, got wind of the cook's sexual preferences, and soon the hostel was being transformed into a male brothel, with drunken orgies every night. The ex-army major had a nervous collapse and had to leave for a psychiatric hospital, where he died not long afterwards. The local woman cleaner who came in each morning to help me with 'the rough' was aghast at some of the scenes she witnessed in the early morning, when his 'early risers', as the cook tactfully referred to them, woke up with a full head of steam. As a consequence, there were not so many evidences of wet dreams on the sheets I had to smoothe every morning when the itinerant labourers had departed for their honest toil.

But things began to get out of hand at nights. Several times, the police and the M.P.s had to be called in, and I wondered, with a thrill of amusement, if we would be charged with keeping a 'disorderly house' – at a Y.M.C.A. hostel! The old male cook was almost completely gaga, and could not have cared less: he had told me some horrifying tales of his encounters with the British police in the 'gay' nightlife of London and the provincial cities when he was on tour with 'Sunny' or 'The Desert Song'.

But I felt that things were perhaps getting a little too hot, so I moved into very comfortable digs in the village. It was at Cliburn, too, that I first met Italian and German Prisoners of War, with many of whom I struck up romantic friendships. It was my way of putting my pacifism into practice, and of healing the breach between the nations. It was also marvellous practice for my Italian and German. They taught me a lot of naughty words I had not learnt in Dr Mennie's classes. With the Italians, I sang choruses from grand opera; with the Germans, I performed all the folksongs dear Miss Robinson had taught us at school – *'Muss i' denn'*, *'Ach, du lieber Augustin'*, *'Ein Jäger aus Kurpfalz'*, and, of course, *'Die Lorelei'*:

Ich weiss nicht, was soll es bedeuten,
Dass ich so traurig bin . . .

Anything but the Horst Wessel Lied. . . . With all that linguistic exercise, I soon became very fluent, while overhead the Nazi bombers droned impulsively towards Glasgow or Belfast.

My peregrinations continued. I had to be on the move all the time. This explains my love of travel, in part at least; the only way I can conquer the pervasive melancholy of my character is through a constant change of scene. Years later, Joe Ackerley showed me his address book: mine was the only entry with page upon page of different addresses. I hate to feel 'settled' anywhere. As soon as I get tired of a place, or if people are too nasty to me, I fold my tent and depart under cover of night, often leaving valuable possessions behind me.

That was how I came to leave Cliburn, in the small hours of the morning, in a lesbian friend's taxi. I was on the run again, until the damned Ministry of Labour in Wawn Street caught up with me and sent me to some other destination. But on two occasions, I chose my own work.

The first was a spell as farm labourer at the George Lansbury Farm, known as The Lansbury Gate Farm at Clavering (Lower Ford End), Essex. It was run by the War Resisters' International, and it was named after a celebrated labour politician and pacifist, whose beautiful grand-daughter, the unusual actress Angela Lansbury, is now a Hollywood and Broadway star. I did not know it at the time, but my hero Max Plowman had lived not far away, at Langham, near Colchester, where he died in May 1941. This was also the headquarters of the *Adelphi* magazine and The Adelphi Players, run by John Middleton Murry, another of my heroes at that time. (At the age of sixteen, ecstatic at the sudden realization that I was homosexual, I had taken his autobiography, *Between Two Worlds*, out of the South Shields Public Library on finding the entry 'homosexuality' in the index: with what excitement I devoured those important pages!) Middleton Murry published several of my early poems in the *Adelphi*, and wrote me a number of kind letters. It was through Murry that I was taken on at the Lansbury Gate Farm.

It was a happy, hardworking community, but it soon became evident that I was no good at all at farming. I used to mix the mash for the fowls and the pigs, and tried my hand at milking, with no success: the cows looked round at me with undisguised expressions of scorn at my incompetence. I mucked out the stables and the pig-styes, and for a while I took great pleasure in grooming the farm horses, until it was discovered that the job aggravated my constantly worsening asthma. Sometimes I would wake up at night and feel as if I would never draw another breath. I had to get up and sit in a chair, sleepless, trying to do deep breathing and avoid the horrible feeling of imminent suffocation. I used to sniff snuff to make me sneeze, because sneezing seemed to give my constricted chest a temporary relief. In the mornings, I was in no condition to work, but I used to go out into the fields hoping the fresh air would help me, hoeing and weeding-out endless rows of turnip seedlings or banking up potato clamps in the mist and frost of the featureless Essex countryside.

On one of my weekend trips to London from the farm, I got caught in an air-raid, just before closing-time. I had 'done the "Dilly" ' without any luck, so when the sirens went I popped into the nearest bar, though I only had about two bob in my pocket. I sat at the bar, which began to empty as the bombs started falling. My drink was a glass of Algerian wine, the cheapest I could order. The bartender, an amiable Irishman, shouted time and said I could stay inside until the 'rumpus' as he called it was over. He locked the door and checked the black-out shutters. One or two old soaks were sitting at tables, taking advantage of this unofficially extended drinking time to swill another warm beer – the drink I hated most after whisky.

There was only one other person seated at the bar, and I could tell at once that he was not 'gay'. He looked like a rather raffish business man, but he had a look of sardonic amusement on his face as he said to me: 'What's that muck you're drinking?' I told him. 'Here, have a proper drink on me,' he answered, looking at my hands that were starting to shake with fright as the bombs kept falling. He produced a silver flask from his Burberry and poured me a stiff brandy. We started chatting, and soon found we were both interested in writing. I told him I was a poet. 'Would I have read anything by you?' he wondered – the sort of question I never know how to answer. If I said 'No' it might be taken as an insult, and as my work had appeared only in the obscure plaquette, *Indications*, I hardly dared hope he could have seen it, so there was no point in replying 'Yes, perhaps.'

I told him my name, and in reply he said: 'I'm Ian Fleming' – a name that meant nothing at all to me then. I told him why I was not in uniform, and to my surprise he commented 'Good for you'. Was he being ironic? I supposed so. But at least he had not punched me on the nose or called me a traitor to my King and Country, which were the usual reactions from strangers.

He went on to ask me what kind of poetry I wrote, and I tried to explain my Europeanized English poetic style, with its heavy reliance on foreign models rather than on British poets.

'Can you recite some to me?' he asked. In those days, I had a good memory for poetry, especially my own, so to the accompaniment of whistling and exploding bombs I began to recite what I naively considered to be one of my most inscrutably hermetic poems, in a very mysterious yet dramatic manner, and with infinite slowness that I condescendingly imagined would allow him to catch one or two ambiguities of the eighth type in full flight:

A child laid ringed hands
On the adamantine rails.

There is a cottage buried in the lines
Abandoned and with showy curtains.

Dragons and aromatic monsters
Go scalded there with their own bad breath.

Parents come to pose a long-delayed wreath
And a friendly inspector has a word for them.

But as they pass down Bright Street
The neighbours back into their dark pantries.

The grave like water beats:
A heart is in it.

The dead child looks round his grief,
And sees a rose.

The Irish bartender, Terence, was gazing at me pop-eyed, and the little audience at the tables seemed transfixed in a long silence – my poem had stopped the bombs falling, and just as I reached the end the all-clear sounded. Everyone applauded, but whether for my poem or the all-clear I could not tell – perhaps for both, I hoped. 'You stopped the Luftwaffe!' Terence cried, open-mouthed. Smiling, I batted modest lids on self-approving eyes.

'That's really quite sinister,' said my companion at the bar. 'I suppose the word "cottage" has more than one meaning?'

'If you like,' I replied rather huffily, thinking he was trying to 'send me up'.

'And I expect the "inspector" is both a train inspector, a ticket inspector that is, and a police inspector?'

'It is not to be taken literally,' I answered. 'But the cottage was one I stayed in for a few weeks right beside the railway track from Newcastle to Carlisle, just outside Haydon Bridge. I was so miserable there, I often felt like throwing myself in front of the blacked-out expresses – which, if you like, are the "dragons and aromatic monsters" with their throat-rasping steam or "bad breath". The "inspector" could be anyone in authority, come to take me away to jail or the loony bin.'

'Your poor parents,' – his voice trailed off in a sigh. This veiled remark was, I thought, quite perceptive for a non-cryptic poet.

'Actually,' I went on, 'I've often thought that my kind of impenetrably hermetic poetry could be used in wartime as an absolutely uncrackable secret code. Messages could be sent in what is for most people utterly nonsensical poetic form, something like modernized Góngora or Mallarmé, and that could only be interpreted at the other end by another hermetic poet. If the message fell into enemy hands, it would be completely incomprehensible. And if the poet himself fell into enemy hands, he would not even have to swallow the paper it was written on in invisible ink.'

There was a long silence. As we made for the door, my companion said: 'That's a very interesting idea. Let me have your address, and I'll get in touch with you about it.'

I thought he meant that he would show my poems to some editor, so I gave him the address of the George Lansbury Farm. When he heard the name, Fleming commented: 'A damned good socialist.'

'And pacifist,' I reminded him. 'None of your turncoat James Maxwells!'

He gave me a funny look, then we shook hands and parted in the blackout. I never heard from him, but years later I learned that Ian Fleming had been in the Secret Service during the war, something to do with secret codes, in fact.

In my first book about Japan, *These Horned Islands*, I describe an early-morning train journey between Hakodate (where I had got off the ferry from Aomori in Honshu) and Sapporo, the chief city in Hokkaido. I went to the 'Nippon Shokudo' dining-car for breakfast, and was amused to find a typical Janglishism on the menu – a ham omelette whose name had suffered the ritual contraction so beloved by the Japanese ('pascom' for personal computer is one of the latest). The item on the menu was billed as 'Hamlet'. So I had a 'Hotto Sand Hamlet' – a toasted sandwich of ham and omelette. In one of Fleming's books, written after his first visit to Japan – it was the year after I'd left Sendai – I found the word 'Hamlet' used by him to describe a ham omelette. William Plomer at Cape's, who had reviewed my book for Joe Ackerley, had given Fleming a copy of it, and he had plagiarized my little discovery, with its slightly hermetic ring. I wonder if he remembered the poet he had talked to about secret codes that night in the bar, during an air-raid whose bombs I had stilled by the magic of my voice intoning those cryptic phrases?

I was lucky to make a close friend of Angela Petter, who lived in a small cottage not far from the farm. She, too, was a pacifist, and a writer. We talked about poetry and literature and music, and she introduced me to Hugh Ianson Fausset, who at that time was writing his fine biography of Whitman, my favourite American poet. I remember we discussed Whitman's homosexuality, and Hugh agreed that he was 'so', but believed that the good grey poet had not indulged in any 'dirty' sexual habits. I felt dubious about that; in sex, is anything 'dirty'? I did not think so, except in the minds of others.

My old friend from university, David Paul, came to stay whenever he had a weekend leave – for he had unwillingly joined the army – and in the end he and Angela were married: I was godfather to their delightful daughter, Helena. But that was still two or three years in the future. . . .

At New Year, I was given a few days off – I had had to work all through the Christmas holidays – so I went up to London for a couple of days. I was strolling along Coventry Street, outside Lyons, when a well-dressed young gentleman caught my eye. He was tall and quite nice-looking, obviously from the upper classes. Without speaking, we began to walk side by side towards Piccadilly; whenever I made a gesture, he would copy it. This was one of the ways homosexuals used to recognize one another. Eventually, I found myself in a well-appointed flat, with a grand piano, somewhere in either Jermyn Street or Half Moon Street. Without a word, we undressed and got into the luxurious double bed, where we made delicious, gentle, tender love until about three o'clock in the morning. Then he said I had to leave. He gave me thirty shillings for a hotel room, which I gladly accepted, as I had only about sixpence and my return rail ticket from Liverpool Street. I went out into the blackout, where a few New Year revellers were still wandering. By the time it got to four o'clock, I decided it would be a waste of money to get an hotel room, so I spent the next two hours strolling among the pimps and prostitutes of Piccadilly Circus, watching their manoeuvres as they accosted servicemen: American sailors, floating along with a rolling gait in their sexy, smooth serge bellbottoms, were particularly desirable. I discovered that the two-button flap at the crotch was repeated in the underwear. These two-button flaps seemed to me wonderfully exotic and enticing; today's American sailors no longer have that aura of male mystery and glamour. My poem, 'Wild Wilbur' from *The Drowned Sailor* (and reprinted by Geoffrey Grigson in one of his anthologies) was about such an American sailor whom I met in Falmouth.

For my next stop was the West Country. I thought that the air of Devon and Cornwall would be good for my asthma, so I answered an advertisement for a tutor in a family living at Praze Downs in Cornwall; I think the ad was in *The New Statesman*. I was accepted, and arrived to teach various subjects I knew next-to-nothing about – geometry, algebra, geography – to two girls and a teenage boy. I stayed at a farmhouse a short distance away, where the farmer's wife fed me on a diet of Cornish pasties composed mainly of potato. But I had some free time in which I did some paintings of the place, and I was able to make trips to Camborne, Truro, Penzance, Newquay, St Ives and Carbis Bay, where I met Ben Nicolson and Barbara Hepworth and visited the studios of various other local artists. But the air of Cornwall did not suit me at all: I seemed to be getting worse. So again I packed up, and in a state of desperate ill-health dragged myself back home to South Shields.

A Day on the Thresher

1945

Jethro, the boss, has a black patch over his left eye. He stands on top of the thresher and tosses the sheaves, after the binder-twine has been cut, down into the maw of the treacherous, old-fashioned machine.

I was standing beside him all day, cutting the twine on the sheaves and throwing the sheaves to him to shove down into the thresher's roaring, ever-hungry maw.

'Bloody fool of a gentleman farmer did this,' he shouted at me, grinning. 'Put a pitchfork through me eye. Up Alnwick way. Wanted to keep on working as well, the mean bugger, frightened he wouldn't get his stacks finished by dark, the rotten bastard. Got 'is pound o' flesh, 'e did!'

Two men are throwing sheaves up to us from the old stack, which is slowly getting lower. The sweat is soaking their shirts on this August day and the chaff and dust stick to their wet faces. After three hours without a break, they are obviously tiring.

'Do 'em good, a bit of 'ard work,' says Jethro, laughing at himself. He is a tall, broad, swarthy man. His father had been a gipsy, a true romany. Jethro is now 'settled', which does not mean much, as he tours all the farms in this county and the next with his own thresher, picked up for a song at some market fairing. He is feared and respected by all the farmers, and that's saying something. 'I got 'em by the short 'airs,' he chortles. He could let them down by arriving a day late, or when the weather had broken. While Jethro's on his thresher, he's the king of the castle, he's the one who bosses the boss of the farm labourers.

The farmer, old Matthew Potts, a sour-faced, stingy, bent old rogue, a tough character well-known in every livestock and grain mart in the county, is standing on the new, slowly rising stack behind us, slowly building it up round the sides, then filling in the middle, layer after layer, with crabbed, liver-spotted, trembling but experienced hands. He must be seventy if he's a day. But his attention to the good building of the stack of straw does not prevent him from keeping a wary, shrewd eye on us from under the broken peak of his ancient tartan cap, to see that everybody keeps hard at work. Indeed, on a threshing day, there's no stopping. The old lad wants his money's worth, and he doesn't intend to pay a penny overtime.

A small boy, Terry, with a nose like a cherry, his carrot hair grey with dust and thistledown, is trying to cope with the shifting heaps of chaff that pour relentlessly from underneath the shuddering machine. His clothes – a lumberjacket, an old khaki army shirt of his brother's, torn breeches and wrinkled wellingtons patched with bicycle puncture outfits – are all too big for him, and he looks a proper clown as he flounders desperately with an enormous, almost toothless wooden rake among the drifting mounds of chaff without making much impression on them. Old Potts is paying him sixpence an hour. Luckily for Terry, the corn stack is almost finished, so that the thresher will soon move on to another stack, leaving behind the accumulated chaff and straw.

Meggie, the sonsy land-girl, is humping the 'bottles' of straw from the thresher to old Matthew on his stack. She staggers back and forth ceaselessly, except when the twine in the thresher snaps – it often does – and the 'bottles' come out in loose masses of jumbled straw, which she wearily pushes to one side among Terry's chaff hills. Old Potts places the bottles round the edge of the stack as if he were arranging three-piece suites, or big, blond cushions, making the new layer slightly overlap the lower, so that the sides of the stack will be neatly inward-sloping towards the bottom – helps to keep it dry in rain and snow.

Andrew and Jack, two of the regular farmhands, know the rhythm of work demanded by Potts only too well. They keep silent, a bit grim and resentful, at the other end of the thresher, weighing the grain into 12 cwt sacks then hoisting them by the 'ears' on to their shoulders and dumping them in an orderly fashion on the lorry.

Angus, a raw young fellow of seventeen, is Jethro's mate, has travelled all over with him, drunk him under the thresher many a time and slept the night there with him. He's a hard case. Angus and Jethro take turns working with me on top of the thresher, and when Angus jumps up on top to give Jethro a 'spell' I can feel at once the subtle change in pace. Nobody gives me a spell. I have to keep up with either of them without stopping. Angus is a lot nimbler and faster than Jethro, and working beside him I can feel the electric energy throbbing in his powerful body, the neat turn of his belted waist, the biceps bulging his rolled-up faded pink shirt. But he's all right: from time to time he tells me to take a blow, and, as if it were nothing, does the work of two men, all the time laughing and talking fit to beat the band, never winded. 'Man lost 'is leg doon there 'tother week,' he shouts, pointing to the machine's grinding maw. 'Right up to 'ere it took 'im off' – pointing to his prominent groin. 'Nearly lost 'is little willie.' He roars with laughter that is slightly mad. 'Watch out fer yersel', Jim, divvent lose the family jewels!' He has to bawl at me to make himself heard in the ferocious din.

Just now, Jethro is giving little Terry a hand with the ever-invading chaff, but he is ready at any moment to rush to the thresher, or the filthy, smelly tractor that drives it, if something goes wrong. Often the driving-belt slips off the huge flywheel, or the twine tying the bottles snaps. ' 'Urry up, Jeth, ould Pottsie's nigh pissin' hissel'.' Indeed, the old sourpuss is gnawing his gums in frustration; he puts his false teeth in only after work. I can seize such unscheduled pauses to take a swig of cold tea from my can, and brush the thistledown from my eyelashes, the sweat and dust from my eyebrows and neck.

Angus likes to act the foreman ganger, to the veiled annoyance of Potts' regular farmhands working on the sacks. When Angus isn't busy with the machinery, he will give them a hand, making them work twice as fast for a few minutes as they swear at him out of the corners of their mouths, keeping an eye on Potts, who won't allow bad language from his men.

When it is Jethro's turn to look after the machine, Angus stands away from the stack and smokes – something else old Pottsie does not approve of, for what if the stack caught fire? Angus laughs in his face. He just stands with hand on hip, in an oddly feminine stance, watching us all critically and not very kindly – pityingly, really – and shouts uproarious insults at Meggie, who can give him as good as she gets, and better, in the way of 'language'. She sometimes makes old Matthew Potts' face blench with her blasphemies, that are more comic than irreverent. 'Now then, Meggie,' he warns her, shaking a crooked, arthritic forefinger at her. 'Remember God's listening.' He is a pillar of the local Ebenezer Chapel.

'Silly old fart,' grumbles Meggie. ' 'E 'ad 's 'and up me shirt i' the kitchen last night. Then Ethel come in.' Ethel is his wife, a hefty cheesemaker and bread-baker, and something high up in the W.I. 'Ye'd think 'e'd got a 'lectric shock.'

Roaring with laughter, Angus leaps on top of the thresher again and starts working with maniac energy. After a while, he unbuttons his breeches and pisses over the side, sending a seething, steaming stream from a prick like a hosepipe in a soaring arc above Meggie's headscarf with its pictures of the Royal Family at the corners.

'Ye filthy fucker!' she yells up at him. 'I'll come up and cut that off if ye're not careful.'

'Ye're jealous!' crows Angus, ''cos ye can't piss standin' up!' And so the long day wears on.

All day, every day, day in, day out. All morning, from eight o'clock to twelve, and all afternoon, from one o'clock to five, the work goes on. Potts won't let us take a snack mid-morning and mid-afternoon, like most farmers do. The tractor stinks and splutters, the thresher thunders and shakes and shudders and sends out clouds of dust and slowly drifting thistledown. The din is deafening.

The men on the wheat stack toss up the sheaves with one unchanging motion. Meggie impales the bundles of straw as if she were bayoneting a Nazi, hoists it on her shoulders, walks a few yards to the new straw stack, throws it up to old Potts who fussily sets it in place, then walks back to the thresher in time for the next bottle. There are dark circles of sweat under her arms and between her capacious breasts in their aertex land-girl's shirt.

I slash the twine round the sheaves with a worn pocket-knife. Jethro takes over and starts feeding the machine. Andrew and Jack unhook the full sacks, hook on empty ones, weigh the full sacks and heave them on to the waiting lorry. The mindless monotony of it all is so spellbinding, I sometimes feel I am working in a waking nightmare.

'Watch out, Jim,' Jethro warns me. 'That's 'ow lads tumble into the 'ole.'

The driving-belt jumps off the flywheel, nearly hitting Andrew, and Jethro jumps down to fix it. In the sudden silence, we hear a strangely sweet, musical, harmonious note filling the sky before it slowly dies away in a despondent growl. The all-clear. We were so busy, and the noise was so loud, we never heard the air-raid warning.

'I wonder if it were one 'o they doodlebugs,' mutters Jack.

'Naw, they can't reach this far north,' says Jethro. 'We got ol' 'itler on the 'op, men!'

The thresher starts up again, screeching, swaying, shuddering with a frenzied abandon. The work starts again.

All this under a low grey sky, in the field beside the road, where the armoured waggons and the cars flash past, their occupants like dummies for a moment watching us work our guts out, and on their faces a look of interest that never varies.

When I get home at night, I collapse in the chair and start shaking all over. I feel I'm still on top of the thresher. And I can't stop shaking. I can hardly hold my cup of tea. My mother holds it to my lips until I've swallowed a few mouthfuls. Then the shaking stops. It's like this every night. And I'll be shaking in my sleep, dreaming I'm falling into the hole.

Towards Hiroshima and Nagasaki

1945–6

My parents were alarmed by my thinness and pallor. I had given up prostitution and 'the gay life' – at least, for the time being. I felt too ill to do anything, or anyone. My mother suggested, with my father's approval, that I should visit a local doctor who was said to be good with cases like mine. He was Dr Grant Sinclair, whose surgery and very comfortable home were in Dean Road. 'He's a bachelor,' my mother informed me, and my father looked away rather quickly.

Grantie (as I came to call him when he became my good friend) had me X-rayed, and I was referred to specialists at the Ingham Infirmary in Westoe Road, and at the Newcastle Infirmary – where I had once spent a few days at the beginning of the war with Wittgenstein, working alongside him as a very incompetent ward orderly. I could not stand the sight of blood, so I had to leave after three days. I remember Wittgenstein despised my pacifism, but when I met him occasionally in town at the public toilet behind the Y.M.C.A. in Eldon Place, a favourite haunt of cruisers, he was more friendly.

It was discovered that I was suffering from a chronic form of asthma that could be fatal: the word 'emphysema' came into my existence, which the COD defines as 'enlargement of air vesicles of the lungs; swelling caused by presence of air in connective tissues of body, from Gk *emphusēma* (*emphusaō* puff up)'. Apparently what had always been considered as adolescent asthma had long been an emphysematic condition, and it was rapidly getting worse. 'You silly ass!' Grantie told me, 'you'd never have passed an army medical with that condition in your lungs!' I explained to him that I had wanted more than anything else to make a personal protest against war. He was not impressed. 'You daft bugger! Just one look at you and they'd have turned you down, with that hair, and that face, and that walk!'

'I'm aware of all that,' I told him. 'But it's all beside the point. You don't seem to realize that a man can be both a poof and a pacifist. Being "gay" does not mean I lack all seriousness. Even your flaming screaming queens have important opinions of their own, and are not devoid of sincerity. I may put on a mask of gay abandon, and if it deceives people I can't help that. But underneath that mask I'm a completely different person – a real man, and a real poet – even though I do say it meself.' I could not resist giving those last words a mincing intonation, with a careless flap of my limp-wristed right hand. Grantie was a conservative, but he accepted it all, all I appeared to be on the surface, and all I kept secret in my heart. He often invited me for drinks after his surgery in the evenings, and we would sit up half the night listening to his vast collection of jazz and classical records, and playing four-handed duets on his grand piano. I dedicated a poem to him, 'Music at Night', which appeared in my first Oxford University Press book, *The Submerged Village*. And ours was a genuinely platonic relationship.

My emphysema was aggravated by hay fever, so first I had to go to Newcastle to take allergy tests, and it was found that I was allergic to practically everything I had been in contact with during the last five years – cat fur, horse scurf, tree pollen, ragweed, house mites and heaven knows what else. I had an extremely painful series of intra-muscular injections to cure the hay fever; they worked, and I have never again suffered from that distressing affliction. I was given a long course of therapeutic massage at the Ingham Infirmary by a truly wonderful blind young man, an expert masseur who could sense the slightest changes in my mood or in my physical condition. 'Been overdoing it again, haven't we?' he might comment drily. But he assured me that my ribcage was still flexible, not like some of the patients he had, in whom it was absolutely rigid. During his long, soothing massages, he was patiently teaching me to re-learn breathing. I had been breathing with a small section of the top of my lungs, instead of using the whole lungs, and he was soon having me breathe calmly and steadily with my stomach, with my diaphragm. After a few weeks, I stopped gasping at nights, though it took long practice to concentrate on my new style of breathing until it became automatic. My asthma and emphysema were completely cured, and I have never suffered from them again, expect for a short period when I was Poet in Residence at Amherst College, Massachusetts – and there I think the causes were mainly psychological, because of the contemptuous way the supposedly intellectual teaching staff treated me: 'But He's a Homosexual!' screamed the title of an essay about me written by the Professor of English in the first issue of a literary magazine published in New York that I think was called *New Writing*. It was carefully placed on my bedside table at the Lord Jeffrey when I attended my interview in Amherst, but it did not deflect me from my determination to get the post in that narrow-minded little academic community.

As soon as I had recovered from my treatments, Wawn Street was on my tracks again, and I was dispatched to my final slough of despond, the Ponteland hostel run by the War Agricultural Executive Committee ('the War-Ag' as we contemptuously referred to it and its incompetent directors, later arrested for misappropriation of funds and other irregularities).

This was another dump for the undesirables of Tyneside – petty crooks on probation, handicapped elderly men, unemployed pitmen, 'walking wounded', shell-shocked merchant navymen, school leavers with nowhere else to go – and again I was the only conscientious objector. There was an atmosphere of delinquency and furtive crime. Our lockers were constantly being broken open by some desperate Borstal youth; money, clothes and other possessions kept going missing, and nothing was done about it. There was none of the gaiety of the Y.M.C.A. hostel at Cliburn, though there was considerable larking around after lights-out – sexual activities in which I took no part: at twenty-five, I considered I was past it, 'all passion spent' and all that. In my spare moments, I got on with my reading and writing, as far as these were possible in that crowded, noisy camp. There was absolutely no one I felt in sympathy with, except for one witty ex-miner who told me he was suffering from a 'barking ulcer' and so was exempt from military service. He described to me how he had developed and nurtured his ulcer to deceive the doctors at his army medical. 'Thousands do it, and get exempted,' he told me. 'Why don't you?' I felt it was useless to explain my motives in refusing to be conscripted.

The war in Europe was obviously drawing to a close. My friends in the army, navy and air force kept sending me Forces Letters – some of which must have puzzled the censor when he opened them – from North Africa, Italy and then from France. I still have all those letters written on those strange little forms, from Bill, Terence, Herbert, Tommy, Gerald, Andy. . . . One day, I hope to use them in some other work. Sadly, so many of the writers are now dead.

Other friends and old classmates were dying in battle, or in air raids. I wept for the absurdity of it all, for all that unnecessary courage and useless patriotism.

It was while I was at Ponteland that I saw my first British casualty. We had been sent out from the hostel one bitterly cold day to 'knock muck' on some farmer's fields. There were four of us: Basil, a sort of seedy down-and-out who had once been a bus conductor before it was discovered that he had been pocketing some of the fares; Teddy, an ex-Borstal lad, raw-boned and perennially cheerful in a particularly depressing way; Mavis, his inamorata, a former chorus-boy, and myself. We had worked off and on all morning, with many a break for tea and entertainments – Mavis singing 'Roll out the Barrel' and giving hilarious imitations of Vera Lynn, 'the Forces' sweetheart'. We were expecting the farmer to bring us hot tea for lunch – 'an' mebbe a roast turkey wi' all the trimmin's' laughed Teddy – so we sent Basil to wait for him at the roadside just before noon. Basil went off, silent and sullen as ever, and disappeared behind the dry-stone wall beside the gate. Time passed, and we saw the farmer's car stop by the gate, then drive off. The tea had been delivered – 'with some dainty puff pastry, we hope,' lisped Mavis. We waited a while, and as Basil did not appear, we got impatient. ' 'E's scoffin' all the bloody stuff hissel',' yelled Teddy, with a broad grin. I went to see what Basil was doing. When I got to the road, I saw Basil lying on his back by the gate, the can of hot tea upset by his side. He was dead. He had had a heart attack just after the farmer had driven off. We laid some old potato sacks over him, and Teddy ran to the nearest telephone; the hostel van arrived within half an hour and took us all back to the hostel, with poor Basil's body still under potato sacks on the floor. We had the rest of the day off.

Basil apparently had no relatives, or no one who wanted to own him. We all subscribed sixpence for a gorgeous wreath of 'mums and glads aureoled in gypsophila – 'baby's breath', Mavis called it.

'It's a judgment on you all!' This indictment came from a fundamentalist religious maniac. He was not a pacifist. 'We are working in the armies of the Lord!' he would shout as we drove off to some field of beets. 'Hellfire and damnation shall come upon ye!' he cried when he caught any of us creeping into someone else's bed for a bit of humping. 'Sodom is come again!' he would groan, praying on his knees for our depraved souls. 'Shut up, you old faggot!' screamed Mavis. 'Who wants an old pisspot like you to pray for our souls!' Holy Harry, as they called him, went on inveighing against the sins of the younger generation, 'tribe of beasts, buggers and blasphemers!' His alliteration was biblical, but there were some doubts about what the last word meant. 'It's people what drink dead men's shit,' explained Teddy. 'I knew one once in Wallsend.'

We expressed disbelief.

'It's true!' he cried indignantly. 'Every time some old bloke kicked the bucket he used to ask to lay 'im out free of charge. He used to suck their shit. I seen him do it wi' me granddad. Lovely job 'e made of 'im, looked a picture, 'e did.'

'Men loved darkness rather than light, because their deeds were evil,' Holy Harry quoted from his well-thumbed Bible. 'John, three, nineteen.'

He was always trying to convert us, begging us to 'get down on those sinner's knees' beside him and pray for our salvation. I had a hard time trying to convince him that I had no faith at all, that for me God did not exist, and that I did not need the comfort of any religion.

'I could tell from the minute I set eyes on ye, ye were not a Christian,' Harry said reproachfully. 'But I'll pray for your soul, whether ye like it or not.'

'I'd rather you didn't,' I replied. 'There is no salvation for any of us. The sooner you realize that, the sooner you'll stop spouting all that tripe.'

His words had reminded me of something the pious young chairman of the Student Christian Movement had said to me in the Union one day: 'I can tell you're not a Christian.'

I wondered how he could tell. A sort of S.C.M. missionary came to spread the good word among the students. He was a permanent fixture in the Union coffeeshop, where he lay in wait for sinners to convert. We called him Punch, because he had the profile of Mother Shipton. He was stocky and manly and smoked a pipe – a real old-fashioned muscular Christian. When I told him I had no faith, he asked me if I had any plans for the next day.

'Yes,' I replied. 'I'm going to the Kreisler concert.'

He was triumphant. 'You see!' he cried. 'You believe! You have faith in tomorrow!'

Frankly, I couldn't see what that had to do with believing in a non-existant God, or in a God who, if he did exist, as Punch assured me he did, was a spiteful and cruel old man I would have no desire to know in real life.

'I believe,' said Punch quietly, looking me in the eyes. 'I believe in the resurrection.'

I did not bother to argue any more with him. Anyone who believes in the resurrection will believe in anything.

Ponteland, Tyneside, 6 August 1945. I was waiting for the bus to take me back to the labour camp from the farm where I had spent the day working on the top of an ancient mechanical thresher. I was with a group of fellow conscientious objectors from another hostel, and the farmer had brought us a copy of the evening paper, the Newcastle *Evening News*, with the news about Hiroshima. At that moment, we did not grasp the enormity of the disaster. Slowly, however, we realized that this must mean the end of the war in the Pacific. We had had V.E. day, which in South Shields at least had been a damp squib of celebration. My parents had sold their house in

West Avenue, and we had moved to a flat above the shops opposite the Town Hall, in Fowler Street. From our bay window – I had been given the day off from the hostel at Ponteland – I watched a few depressed-looking soldiers sitting on the steps of the Town Hall, as if stunned, not knowing what to do with themselves.

Then it was back to work as usual. But we realized that the end of hostilities in Europe and the Pacific would bring our release from the monotonous drudgery that had been our lot – six years of forced labour as punishment for refusing to be conscripted into the British Armed Forces. Some of us had spent long periods in prison. Others had given up in despair, and joined the army.

Then there was Nagasaki. The full horror of those atom bombs made our own experience of air raids pale into insignificance. But it convinced us that we had been right, that pacifism and total rejection of armaments were the only hopes for the survival of mankind. The tragedy of war was absurd, monstrous, bitter and unnecessary; but after those two holocausts, pacifists would no longer be regarded as a cranky minority. We became a moral force to be reckoned with, especially after the establishment of the Campaign for Nuclear Disarmament, under the inspired leadership of Bertrand Russell.

We had entered a new age. Years later, I was to see a memorial near the Peace Park in Hiroshima honouring the formula $E = MC^2$ arrived at by the idiot genius Einstein, who may be regarded as the father of the atom bomb. It is well that the statue to his theory should be placed outside the park.

By this time, both my father and my mother had come round to accepting my pacifist beliefs. We had become reconciled. For what is the use of working for world peace if you are war with yourself, and with your own loved ones? 'You were right, Jim,' said my father grimly. 'By God you were right.'

In all the endless discussions that were about to begin on the control of atomic weapons, arms limitations and unilateral disarmament, there was one argument the force of whose logic I still cannot grasp. It goes something like this: any country that renounces its atomic weaponry will be at the mercy of those who do not. This seems to prove that men are even more stupid than I thought, for they are ready and willing to risk total, universal annihilation in order to prevent the atomic bombs, the hydrogen bombs, the neutron bombs, the biological and chemical warfare bombs from being dropped, while at the same time piling them up like greedy children jealous of one another's sweets or toys.

Yet men – and their misled leaders – would not be prepared to risk annihilation in order to preserve their freedom from perpetual and growing menace.

Another thing that proves men are stupid: they do not fight in modern warfare because they enjoy it. Like Auden's Unknown Citizen, 'when there was war, they went.' War could not exist without human stupidity. Men fight because the papers tell them to, because their leaders, safely ensconced in atom-bomb-proof shelters, tell them it is their patriotic duty to do so. The people who invent excuses for war have the wily one-track minds of the very stupid. And men are always taken in by them.

Or nearly always. Sometimes they suddenly see through the imbecile deception.

'You were right, Jim,' my father said. 'By God you were right.'

PART THREE

Post-War

The lion griefs loped from the shade
And on our knees their muzzles laid,
And Death put down his book. . . .

Peacetime Fighter

1946–7

Although I was more or less at peace with myself, and at peace with my father and mother, I was still at war with the world, and would continue to fight my personal conflicts for many years to come.

As a pacifist and ex-C.O., it was difficult for me to get a job after the war. It was thought that demobilized soldiers, in their 'demob suits', were the ones who should have the jobs. So I had to look for work in places that were sympathetic to pacifists. My first teaching post was at a Quaker prep school, the Downs School, Colwall. I was to teach French and German to the sons of well-to-do families, boys ranging in age from about nine to thirteen, after which they mostly went on to public schools like Oundle, Rugby and Winchester.

I was comfortably accommodated in two rooms in The Lodge, one of them a ground floor room with large windows looking on a big lawn. W. H. Auden had taught English there before the war, and I had the very rooms he had occupied. On warm summer nights, he would take his bedding out on the lawn and sleep there:

> Out on the lawn I lie in bed,
> Vega conspicuous overhead
> In the windless nights of June. . . .
>
> The bathing hours and the bare arms,
> The leisured drives through a land of farms . . .
> . . . Our freedom in this English house,
> Our picnics in the sun . . .
> . . . And all the birds in Wicken Fen.*

This lovely poem is idyllic, yet pregnant with menaces of the coming conflict, which the poet wisely sidestepped by emigrating to the United States. I would have done the same if I had had the chance.

I never felt that sense of emotional and spiritual involvement with the boys and with the social life of the school as Auden had. At the root of my

* Auden's lines to Geoffrey Hoyland, the headmaster of Downs School at that time.

lack of success was some inexpressible working-class resentment against those privileged boys. But I made one good friend there, the art master, Maurice Feild, a gentle and good-humoured soul, who encouraged me in my painting and music. At Christmas, we went with the school choir to sing to the German P.O.W.s in Malvern: I think it was Bach's 'Christmas Oratorio'. The P.O.W.s listened attentively to their former enemies singing the immortal music of their great countryman. At the end, they returned the compliment by singing an English carol, and then some German ones, carols that brought tears to my eyes as I thought of my German classes under Miss Robinson, who had taught us those very songs. I thought, too, of the classmates who had learnt the songs with me, many of whom had been killed in battle or in air raids. Those strong, virile German voices moved me deeply, and when I gave a speech of thanks in German, I found I could hardly speak for emotion. What useless suffering we had inflicted upon each other! And now we were singing carols of peace and love and good will to all men! What good had our religion of love and peace done to us? Why had we denied its basic beliefs? Were we all hypocrites, those of us who were Christians? I felt full of rage and despair, as well as sorrow.

There was a tremendous snowfall that winter, when I felt I would die of cold and grief and loneliness. The cold went on and on, and in the end I suddenly found myself breaking into helpless sobs as I left a particularly horrible class and trudged through the biting wind to my apartment. Nurse was alarmed (sweet thing!) and put me to bed for a few days of blissful respite from my torment. As so often in my academic appointments, it was the household staff and the secretarial staff who were kindest to me, not my fellow academics, who were nearly always dismissive or openly hostile.

So I was lucky to have a brief affair with a magnificent big Dutch girl who came to be the headmaster's family's au pair. She was an invigorating companion with a perpetual hearty laugh bubbling up from within her generous body, the perfect antidote to my introspection and silence. We spent long hours together in my snowlit rooms, and once walked all the way to Malvern and back when the buses were stopped because of the colossal snows. It was pure joy. She introduced me to Dutch coffee and cooking, and fed me on delicious marzipan cakes adorned with drifts of rainbow coloured sugar. She revitalized me in that long, white winter with her good humour and never-failing sense of the absurd, her personal sun.

The matron and the nurses and cooks all became my friends, and I still think of them with deep affection. When the snows melted, there were immense floods in Worcester, and my Dutch girl and I went to marvel at them, and at the cathedral, where I wrote a poem, 'The Flood', on one of the tombs.

But I was also writing longer works: translations of Henri Michaux and the novel by Jules Supervielle, *Le Voleur d'Enfants,* which, like my many translations of his poems, I did on spec, only to find that Alan Pryce-Jones had done it too, and got it published. So I started on a longer work of my own – a poetic epic called *The Creation,* which was eventually published by one of my students at Leeds University, Robin Skelton, from his short-lived Lotus Press, with a cover by Muriel Metcalfe. The poem created something of a theological controversy – theologians in those days were very authoritarian and uptight – because this creation had no God and arose *ab nihilo*: the first thing I had to create, before I got started on the rest, was fascinating Nothing. It received little other notice, but I gained an insight into King Lear's 'Nothing will come of nothing. . . .'

Summer came round again, and there were Audenesque parties and midnight dips in the swimming pool, with the delightful nurses and cooks. I 'swam' with one foot on the bottom. Eric Newton came to talk about art, and joked that the boys mistook him for Sir Isaac Newton. Under Maurice's guidance, I started to paint a picture of a skull that somehow turned into a Bantingesque landscape.

Another friend on the teaching staff, James Batley, arrived that term, and we soon found common enthusiasms in music and poetry. He was a very tall, affable, witty scholar, and wrote a poem for my departure which is so clever, and sums up so well the atmosphere of The Lodge, that I feel I must print it here. I hope James will forgive me for doing so without his permission, for I have long since lost sight of him:

The Lodge

Beyond the highest of school hedges –
sure shelter against boy and bell –
upon a lawn with rough-trimmed edges,
an Irish yew stands sentinel.
White doors and windows in the centre,
walls hung with clematis and rose,
will strike such strangers as will enter
the house not every schoolboy knows –
The Lodge, where many a legend lingers;
how masters came and went their way;
how tunes were strummed by poets' fingers;
how banquets cheered a youthful day.
Its upper rooms are daily haunted

by spirits, well-disposed or not,
who bump when some cold water's wanted
and rumble when the water's hot:
but water-sprites take swift dismissal
from boys who scamper through the hall,
from Collier's hounds or midnight whistle
or Norman, asking to play ball.
From January to December,
bold youths assail the Lodge's door:
may one or two of them remember
three men who came and went before.

The Inscription

Boy! as you come to your tutorial
forget the passing songs of birds.
Remember those whose true memorial
stands in a few hard-written words.
Here, AUDEN warned his generation –
too late to save it shedding blood.
Here, KIRKUP finished his 'Creation'
within a week and wrote 'The Flood'.
Abandon no chance inspiration
as, through these haunted doors, you dodge
for here, as his commemoration,
James BATLEY wrote 'The Lodge'.

My lovely big Dutch girl was the beginning of my long romance with Holland and the Dutch, for whom I feel a deep affinity; my ancestors were Friesian Vikings, part Baltic Russians, and many people have thought I was either Dutch or Russian or Polish. Maurice Feild and his cellist wife remained my best friends; many of his pupils became well-known artists. Maurice sketched me, and painted my portrait with patient care. His master was Coldstream, and as he explained to me his methods of building up the structure of the face by the application of subtly graded colours, I learnt a great deal about painting and about how to look at the world through a painter's eyes, a way of looking that was to influence my poetry.

But as a teacher, I was a hopeless failure. Children are the most right-wing of conservatives. They soon detected in me someone who did not care for their standards of conduct or their way of life. My classes became chaotic, and I am sure that secretly, unconsciously perhaps, I encouraged their bad behaviour: the incorrigible anarchist within me wanted to make those smug little oafs rebel, and rebel they did. I had let my hair grow unusually long again, and they called me 'Haystack'. In cold weather, I wore a feathered and beaded muff that had once, I was told by an antique dealer, belonged to Queen Marie of Rumania. I must have been the only man in England to wear a muff throughout the war, and I kept up the habit after it. So the boys called me 'Mademoiselle'. Yes, I was asking for it. But on the other hand I could not behave in any other way: I simply could not be strict and severe and manly. I think some of the boys were quite confused about my sex; during bath hours, when I was in charge, there was riotous behaviour, and small boys running past me stark naked from bathroom to dormitory would put their hands on my crotch to check my equipment.

'Yes, he's got one,' I heard a boy say. 'It's a beauty.'

I stayed only two terms. When the parents came to visit the school in the summer term, I was put in charge of the swimming pool, where the boys used to disport themselves naked. Nobody had asked me if I could swim; it was taken for granted that I could, if there were an emergency.

As I stood by the poolside moodily watching the boys enjoying themselves, a mother approached me, and said:

'Why aren't you swimming with the boys, Mr Kirkup?'

'I can't swim,' I replied.

She looked shocked.

'But what would happen if one of the boys – if my Anthony, for example – got into difficulties in the water? What if he were drowning?'

'Madame,' I replied, 'there would be no point in both of us drowning. If he was drowning, he'd just have to drown, I'm afraid.'

I was reported to the Head, an amiable giant, son of the Geoffrey to whom Auden had dedicated his poem. Hoyland had a sense of humour, and roared with laughter when my incompetence was revealed. But it was felt that perhaps it would be better if I were to leave at the end of term.

Maurice told me something about Auden which I thought was very amusing. The post for the staff was laid out every day on a big table in the main building, and if there were any postcards, Auden used to read them all, no matter to whom they were addressed, saying: 'It's wrong to read other people's letters, but reading their postcards is quite all right.'

Hoyland wrote me a kind little letter of recommendation, saying I was leaving of my own will, and that I should probably be more suited to older children. How wrong he was!

My next post, obtained after writing away to umpteen advertisers in *The Times Educational Supplement*, was to teach languages at Minchenden Grammar School, Southgate, London. Here I was equally unsuccessful, and those tough London kids, though older than the ones at the Downs School, were even more ferocious, both boys and girls. My classes were pandemonium. The only way I could keep a modicum of order was to give dictations, which I made as long as possible, provoking exaggerated groans of despair from my boisterous pupils. As soon as the dictation was over, all hell broke loose again. There was a jovial P.T. instructor with a sprightly ginger moustache, ex-army, who came to my rescue many times. He had only to enter my chaotic classroom for a sudden dead silence to fall. It was magical, and I looked upon him as a wizard. But his magic never rubbed off on me. Boys jumped out of the open windows and ran home. Girls pretended to faint, or put love notes of embarrassing frankness into my overcoat pocket – 'I just love your bump,' said one hussy's letter. Boxes of chalk were spilled on my hair. The high chair at the desk where I sat to mark the register in endless uproar was one day bedaubed with glue, and I sat on it for several minutes before realizing something was wrong, and then it was too late: there was a rending sound as I tore myself away from the seat. Lines and other impositions, keeping them in after school, giving them extra homework – all these attempts at discipline failed. In the end, I decided I had to give the most obnoxious and bad-mannered boy a thrashing. As he bent over to receive the strokes of the cane, I suddenly felt sick, but I went through with it, and gave him 'six of the best'. It filled me with horrible shame and sadness, and it was the only time I ever beat a boy. (He was seventeen, more like a grown man.) I had laid on the strokes as lightly as possible, and in class afterwards he told his mates: 'He don't 'arf lay it on strong!' But this false reputation had no effect. I had to leave before I had a nervous breakdown, despite the pleas of the extremely kind and sympathetic headmaster. But out of this dreadful experience I made a poem, 'In a London Schoolroom', which was one of the first of my poems to be accepted by Ackerley for *The Listener*. It was later reprinted in *The Submerged Village*. And my teaching days – at schools, at any rate – were mercifully over.

While I was at Colwall, I received my official release from the Ministry of Labour and National Service. The language in which it was couched was so absurd I have kept the release form as a treasure of English officialese:

National Service (Release of Conscientious Objectors) Act, 1946

Whereas under the arrangements for the release from army service of persons called up for service under the National Service (Armed Forces) Act, 1939, the 31st. day of May, 1946, was fixed as the date for completing the release

> from such service of male persons of all ranks in the age and service group 28, who are released by reference to their group;
>
> Now therefore the Minister of Labour and National Service by virtue of the powers conferred on him by section 1 of the National Service (Release of Conscientious Objectors) Act, 1946, directs that James H. Kirkup of The Downs School, Colwall, Malvern, a conditionally registered conscientious objector, of the same group shall as from the date hereof be released from the obligation to undertake work subject to which he was so registered.
>
> Signed by order of the Minister of Labour and National Service this 6th. day of June, 1946.
>
> (Signature indecipherable)

I marvelled that such a pretentious piece of prose should have emerged from the Regional Office, 281 Corporation Street, Birmingham. I always distrusted communications beginning with 'whereas' and containing words like 'hereof' and 'now therefore'. But I was relieved to know that my long ordeal, which I had tried to enliven and make as entertaining and pleasurable as possible, was finally over. And I felt quite thrilled to be addressed as a 'male person'.

I went to live in a caravan – really a roadman's hut – on the outskirts of Oxford, on the road to Wallingford. It was a miserable existence, but I wrote a few poems, including 'The Ship', about a beautiful old tree in the next field, which was reprinted from *The Listener* in *The Submerged Village*. I wrote a few pages of prose about my life there:

> The dogs have started barking again. It is merely the sight of a strange man with a dog walking in the neighbouring meadow that excites them. But it will always seem to me that their nerve-wracking, monotonous and meaningless barking, so constant, so excited, is the very sound of my own caged restlessness and disquiet.
>
> The man is quite harmless. He is in his rights. He is no trespasser. He has brought a sack with him which he holds in one hand. With the other hand he is tearing up the long green grass and stuffing it into the sack. Soon the sack will be full, and the bareheaded man will call his own quiet dog, and go away.
>
> But even when he has gone, I feel, the dogs will go on barking. For the false peace of my mind has been broken, and even if the dogs are taken far away on long leads by their master, or if they escape and devour the beastly children of the village, or if they are killed by lightning or by my own hand, still they will go on barking in my disordered brain.
>
> And the big Airedale, Nick, when he is not barking, lies outside whining mournfully for his master to return and run in the fields with him. Nick lies all day tied to a stake with a rattling chain, looking up with old, grey-set eyes at

his master's locked caravan door, whining and barking incessantly.

Two enormous black dogs are shut up together in a small old hen-house with little glass windows, through which one can occasionally see them gazing down their sleek, black, grey-speckled muzzles out of brown eyes that are not more than eyes: they express nothing. But if anyone passes through the meadow where our two caravans stand, or walks along the road past the distant farm, or shouts to the miller at the mill across the stream, they know, and they bark, bark, bark. I can do nothing for them. In fact, if I show myself outside my caravan, when they are for a moment silent, the sight of me makes them begin barking again. Their master cannot silence them either. He has no real control over them, and his thin, elderly figure and weak, worried voice have no authority over them.

This afternoon, it was so peaceful. Their master had gone away to do his shopping in the city, and no one was stirring in the rain-swept fields. The rain beat gently, firmly on the roof of my little van, so resonantly, and I sat still, hardly daring to breathe, and wondered at the peace, so unusual in the country. The hens were all gathered together under the vans, silent and critical, tilting their heads disapprovingly at the rain. The two cats, the pure white one – the kitten, and the tortoise-shell one, lie asleep together under a broken box. The white she-goat and her white kid were in the long grass and nettles at the other end of the meadow, munching peacefully. The ducks were far off down the river.

I held my breath and waited, listening to the sound of the rain on the hollow roof, hearing it almost with a sensation of physical massage. Occasionally a bird chirped, sang a few notes doubtfully, a hoarse cuckoo's voice with its June note passed through the raindrops like a flat stone skipping and skimming the surface of a pond, scattering little splashes of sound.

Sometimes the wind made the trees roar like little anchored seas of foliage, and through the van's tiny windows I could see the leaves turn white and then dark again. And always on the roof the low, soothing drum of the early summer rain, drowsing the grief and madness out of my brain, making my taut body loose, my fierce muscles suddenly relax. And it was cool, so cool, after all the heat of the past week.

Slowly, I became less and less aware of the presence of the dark dogs behind me: they were no more than threatening shadows which could be disturbed by a single footfall, and would let hell loose at the sound of a distant voice. Even the little brown spaniel bitch, with her eyes like a rich, spoilt child's, and long ears reminiscent of Victorian ringlets falling over her smooth, sloping shoulders, had stopped howling and whimpering, as if stunned by the silence, in the darkness of the other van.

This impressionistic prose passage, written, like so much of my work at that time of paper shortage, on the 'Weekly Time Sheets' my father had to fill in at 'Binns Limited', gives some idea of my state of mind. Grief and madness? Caused by the departure to Canada of a young actor I had fallen in love with, and who, because of his own unhappy experiences with the police, had decided to emigrate. On the day he left London airport, I wanted to see him off. But instead, he gave me a ticket to 'Oklahoma', which had just opened at Drury Lane. I sat there in the upper circle, watching the show as if it were something taking place on another planet, while my mind was all the time on the one I would never see again, flying first to Prestwick, then to Shannon, Gander and Toronto. He wrote me many letters, begging me to join him in Canada. But we never met again; the idea of living in a place like Toronto filled me with premonitory, fearful tedium much worse than the pain of lost love. He had spent a few days with me in the caravan before his departure, and now his presence seemed everywhere. And those damned dogs were like the hounds of Diana tearing my heart to pieces. Once or twice, students came out of curiosity to see me, for my work was beginning to appear in leading periodicals and poetry anthologies. I have forgotten who they were: they were like ghosts. I could make no contact with them, and I was filled with a terror of being bored by their chatter, their inquisitive eyes, their even more awful questioning silences. I had to leave the van; it was killing me.

I went home to South Shields for a few weeks to try to decide what to do with my future. I had made applications for grants and prizes without success. Indeed I am the sort of person who is temperamentally incapable of presenting my case convincingly before your usual band of bureaucrats in charge of financial support for struggling artists. I think there should be a special system of grants for those incapable of applying for them in the proper manner. And now that I am old enough not to be 'promising', I suggest that there should be grants for writers over sixty-five; many of them need assistance just as badly as the 'under thirty' group that is always favoured. If ever I have enough money to leave to posterity, I shall endow a foundation to distribute grants to all poor old clapped-out writers who still have the sacred fire within them but cannot put pen to paper when it comes to filling in forms and composing persuasive letters to condescending committees of academic libertarians and influential moneybags. For an artist over sixty-five, just to be released from the burden of having to fill out an Income Tax form would be an inestimable relief, a benefit beyond price. Even in Eire, the tax-free artist has to fill out his tax forms. . . . But I digress. . . . Back to the not-so-distant past. And to some important materials culled from our local newspaper, *The South Shields Gazette and Shipping*

Telegraph for Friday 17 October, 1947. Front page, headlined right-hand column:

'My dear Sir' – Jap to his prisoner
Ex-prisoner of war William Morton of 119 Whitehall Street, South Shields, describes as 'the height of cheek' a letter he has received from a Japanese.

The Japanese was one of the administrators at a P.O.W. camp in Aomi, near Tokyo, where Mr Morton served part of his three-and-a-half year 'sentence' following the fall of Singapore.

Regards to Family
The letter reads:

My dear sir, two years have passed since I bade farewell at Aomi station. I beg to pay my highest esteem and courtesy for your hard work while you were at Aomi for a long time and at the same time I am anxious to know about your welfare since then. We Japanese are endeavouring to bring about a spiritual revolution in speeding the establishment of a democratic, peace-loving and cultural nation.

I trust Japan will become a comfortable land in the near future and I hope you will have a good chance to visit Japan to inspect her old customs and manners. Please give my best regards to your family.

The letter is signed T. Kondoh.

At Aomi Mr Morton was one of a party working at furnaces in which the heat was so intense that work could only be done on a half-hour shift system. Prisoners who straightened their backs at work were rewarded with a blow from a shovel.

The day after Mr Kondoh's letter appeared in *The Shields Gazette*, the matter was taken up by other local and national newspapers. I traced this version in *The Journal* of Newcastle on Tyne, of Saturday 18 October, 1947, which was also given front-page headline treatment:

Jap writes 'dear sir' to ex-P.O.W.
The Japanese gave William Morton, of Whitehall Street, South Shields, three and a half years of misery. When he was taken prisoner he was forced to work as a furnace hand in a war plant.

If he halted for an instant, he says, he was hit with a shovel, or anything else that came handy to his Japanese gaolers.

Now he has received a letter from the Japanese president of the company whose plant he was made to stoke.

'My Dear Sir,' it starts, and invites him to return to Japan to 'inspect her old customs and manners'.

Morton's reaction: 'I would like to have that Jap here now. It beats the band for impudence. I can't reply because no censor would pass what I feel like writing.'

After reading these letters and comments from Mr Morton, I decided to write to the newspapers concerned to put forward a more conciliatory point of view towards our former enemies. I fully realized that this action would cause great distress to my parents, who had a working-class fear of any kind of press publicity, and that the consequences to myself might be dangerous. But I had to write it:

138, Fowler Street,
SOUTH SHIELDS
18th. October, 1947.

To the Editor,
The Shields Gazette
Sir,

Many people must have been gratified by the prominence that you gave to the courteous letter from Mr T. Kondoh in Friday night's *Gazette*. But most sensible people will regret the tone of Mr William Morton's accompanying remarks. It is surely a dreadful mistake to interpret the friendliness, the obvious willingness to make amends, and the dignity of this letter as 'the height of cheek' and 'an insult'.

Mr Morton and other Prisoners of War of all nationalities must have known bitter humiliation and suffering at the hands of those who during the last war were called their 'enemies'. Those, like myself, who did not have to undergo the horrors of the prison camp, can never adequately conceive the inhuman depths to which humanity, in the name of Freedom, and driven by politicians and profiteers, can sink, and it may be said that we are in no position to offer opinions on this subject.

But in this uneasy post-war era, when the real terrors of war – famine, disease, and the universal lowering of all spiritual values – must constantly by their continued presence remind everyone of the futility of any war, however 'just' the political press may call it; when in addition we have today the threat of atomic extinction hanging over every minute of our lives, menacing us not only with personal loss, separation, hardship, military stupidity, bureaucratic tyranny, and the arrogant hypocrisy of the Church, but also with the annihilation of civilized living, culture, and all the pleasures that a good life can give us: when we consider all these things, we must realize that it is the duty of every one of us to forget the follies and the anger and the national pride of the past, and to meet our fellow human beings, whatever their nationality, or creed or colour, with forgiveness, trust, forbearance and respect.

During the last war, the countless atrocities committed, the devastating 'inhumanity of man to man', were not only confined to those who were labelled our 'enemies'. We are all guilty, and trying to forget our sense of guilt in lives of unspeakable dreariness and uselessness, and which will always remain lacking in the true joy of life unless we have a real change of heart, and love our neighbours as ourselves. Only complete forgiveness of the past can make mankind whole again, and it is only if all men will stand together in mutual sympathy and understanding that the noisy misery of another war can be averted.

Whether we are Christians or not, the words of the Lord's Prayer – 'And forgive us our trespasses, as we forgive them that trespass against us' – should be always in our hearts and minds, and we should really *act forgivingly* if we are to be forgiven.

It is that very quality of forgiveness that Mr Kondoh shows in his letter. However difficult Mr Morton finds it, I hope that he will answer it in a similar spirit.

Yours etc.

James Kirkup

However, Mr Morton had stated that his feelings remained of a very different kind: the issue of *The Gazette* of 17 October tells us:

> Mr Morton, a linotype operator working in Gateshead says: 'I think that the letter is an insult and that the principal idea behind it is that of reminding Britons they were prisoners. I would like to reply with an equally insulting note.'

There were a number of replies to my letter, all supporting Mr Morton. The men of the cloth, who might have been expected to defend peace and forgiveness for our enemies, were conspicuously silent. I began to receive vituperative letters and threats of death from anonymous writers, which I was able to conceal from my parents, who were already deeply shocked and distressed by my letter. My father looked at his grimmest, his face white, his lips set. He was derided at work. But he said nothing about the matter to me. Only my mother gently reproached me:

'Oh, Jim, son, why did you do it? Don't you realize you've given us enough pain and trouble already? I can't go out to the shops.'

But I had done what I knew had to be done: I could not let that letter of Mr Morton's pass. Here is a representative letter from those written in reply to mine. Of course, there may have been some letters in support of my plea, but if there were the editors did not allow them to be printed.

A Mr Alex Waltenberg expressed himself in this way:

> I was surprised to read Mr Kirkup's letter. I was three-and-a-half years in a Jap prison camp and saw P.O.W.s tortured to death.

> It is time Mr Kirkup took his forbearance and respect to Japan. Mr Morton was right in speaking as he did.
>
> Someone should put an end to Mr Kondoh's writing such letters and opening up wounds which are healing.

Ironically, it was men like this letter writer who were preventing their old wounds from healing by organizing Prisoner of the Japanese associations in order to keep their bitter memories and hatred of the Japanese alive.

But Mr Waltenberg's letter is curiously prophetic when he tells me to go and live in Japan myself. At that time, I had no idea that one day I might actually live there. Indeed, in those days it was still impossible to leave England for Japan unless one had some official reason for going there. But twelve years later, in January 1959, I did in fact travel to Japan and started a new life there.

Finally, a reply was sent to *The Gazette* by Mr Morton, the person who had originally attacked Mr Kondoh's letter. Under the headline 'Ex-P.O.W.s Who Can't Forget' the following letter from Mr Morton was published:

> In reply to Mr Kirkup, who wrote that he hoped I would answer T. Kondoh's letter in the same spirit in which he himself believes it was sent, I would like to say that, personally, I am pleased at the publicity which my letter received, because I wish to show the British public that what we suffered out there can never be blotted from our minds by such a letter as has been sent to the men at home. Since receiving the letter I have tried hard to understand why the British Government allows these letters to reach England.
>
> To some ordinary people, the letter was quite in order I suppose – the only thing they don't understand is that behind that letter is the same fiendish brain which would burn women and children and snuff out the life of a man with the same deliberation as one would blow out a lighted candle.

Another letter appeared, this time written by a Malay living in South Shields who had apparently served with the British in the war in Malaya. This is what he wrote:

> Following the publication of the letter from an ex-Jap soldier, and after reading the sorry attempt by Mr Kirkup to make light of this gesture, I feel I must give some facts.
>
> I served nearly six years in Malaya and Siam and during that time I served with Malayan and Chinese units and also met many Japanese.
>
> There is no friendliness between Jap and Briton. I am sure many of our Merchant Navy personnel can tell of restrictions they were subjected to before the war by the Japanese secret police.

Secondly, I would like to eliminate the belief that humanity sinks low in prison camps. To believe this is utter nonsense because under these circumstances a man is a man and his neighbour is as dear to him as his wife and children.

The thought that the Jap's letter was intended as an act of forgiveness should be forgotten; it was an attempt to laugh at Britons in our present difficulties.

Furthermore, I understand there is a movement to form a society of ex-Jap P.O.W.s. I sincerely hope that Mr Kirkup may meet some of the unfortunate ex-prisoners to hear their views.

Tak San Lagi's
South Shields

This letter appeared under the heading: 'Jap Letter was Meant as a Sneer'.

The Newcastle *Journal* did not print Mr Kondoh's letter in full, presumably because the editor was afraid of the good impression its generally friendly and reconciliatory tone might produce. All the letters printed were of the same type – emotional, distorted, hysterical and bitterly prejudiced. So I felt it was useless to continue the argument in newspaper columns, as well as dangerous to the members of my family. I was called a fascist and a traitor and a spy for the Comintern and other absurd things. My mother and father were abused in public, my father was attacked at work, and I myself was attacked and vilified in the streets. But I did not mind, except for the pain and distress to my parents. I had long become accustomed to abuse.

A fact that emerges from Mr Kondoh's letter is that he went to the station to see Mr Morton off, and obviously had some regard for Mr Morton. This does not suggest tyrannical brutality, but courtesy and kindness and concern.

It is my feeling that the returned P.O.W.s in Britain exaggerated, for the purposes of press sensationalism, much of what they had experienced, and by constant repetition of these inflated charges came to believe in their fantasies, still kept alive by P.O.W. associations. It is quite obvious that in wartime beastly and inhuman cruelties occur, as they did among the prisoners of British and Allied troops (particularly the Scots, who were guilty of My Lai-type atrocities in Malaya and, more recently, in Northern Ireland). But such are the inevitable consequences of war, which in itself is brutal and violent and not at all gentlemanly.

Not all British people were hostile to the Japanese after the war, though I was one of the few who had a good word to say for our former enemies. Laurens van der Post wrote some books and short stories about his experiences as a prisoner of war of the Japanese, works composed with artistic restraint. Indeed, his *Merry Christmas, Mr Laurence*, after being made into a ridiculous movie by Oshima, has become very popular with British P.O.W. clubs.

On the other hand, I read a most disturbing account by a Japanese who had been a prisoner of war of the British in Burma. This book, by Yuji Aida, was translated and published in England by the Cresset Press under the title *Prisoner of the British*. The cruelties and humiliations described in that book should be read by every Briton who suffered under the hands of the Japanese and believes that the British never do such things. Mr Aida's book is a shocking account of the brutality of men in wartime.

Of course, if we allow war to exist, we must expect the kind of human conduct that is 'not cricket'.

I hear continually from the lips of men
Who fought in wars, who slaved in prison camps
Of captors' cruelties, starvation, lingering death,
Of tortures, atrocities, inhuman rage.

We are all prisoners of one another,
And all our captors are ourselves.
We are all beasts. But beasts
Do not disgrace each other as men do.

I, too, remember brutal overseers
In the labour camps of Britain, men
Who could only relish power
If they could degrade, mock, punish

With violence as sad as any commandant's,
With anger that revealed the heart of war.
I remember also those who sheltered me,
Although they had no cause, and suffered for it.

I remember those in foreign camps
Who allowed themselves to love their captors,
And were loved. On both sides
A common brotherhood survived.

Not for us to rant of war's bad taste,
To issue pleas for decency, fair play.
– If we permit our governments to arm for peace,
We sanction war, and must expect unpleasantnesses.*

Hiroshima

*'Not Cricket' from *Paper Windows: Poems from Japan*, a volume of my poems published by Dent, London, in 1968.

Cruelty has no standards: there is no lesser cruelty or greater cruelty – there is only cruelty.

We cannot say that the cruelty of Japanese commandants or the cruelty of Nazi extermination squads and concentration camp guards was any worse than Churchill's unprecedentedly inhuman bombing of helpless civilians in Hamburg and Dresden, or that German bombings of British cities was any worse than the wholesale fire-bombings, not to mention the atom bombings of the Americans against Japan. Neither can we claim that Japanese mistreatment of P.O.W. labourers was any better than the callous repatriation to certain death under Stalin of the Russian P.O.W.s from post-war Britain by Churchill and Macmillan, those arch-patriots and arch-conservatives. And what about the Jews who sailed on the eve of war on the 'St Louis' from Hitler's Germany but were not allowed to land at Havana, and were rejected by the USA? They were sent back on the same ship by our democratic ally to the death camps of Nazi Germany and Poland. Even when, in 1943, it became evident that the Germans were slaughtering Jews by the hundreds of thousands, Churchill would not lift the restrictive quotas on Jewish immigration into Britain. Yes, cruelty has many forms.

In February 1972, I was leaving Japan after many happy years. But before I left Nagoya for Britain, I decided that I would reveal to the Japanese how Mr Kondoh's letter of good will had been received by his conquerors. I gathered all my materials and made them into the final chapter of a book of essays, *The Britishness of the British*, edited and annotated by Professor Kawasaki Toshihiko, my learned colleague in the English Department of Nagoya University, and the book was published by Seibido Publishing Company in Tokyo, and recorded by me, before I left Japan. I intended to spend four or five years in Europe and the USA before returning to take up my next Japanese post in Kyoto.

The book was an instant success with students and teachers, and with Japanese readers in general, and became a bestseller, reaching hundreds of thousands of sales. It caught the attention of the media, and soon newspapers and magazines were carrying articles and reviews about it, concentrating on my final chapter, 'How the British View the Japanese', in which all the letters were printed. I donated a copy of the book to the Reference Library at South Shields, in the hope that some of those indignant letter-writers might read it. If they did, I received no reactions.

But the publication of my essay in Japan brought unexpected and very gratifying results. While the furore about my letter in the British press remained completely unknown to Mr Kondoh and his family, when a long report of my defence of the man appeared in the *Asahi Shimbun* the newspaper was deluged with letters and telephone calls from readers, informing us that the man in question was Tetsuji Kondoh, former president of Denki Kagaku Kogyo Electrical Chemical Company at Oomi Town – not 'Aomi' – in Niigata Prefecture on the Japan Sea coast. But it was also revealed that Mr Kondoh had died twenty-one years before: that is, only a few years after he wrote his good letter to Mr Morton.

The *Asahi Shimbun* arranged a meeting for me with Mr Kondoh's widow at my hotel in Tokyo, shortly before my departure for Britain, and Mrs Kondoh, a beautiful, gracious old lady, gave me much priceless information about her husband.

During the war, the electro-chemical firm in the southern part of the prefecture facing the Japan Sea had some 1,000 British prisoners of war working there, producing carbide. Mrs Kondoh recalled: 'My husband used to remain at the plant, which was furnished with a large P.O.W. camp, very late at night – for example, to keep the bath heated until all the captives had finished washing.'

Acknowledging the kindness of the camp administrator, many P.O.W.s visited Mr Kondoh's house after they were freed following the end of the war.

'We had really busy days preparing dishes for serving the foreign visitors,' went on Mrs Kondoh. 'We served, as much as we were able, fresh vegetables – and pork and beef from livestock raised at our company's farms – as they apparently needed those foods.'

One night in September 1945, they were taken by train to Tokyo for physical examinations and other procedures required for repatriation to their homeland.

Mr and Mrs Kondoh and a nephew of the couple went to Oomi Station on the Japanese National Railways' Hokuriku Line to see them off.

'What impressed me most at that time was the scene of many war prisoners who extended their bodies out of the windows of the train to shake our hands or wave goodbye to us,' said Mrs Kondoh, with tears in her eyes. 'One of them was loath to let go of our hands even after the train began moving.'

During the Yuletide of 1945 and the following several years, 'we received many Christmas cards sent by the former P.O.W.s in Great Britain,' Mrs Kondoh added.

I was very pleased to hear that many British P.O.W.s acknowledged the kindness extended by the Kondoh family, although it was regrettable that his letter met with such bitter criticism in my home town. Mrs Kondoh presented me with an exquisite vase painted by her husband. All this, and much more, was reported in the 11 February 1972 issue of *The Asahi Evening News*, the fine English-language edition of the *Asahi Shimbun*.

So, in my own small way, I did my best to heal a rift and to overcome misunderstanding and prejudice between former enemies. It was a continuation of my war with the world – but, at least on my part, a peaceful war.

When I got back to Tyneside, I received a letter from Mrs Kondoh saying that copies of *The Gazette* letters, my book of essays, and all other materials had been offered by her and her family at the household shrine of Mr Kondoh, with offerings of fruit, flowers, rice and *saké*, in honour of his memory. I felt that this was a perfect and harmonious conclusion to an episode that had engendered so much hostility and sorrow.

Why have I reprinted these old letters and cuttings, relics of a bitter controversy which took place forty years ago, before I ever had any thought of one day living in Japan? I see them as a tribute to my parents, who were so despised and abused because of them, and because of my persistence in questioning the correctness of the British attitude towards the Japanese. The materials were all preserved by my father, and I found them among his papers after his death, just before I first went to Japan. They both hated any kind of publicity, and my exposure in the local and national press caused them great anxiety and suffering. I remember my mother using an old Irish expression which she had learned from my Irish grandfather when she found my letter in *The Gazette* and in the *Journal*: 'Jim, your name is up!' This probably derives from the use of names in eighteenth-century Irish broadsheets or ballads, for in those days the mention of any person's name in a poem – whether by Rafferty or Kavanagh – brought fame or notoriety to the person whose 'name was up'.

I think it is necessary to reprint the letters because prejudice against the Japanese is steadily reviving. Dislike of the Japanese and deep jealousy for their successes in technology and trade are increasing everywhere. Critics forget the great qualities of the Japanese that made their extraordinary advances in the modern world possible – hard work, cheerfulness, determination, persistence, single-mindedness and a dawning inventiveness all helped to bring Japan out of misery, militarism and suffering into a more sane and prosperous existence as members of the free world trade community.

However, in recent years there has been a regrettable tendency in Japan towards a revival of right-wing nationalism, and increasing defence budgets suggest a resurgence of militarism. Nakasone's visits to the shrine of the war dead, where many war criminals are memorialized, is a sinister development – though this summer (1986) out of respect for the feelings of China and Korea and other S.E. Asian nations who suffered under the Japanese invasions and the abominable cruelties of the *kempeitai*, Nakasone and his cabinet forwent their visit to Yasukuni Shrine in Tokyo. I hope the letters I have printed may make the present generation of Japanese remember the follies and disasters of the past, and so keep this rising militarism and nationalism at bay.

The despicable use of the racial slur 'Jap' and the contemptuous expression, 'Jap-happy' are today less prevalent than they were in the immediate post-war period, but they are still occasionally thoughtlessly employed in newspaper headings and in conversation. There seems to be a tendency for this kind of insult to increase, now that Britain, America and the nations of Europe are attacking Japan for its economic genius and technological superiority.

However, I have been encouraged by the publication, in a magnificent illustrated edition by Collins, of Ronald Searle's drawings of his experiences during the Second World War in Singapore, Malaya and on the 'Railway of Death'. These pictures are not caricatures, but portraits of real people, the sort of Japanese men one can see today in streets and trains and on election posters. Moreover, his prose commentaries are balanced and unprejudiced, a far cry from the hysteria of Mr Morton and others. The copy of the book that I saw had been sent by Searle to a colleague of mine at Kyoto University of Foreign Studies, Professor Jun'ichi Kikkawa, who himself had been a prisoner of the Russians for many years in Siberia. Searle's generous spirit of forgiveness shows the quality of mind of a true artist and humanist. He tells us of Japanese who were kind and sympathetic, like the young artist officer who brought him painting and drawing materials. Searle dedicated his book to Professor Kikkawa with kind and thoughtful words, expressing the hope that those who were once enemies should now for ever be reconciled. We have come a long way from my letters in *The Gazette* and the *Journal* in 1947, so I feel there is hope for us yet.

A Post-War Outsider

1947–8

South Shields is a peculiar and depressing place. It has also a certain pathetic charm. Without the sea and the River Tyne it would appear to be without dignity and meaning. The sea, that is always there, its horizon barring the ends of many streets, is what I turn to in hours of boredom and exasperation. Without the sea, it would be impossible for me to go on living in this town, in whose streets the sand grates underfoot, like spilled sugar, symbol of my enervation and frustration.

A large industrial and sea-going population is centred here at the mouth of the noble Tyne. I myself come from an old family of master mariners. But most of our workers are employed – if they are lucky enough to find work – in the pits or the shipyards and the new factories that are appearing everywhere with a somehow unbelievable air of permanence. The ghost of the thirties – slump, depression and unemployment – still haunts our streets and our homes; but the Tynesiders stoically endure, for endurance in the face of hardship is one of their best qualities. It has to be. This region is the forgotten ghetto of Great Britain, a pocket of deprivation and poverty neglected by the Government, and subjected to all kinds of trials and humiliations both in wartime and in peace. During the war, for example, ours was the region where rationing of even basic foodstuffs was most severe. Ours is the region from which most young men have gone to their deaths in two world wars. No wonder there is an air of bitterness and resignation in the pubs and shops.

But still the Tynesiders remain, hanging on to family memories, to fading hopes for the future, silently praying for a miracle to happen. It is not only apathy that prevents many families from emigrating to Australia or Canada, like thousands of others between and after the wars, or even from moving to the better-paid and climatically more congenial South. A strange nostalgia attacks those who depart. They experience an aching longing for the sight and smell of the sea and the sands of their native coast. They dream of the great bend in the river between its mouth and Newcastle. They remember fondly the great forests of cranes over the shipyards, the slate-roofed, ribbed acres of grimy and often unbearably monotonous working-class streets and gloomy back lanes, the playgrounds of the children of the poor, and the front doorsteps that are the salons of the unemployed. They desire to hear again in its proper context the authentic Geordie twang in the stuffy, ornate Victorian pubs, or in their even more dismal contemporary plastic and formica versions; to listen to those with the gift of the Geordie gab in trains and buses, at the football, wrestling and boxing matches, at the greyhound tracks, and at the gates of dockyards and factories at 5 p.m., when the men pour out with their little bundles of 'oven wood' for the kitchen range.

For Tyneside knows how to talk its own language, and so it is a very sociable place. In queues at the butcher's or the grocer's, Tynesiders, especially the women, express their candid opinions in earthy language that always has a stylish fluency. You can hear them at the Labour Exchange, as they queue to sign on for the dole, and on the ferries, giving intimate details of their family lives with an endearing frankness. There is a kind of desperate, communal gaiety underneath the grim exterior, a cheerfulness of heart against all odds, that I have often heard expressed on crowded buses or in packed pubs (and, during the war, in the air-raid shelters) in the phrase: 'Howway, hinny! Howway, man! We're aal tegither like the folks o' Sheels!' There is a gallantry and courage in that attitude. But then I ask myself: 'Why should such courage be necessary?'

And although I admire this cosy familiarity and this devil-may-care local pride, it eventually gives me a feeling of being stifled in some hideous, black-shawled, beer-and-fish-smelling bosom.

But there is always the sea to turn to for a breath of fresh air and a change of one's gloomy ideas. Most of the inhabitants, apart from the sailors and sea captains, appear to ignore its existence, excepting on fine summer days, when the long but rather littered beaches are black with children and families from all parts of Tyneside, for we have the best 'plodging' and bathing beaches in the North East.

I well remember, as if it were yesterday, how, as a child, these excursions to 'the sands', with luncheon sandwiches and teacakes for tea in a napkin-covered basket used to fill me with what seems now to have been an almost unbearable happiness and painful excitement. The approaches to the beach were such a fascinating prelude to later joys. There were stalls of fresh crabs, prawns, shrimps; winkle stalls presided over by old, black-shawled ladies with sheets of pink paper stuck with regular rows of pins that we used in order to 'winkle out' the scraps of meat in those tiny, tasty shells. There were the little whitewashed wooden cabins that sold ice cream and sticks of mint rock with 'A Present from South Shields' printed all the way through them. There were great sheaves of crisp, empty vanilla cones flowering in exuberant Ich Diens from tins and vases, ready for filling with fresh, homemade Italian ice creams from Mancini's or Notarianni's in Ocean Road. In that street there were the shops that sold an incredible variety of tin pails and wooden and metal spades (the latter considered highly dangerous by some over-anxious mothers) for digging in the shingle and constructing sandcastles that, however big we built them, were never big enough and were washed away by the incoming tide at the end of the long summer afternoon. The front of another shop would be covered by whirring, flickering, bickering celluloid windmills in all colours of the rainbow, with paper kites, model yachts, diminutive rowing boats, beach balls, balloons, paper hats, rattles, whistles, streamers, dolls, paper sunshades and celluloid ducks and whales.

Then, on reaching the beach, the agony of finding 'a nice place to sit down!' We would spend precious moments trudging over the sand between the perambulators and family groups, green canvas bathing tents and deck-chairs, until our shoes were full of hot sand, trying to find a spot that was not too littered with chip papers and bread crusts and broken glass and banana skins, a place not too far from the hut that sold hot water for making our pots of tea, and yet sufficiently removed from the shrieking, singing, dancing and ball-throwing 'trippers' (not local Shields folk at all!) whose children, we were told, were 'not nice' because they were always throwing and kicking sand in people's faces and over the tablecloth neatly arranged on the little sandy plateau we built as a teatable. Throwing sand on the beach was the very worst of crimes, though smashing bottles was another serious offence.

Though I was so happy at the beach with my mother and father, I have never felt so lonely. I did not like organized games at all, but I used to watch with longing the teams of children playing rounders or wrestling in the soft sand. No one ever asked me to join those games, and I was too shy to ask if I could be admitted to their communal fun. So I spent my time paddling in the shallows (I had always refused to learn to swim), enjoying the sucking sensation of the retreating wavelets as they drew the sand and shingle from between my wriggling toes. I collected shells and pretty stones and seaweeds, whose brilliance soon vanished as they dried and lost their seawater lustre. I built bridges and castles and mazes in the damp sand at the water's edge. No other child ever offered to help me. Once I stuffed the front of my bathing suit with dry sand, giving myself an enormous belly, and was gratified by the smiles and laughter that my grotesque appearance produced. And at times, after reading another chapter in *Treasure Island* or *Gulliver's Travels* or *Little Women*, I would rest my eyes a while, dazzled by the brilliance of the sun on those beloved pages, and feel suddenly a curious detachment from everything and everyone around me. I entered into a kind of trance, a gentle daydreaming that took me far away from my surroundings. Then, just as suddenly, I would come to myself again, to all the noise and colour and the distant pounding of the surging surf, the cries of gulls and children, and look guiltily about me, wondering if anyone had noticed my abstraction, and trying to remember where I had been in my absence from immediate reality – an absence that could only have lasted a few minutes, but that afterwards seemed to have been an eternity. I could detach myself from the world like this quite easily, at will. But I was always thankful to get back to the lively bustle of real life and the normal world, because I wondered sometimes if I should depart never to return.

The sea was the very expression of my loneliness, the image of a separateness I still could not understand. Even today, a man without illusions, I often wonder why I prefer being alone. I no longer go to the sands in summertime. Autumn and winter are the times for me there, when I am the only visitor – an only visitor perhaps hoping that one day there will be a similarly lonely wanderer along the stormy northern beaches and cliffs, the mile-long pier. I do not miss all that exuberant, lusty, happy-go-lucky atmosphere of my childhood, when we were all more or less on the fringes of poverty but knew the luxury of being able to enjoy ourselves simply and without expense either of money or spirit.

In summer now, as I observe the beaches from the promenade or the top of the cliffs at Trow Rocks, the crowds seem to be all 'foreigners', trippers, no longer 'all together like the folks of Shields'. The folks of Shields have gone, perhaps, to the Costa Brava or Majorca. Yet the crowds on the beach and in Ocean Road are obviously more prosperous than in those lean years between the wars and in the drab period before the Festival of Britain in the early fifties. They are better-dressed, too – smarter, more up-to-date in their hairstyles and their slang. But something has been lost since the endurance test of the Second World War: people have regrettably 'had all the stuffing knocked out of them'.

There are more 'amusements', more bright lights in the streets and along the prom, but no one seems to be enjoying life as they used to in my childhood. Despite its brilliance, the summer is melancholy. I cannot bear the sad hilarity of beach parties, but sunbathe in the lonely little Frenchman's Bay further down the coast.

It is in autumn and winter that I love the sea the most, and when my own solitude seems limitless as that bleak horizon. That is when the sands and the piers are deserted, and the caves and the clifftops and the little rocky bays no longer invite summer visitors. It is in those seasons I like to wander, all evening and sometimes all night, in rain or wind or snow, or in warm autumn fogs, with the ever-changing, changing sea as my companion.

But the half-abandoned fairground is still alive, faintly buzzing and hissing in the distance, like some half-dead fly left over from the summer. One of the arcades is hung with large notices that exclaim, in jovial red capitals: 'Should a man gain the whole world and lose his own soul – without a bit of fun?' I often wish that someone would start smashing up the whole place, and the whole town behind it, demolishing with superhuman power whatever the bombs had left standing.

There was that glorious night when a couple of drunken Norwegian sailors kicked the footballs of the 'Score a Goal' stand right over the promenade, across the beach and into the raging sea; but, alas, such things do not happen often.

Yes, though it is October now, the roundabouts still turn, in fog and cold, and shine like little oases of humanity among the strings of green-blue arc-lamps that indicate the riverside roads and cliff-edge housing estates. And in the drab, desolate streets and quays, under an iron forest of cranes and rigging, people out of doors at night turn from the ghastly pallor of mercury-vapour-lamp-blighted faces of the passers-by to the warmer conviviality of bars and picture palaces, coffee-stalls and fairgrounds.

The fairground at South Shields lies between the Coast Road and the broken balustrades of the concrete promenade, broad, checkered grey and pink. The 'prom' overlooks the sands and the unlittered sea, and dies away with an unfinished look among a cluster of huts and small cafés that in summer sold hot water for making tea, and forbade visitors to eat their own food at the tables. At the Trow Rocks end of the prom, Frankie's Café and other shacks still sell ice cream and chips in the sharpening autumn nights.

The promenade is unlighted, wide and featureless. At frequent intervals are placed urine-stinking shelters often occupied by silent courting couples. Occasionally, a trolley bus hisses along the road, a lighted block of glass. Listen carefully, and you will hear the sea rustling with a dry, uninteresting sound on the polluted beaches, the dunes sharp with grey-green marram grass, broken glass bottles, bits of barbed wire from wartime defences.

It is low tide. The moon behind a lattice of clouds lights faintly a patch of colourless sea that can just be seen to be moving, stirring, swelling out in the darkness, the North Sea mournfulness. The lighthouse beams revolve with rhythmical monotony – three brilliant flashes, then darkness, as the lantern rotates with an almost audible tinkle of grinding glass; then the three strong, even strokes of light again, illuminating like lightning or gun-flashes the low, distant cliffs of Tynemouth and Trow Rocks, and the dead façades of harbour-facing houses.

In the river-mouth, between the two long arms of the piers, and just off the little pier called the Groyne, there is the dredger, lit with its own constellation of lights, dragging buckets full of mud and sand and slime from the silting depths of a costive river bed. Often in the night, I used to wake up and hear the rattling of winches and the squeal and clash of iron buckets and the infernal growling of their endless chain. It was one of the sounds of Shields. The dredger is working all night, lurking and roaring like a medieval monster, some marine Lambton Worm, in its harbour den.

The autumn fogs have begun. Ships glide with almost unmoving slowness into or out of the river, blowing welcome or farewell on their melancholy sirens, and extending long, withered arms of smoke into the thicker smoke of the coal-fired sky. From the headland at Boldon colliery comes the regular hoot and moan of the fog horn.

But these sounds penetrate only faintly the noise and brilliance of the fairground. Here, the loudspeaker on the Universal Dodgems, the only 'amusement' left, blares out the voice of Larry Parks in an interminable Jolson Story, or lets Bing Crosby croon in one's ear, at once terrifyingly loud and cosily intimate. Every five minutes the record is interrupted by the voice of a gum-chewing young woman in charge of the microphone, who in an echoing, sepulchral voice utters the words: 'Drivers out of the cars please.... I'm arskin' yer ter leave the cars please.... Drivers out of the cars *please*....' The formula is invariable, coughed out in a voice so synthetic, it is barely intelligible. The occupants of the cars, generally pairs of young men wearing white silk scarves and blue serge suits and young girls with faces of discontented, half-tamed wild animals, stagger out across the metal floor while others scramble for seats. The girls' lipstick looks almost black in the lurid neon lighting, their cheeks deathly pale with patches of mottled purple round the made-up eyes. One half expects to see them all suddenly electrocuted as the little cars begin again to trundle round the reverberating track, colliding and bumping to the accompaniment of yells and screams, the bent metal trolleys spitting greenish-blue sparks from the overhead wire netting from which they drink electric energy.

The Dive Bomber, The Octopus, The Whip, The Ghost Train, The Noah's Ark and The Gondolas have all been dismantled and hauled away in large lorries to hibernate until spring; or perhaps there are less chilly and more profitable winter pitches than this. Crowds of people, mostly teenage boys and girls and elderly men, stand round the brightly-lit arena where the dodgems bumble along with their modern charioteers.

People stand for hours and watch for the inevitable collisions, and display no emotion at the shrieks, giggles and shouts of the 'accident victims'. Some groups of raw young conscripted soldiers and even younger girls lean against the railing with their backs to the lamp-festooned canvas top, and accompany the songs issuing from the loudspeakers in weak, shrill, nasal voices, or indulge in slapping, tongue-showing, pushing and other faintly amorous games. Some people, solitary and sad, stand like statues in the discreet seclusion of the shrubbery that marks the distant outskirts of the fairground radiance, smoking and yawning and looking around with faces devoid of expression. The Giant Wheel, not yet dismantled, hangs over the cinder paths, as vague and blank as another moon, a starfish skeleton, an enormous slice of lemon or an enlarged reproduction of a crude diatom case.

Between the two amusement arcades lit by fluorescent lighting are one or two pathetic, grubby coconut shies, looked after by old women or very young boys. The usual worn, grimy piece of rough matting lies about a yard inside the shy, with a blackboard beside it which says: 'Ladies Stand Here'. But not even this sexist concession can induce the girls to try their luck.

Next to the coconut shies, in complete darkness except for the light that falls from its more prosperous neighbours, is a football goal, with two footballs lying on a strip of raggy mat. The balls are black, shapeless, greasy, heavy and soft, but if you pay sixpence to the blue-faced young woman in a cheap fur coat who is apparently the *gardienne du but* – but a goalkeeper who lets all the shots through – you may enjoy the privilege of kicking them into the empty, sagging net.

The amusement arcades are filled all evening with vivid fluorescent whiteness of light that seems to burst with terrific violence through the wide doorways and the many cracks in the wooden structures, their weathered planks warped by sea spray, their thin white paint blistered by wind and sun. Viewed from the semi-darkness of the promenade, the ramshackle buildings seem about to explode with light at any moment. Inside there is a perpetual din: rattling, ringing pin-tables, football games, try-your-strength machines, mechanical cranes picking up a few liquorice comfits and depositing them with a modest clatter in the player's metal tray. There are juke boxes and punch-balls. Dejected hoop-la that nobody plays: it's too old-hat now, reminiscent of church fêtes and Sunday school outings.

Instead, there are the favourites, the pin-tables, gaily, crudely painted with the empty idealizations of American funnies – young men and women exhibiting healthy torsos and rugged profiles, all engaged in some violent occupation, usually involving guns and fast cars. The machines are dazzlingly lit, and ring and rattle and buzz with deceptively busy sounds. Here are all the popular types of pin-table – Dux, El Toro, Home Stretch, Silver Flash, Touch Down, The Spinner, For Valor, Stop and Go, Long Beach, Rink, Super Charger, Dancing Dan – as well as the more functional, less decorative and hardly ever patronized Bumpers.

These machines can be studied as intensively as racing form or pools coupon combinations and permutations. The practised player knows just how far to pull out the plunging knob that releases the ball, and becomes an expert at 'tilting the case', though this is really forbidden by the regulations. Players who go beyond the limit see a warning panel light up saying 'Tilt!'

The dazed-looking attendants circulating with pockets bulging with pennies that they jingle incessantly seem not to see these illegal manoeuvres, which are very common. Perhaps they know that it does not really matter, for no one ever wins anything. Nor do most people ever seem to score a sufficient number of points to be entitled to a free game. But youngsters spend many shillings every night in pursuit of the elusive numerals, trying to break the ten thousand barrier.

Older people, old age pensioners with nothing to do, rarely waste their money on the tables, but stand by, watching the efforts of the younger generation with sympathetic, scornful or even envious smiles. At the shining, chromium-plated mechanical miniature cranes in their glossy coffins no one ever wins a celluloid doll or a bottle of Brylcream or a plastic hair slide representing four pink dogs walking one behind the other. If you are very lucky, you may win a box of Swan Vestas, or catch a liquorice comfit in the crane's paralytic claws. You are not expected to win big prizes, as a card on each machine takes the precaution of stating: 'For Amusement Only'. Everyone here is a loser – unemployed youths, men on the dole, women with no prospects, pensioners living alone on a few quid a week. You cannot win. I am as luckless as the rest in this backwater ghetto of Tyneside, the black hole of Britain, as it always has been. I have no job, no friends. I cannot get my poems published, I cannot write a bestselling novel. A dull animosity seems to surround my days. From time to time, some inexplicable rage or resentment seems to afflict certain people at the very sight of me. I know it is because I am not like them, because I look out of place here, a loser among losers, yet not one of the lads. I feel an almost unendurable hatred for Tyneside: all I want to do is get away from the stranglehold of this town where I was born, and where I am determined not to die.

It seems as if everything is against me. I have to live at home with my parents, ashamed to be dependent on their charity. I feel useless and hopeless, and, what is worse, almost insanely bored. And I cannot seek relief from boredom in childish machines that are for amusement only.

Boys batter the punch-balls at a penny a time. The ball is attached to a chain, and when the ball is pulled down out of its cage, the sound is reminiscent of a flush lavatory. There is no desire to excite admiration in these would-be-manly punch-ball exhibitions, for the girls ignore them. The boys are only thirteen or fourteen.

Instead, the girls crowd round the Mighty Wurlitzer juke box to listen to Hazel Scott, Pinetop, Mary Lou Williams or Sammy Price, each carving out an individual boogie-woogie base. Why cannot I find my own rhythm, my own personal harmonies, that underlying and unmistakable beat, the base on which these jazz artists erect their most dazzling inventions? The records are all rather dated pieces like 'Beat me Daddy Eight to the Bar', 'Boogie-Woogie Bugle Boy', 'Frantic', or 'Scrub me Mamma with a Boogie Beat'. But for twopence a time, these records are the best value in the whole saloon; there is always a queue, so you can nearly always hear 'The Honky-Tonk Train Blues' at least ten times every night without ever having to pay for it yourself. As I stand around listening to the records – I don't have any money to spend on them myself – a man who must be a sort of bouncer or bruiser, in a shiny blue suit and a broken-peaked cap, makes his rounds, and I catch his eye. At once I get that feeling of the mute animosity of others: he looks at me as if he could kill me, keeps looking back over his shoulder at me as if I were vermin. Is it someone from my schooldays? It is the sort of look I used to get from schoolmaster bullies before they caned me, those pillars of the church, the tennis club, the rugby field – a sheer dislike of my difference. I thought it best to leave the arcade before he created a disturbance. I felt he might attack me, or call the police and accuse me of unmentionable crimes. In my life, there are always those enemies of my innocence, ready to poison my harmless existence, to let me know I am not welcome on this earth – it has been like that since my earliest childhood. I know now why it is: it is simply because I *am* different from them. The very sight of the way I walk or look seems to unleash furies within them.

Outside, I feel no safer. He has followed me to the door and is watching me depart with a look of mingled menace and contempt. I move slowly away, refusing to appear frightened.

As the night advances, the air grows chiller and the fog thicker. The crowds begin to thin. Hungry-looking apprentices wander round the fairground in their clumsy blue denim overalls, eating chips out of bits of greasy newspaper. On the dodgems there are only enough customers for three or four cars now, that amble round the metal-plated floor sedately, crushed into a dreamlike decorum by the unusual crescendo of the loud-speaker and the increasingly inhuman voice of the weary attendant.

When the pubs close, a few tipsy sailors, shipyard workers and miners with drunken girls and loudly-singing women create a brief rush of frantic trade, but after a few turns on the dodgems they stagger away to catch the last bus, at the Wouldhave Memorial.

The foghorn and the ships' sirens now are heard ever more clearly. About 10.30, when the empty arcades close down and the woman at the dodgems shouts 'Goodnight, Goodnight ...' in the lingering, surprisingly softened tones almost of a BBC announcer, the lights go out, the jingling, jigging, mourning, buzzing and moaning stop, and for the first time since nightfall the fairground hears the growing roar of the sea. While we have been amusing outselves, the tide has come in. I wander aimlessly along the deserted pier and back. As I walk slowly home through the sandy, fog-filled midnight streets, the sea's natural sounds and the river's mechanical noises echo like the cries and roars of demented animals in a distant zoo, over the stilled playground of this beaten, luckless northern town.

‘I, of all People’

1948

There are few things more worrying than a pair of worrying parents, and mine were always worrying – not without justification – about what I was ‘going to do with myself’. I was a total flop as a teacher, and further work on the land was unthinkable. The novel I wrote, *The Search for Love*, was at that time considered by publishers to be too short, too Kafkaresque, too explicit, and too peculiar altogether. I was obviously not going to make a go of it as a writer, and I was getting a little too old for prostitution.

For a while, I fancied myself as a male nurse, but when I suggested this to my father, he was horrified: ‘It’s as bad as being a lady’s hairdresser,’ he said – another trade I had thought of espousing. My mother was hoping against hope that I would settle down and get a nice clerking job at the town hall; now that we lived just opposite, I could pop across the road for lunch so easily from the curiously named Ogle Terrace. The very idea of spending the rest of my days chained to a desk in South Shields, even with the enticing (to my mother) prospect of ‘hanging my hat on a pension’ after forty years filled me with such desolate gloom, my mother began to fear I was contemplating suicide, and mentioned it no more. ‘Anyhow, the town hall in South Shields stinks of nepotism,’ said my father.

I wished I could run away to sea, but because of union rules that was no longer possible. Perhaps I could use my languages to become a professional translator? But all the works I suggested to publishers were turned down. I soon found that a translator rarely chooses a work he wants to translate; it is chosen for him by a publisher who has picked up some continental bestseller without the faintest idea of what the style is like, as part of a package deal with a foreign publisher. I have never translated a book or a play I really wanted to translate. As a test of my translating ability, I made a rhymed version of Paul Valéry’s long poem, *La Jeune Parque*, believed at the time to be the world’s most difficult poem (it isn’t), but no publisher would take it – ‘far too obscure’ – ‘what’s he getting at?’ – ‘is this a joke?’ etc.

My dear father with his job at Binns' Department Store, had had his self-confidence restored after a lifetime of unemployment or uncertain work. With typical generosity and unusual adventurousness, he made me an offer: we had sold our house in West Avenue at a small profit, and he suggested that with the proceeds I might like to start a bookshop. A bookshop in South Shields! The very thought was laughable: our town had never had a proper bookshop, and it was my impression that its inhabitants rarely bought books, or even read them. As gently as possible, I explained to my father how impossible it would be to make such a business pay in the North East, and anyhow I felt I should go mad stuck in a shop all day long – even in a bookshop.

My parents realized that I could never make a success of any normal job, because I had the utmost difficulty in getting on with people, and even just in speaking to them. The sad fact was that people bored me; the very sight of the faces in the street made me want never to go out again. Many years later, I learnt that Virginia Woolf suffered from the same intolerable sense of tedium, and that the ugliness of so many people drove her to despair and suicide. That is the one thing I admire in her. I can understand her feelings very well. I have never liked conversation, either: after a few minutes' talk with almost anyone I can only think of how to escape.

My parents wanted to protect me from myself, and from the world. They must have looked upon me as a sort of handicapped child, and they were terrified of my being hurt. Their constant worrying began to eat into my soul, and in the end I saw that the only thing to do was to get away from home. And getting away from home meant only one thing to me – London. Then, perhaps, Paris. For the moment, I was unable to see myself going any further than that. It was hard to explain this to my parents; I knew they loved me, but how could I tell them they loved me too much, that some of their concern for me was unwelcome?

'But are you sure you can manage on your own?' my mother asked.

To my surprise, my father answered the question for her, with a brave smile: 'Of course he can! He'll find something in London.'

They gave me fifty pounds and a set of sheets, and I set off for the great adventure.

London, of course, was not unknown to me. After all, I had worked there briefly as a teacher at Southgate. The school had found me a room in an old lady's house at Arnos Grove, which I found even more deadly dull than South Shields, so I had soon moved out and taken a room at

Finsbury Park, nearer the heart of things, in a cheap working-class lodging house.

Now I intended to live right in the heart of London. When I arrived at King's Cross, in those days a terminus of almost impenetrable murk, I took a room in a small hotel nearby while I looked for accommodation. The hotel manageress gave me what I thought was a rather strange look, but showed me a room with a big brass bed, a chipped ewer of water and an unmatching washbowl on a corner table and a miniature gas fire that had to be kept fed constantly with pennies. The room had a strange smell, a mixture of urine and face powder. But it was cheap, and I took it for a couple of nights.

My first night there was hell. I was kept awake by the unending tramping up and down stairs of prostitutes and their customers, by the banging of doors, and by the groans, screams and arguments of clients. Moreover, when I woke up in the morning I found myself bitten all over by bed bugs. After a cup of tea at the ABC, I went to Charlotte Street, where I knew there was a newsagent on the corner of Rathbone Place, opposite The Marquis of Granby. In the windows of this newsagent (which later appeared in Iris Murdoch's *Under the Net*) there were scores of small ads: second-hand musical instruments, 'French lessons', antiques, colonic irrigation, 'strict disciplinarians', books described as 'curious', puppies and kittens and bed-sitting rooms were among the extraordinary variety of things and services offered here.

I picked the cheapest room I could find – thirty shillings a week – at an address given as 77a, Tottenham Court Road 'above the shoeshop'. When I finally located the house, I found it had a front door round the corner from Tottenham Court Road, facing the ruins of the bombed Whitefield Memorial Church, where the author of 'Rock of Ages', the Rev. Augustus Toplady, has a plaque: he was buried there. Further up the street was the Scala Theatre. I rang the doorbell, and after a long wait heard someone coming down the stairs.

The door was opened by an overwhelmingly statuesque black lady with her head wrapped in a voluminous and complicated silken turban. In fact, she was not black, but, as she liked to remind me, *café au lait*. She looked at me with lids lowered on assessing eyes, her rich mouth puckered into a disdainful *moue*. Yet somehow under that mask-like face there was the sparkle of laughter and warmth. I fell in love with her at once. But would she ever accept the likes of me as her lodger?

'I've come about the room,' I said.

She did not reply. She just gave her head an elegant sideways tilt, motioning me to follow her up the narrow stairs. I closed the door, and before starting the ascent, she turned to me and said: 'You close the door very nicely.'

I later discovered that she judged people's character by the way they closed doors. It's quite a revealing thing, I know, from my own experience of Spanish and Italian door-slammers.

She mounted the stairs with stately slowness, one fine brown hand on the rail.

'Keep three steps behind me,' she ordered, turning her head as I put my foot on the first step. I dutifully waited until she had mounted the fourth step, then started my own ascent. I found she had a magnificent crupper, a real steatopygous derrière of phenomenal proportions, such as I had seen only in photographs in *The National Geographic Magazine*. That impressive behind was discreetly swatched and swathed in several layers of material, and swayed seductively from side to side as she rose on apparently painfully weak ankles and feet compressed into rather tight pumps.

We came to the first landing, where there was an old-fashioned wall telephone, and the door to the kitchen, where two dark-skinned ladies were drinking tea. They just looked at me, wide-eyed, over the tops of their cups.

'Follow me, if you please,' said the lady. 'I have visitors, so please come into the drawing-room.'

I gladly followed her heaving, wagging rear. The drawing-room had two curtained windows looking out on Heal's and the traffic of the Tottenham Court Road. It was directly above the shoeshop. It was furnished in stately bourgeois style, with a three-piece suite, a carpet and rugs, mirrors and pictures of African and other undeterminable landscapes, and a piano covered, like the sofa and arm-chairs, with doileys, lace-fringed, and various knick-knacks and photographs of mainly black people.

'Kindly take a seat.'

I sat on the edge of a hard chair by the window, hardly daring to breathe: would she take me?

'Are you musical?'

'Yes, ma'am.'

'Do you perform upon any musical instrument?'

'The piano.'

'Play me something from your repertoire.'

I fumbled and stumbled my way through a Chopin mazurka. The piano was in tune, and in good condition. When I turned round to face her again, I found her beaming with pleasure, her eyes sparkling, her generous lips parted in a dazzling white smile in which a gold filling glinted darkly. Her hands were clasped in adoration.

'You have the touch,' she announced.

I knew I was a terrible amateur, making up in feeling for what I lacked in technique. Her praise was intoxicating.

'Thank you,' I said. 'But I'm not all that good. I'm self-taught, mostly, and I don't follow the correct fingering.'

'If you will play me some little thing every day', she said, 'I'll let you have the vacant room.'

'That would be wonderful,' I stammered. I had not even seen the room.

'Come this way, if you please,' she said, in the tones of a superior lady floorwalker guiding a customer to the lingerie. 'Keep three steps behind.'

We went up some narrow stairs to the next floor, where there were two small rooms. She flung open the door of one of them with a dramatic gesture.

I looked with dismay into the dark, airless little room, hardly bigger than a walk-in closet. There was a narrow, hard-looking bed, a small table, a hard chair and a dingy curtain behind which were some hooks and coathangers. Over the bed there was a tiny window on an air shaft and a bare brick wall.

'You have Catesby's just next door', she announced, with a flourish of her hand towards the window, 'and Goodge Street Station directly underneath. You will never find a more convenient place.'

'I'll take it.'

'First week's payment in advance.'

I handed her three ten-shilling notes, which she stowed away in the voluminous folds of her robes.

'And when will you be moving in, may I ask?'

'This afternoon.'

'I shall provide you with a rent book at my own expense. May I ask you your name and occupation?'

I told her my name, occupation writer.

'James,' she mused. 'What a beautiful name. A beautiful name for a beautiful face,' she added. Then, with a mischievous smile: 'No lady visitors to your room, please. And', taking another look at me, 'no gentlemen visitors, either, though with my permission you may entertain them in the kitchen. And remember, my room is just below yours, so don't shake the bed too much!'

At this, she went off into gales of laughter, bending down to slap her plump knees again and again, and giving her turbaned head a few helpless shakes that sent the tears of laughter spilling from her big, dark brown eyes. Then just as suddenly she stopped laughing and, trying to keep her face straight, wiped her mouth with her fingers, as if to wipe away her smile, and her face became a mask again, though one full of life and fun. She touched the back of her turban in a charmingly feminine way, rather coquettishly, and said:

'There are some other rules in my house. You must not touch my turban. And you must not touch my bottom.'

'Of course not,' I assured her.

'I know you men,' she warned me, wagging a pink-nailed forefinger. 'You all want to touch my bottom. You men all want the same thing.' (Looking at me and going off into gales of laughter again.) 'Or nearly all of you.'

In this delightfully civilized manner, she was telling me that she had got my number. I refrained from explaining to her that things were a little more complex than she assumed. I did not see why I should give an explanation of myself to anyone, and if they got the wrong impression, that was their fault, not mine. In fact, I rather enjoy creating a wrong impression.

She did not tell me her name. She took me downstairs to the kitchen and introduced me to the two ladies seated there. One of them was Lotte, a vivid Abyssinian girl, refugee from Mussolini's Italy, where she had been conscripted to work in a factory. She had a big, radiant, toothy grin, and stiff black hair standing out straight in a sort of frizzy bob that would become popular in the 1980s. The other woman was a light-coloured West Indian, in her twenties, called Marlene, and she was studying acting and 'the dance'. She was married to a Nigerian. These were the other lodgers. They addressed my landlady as 'Madame Sheba', the only name I ever knew her by, though I lived there off and on for several years. 'My Queen of Sheba' I sometimes called her when we got to know one another better. I never saw her without her extravagant turban. Her bedroom was off the kitchen in a small room the same size as mine overhead, but her bed was bigger, and higher: it seemed to take up the entire space.

I learned that she had come from South Africa, 'where the Zulus are'. She gave her home town variously as Port Elizabeth, Durban and Jo'burg. I very soon learned the rules of coloured people's class distinction in Britain: the light-coloured ones were the aristocracy and, as skin grew darker, social position descended. Lotte was very dark, so she was treated almost as a servant. Marlene was as light as Madame, so she was an equal. Madame

Sheba always judged a person's social standing by the colour of his skin: as mine was practically chalk-white, I became for the first time in my life someone out of the top drawer.

Madame Sheba had no visible husband or lover. Indeed, I think she led an almost nun-like existence. But I later discovered she had a grown-up 'nephew' in Port Elizabeth. It was very difficult to tell her age, for she was well-preserved. She introduced me to the simple cosmetics of the bush – rubbing glycerine on face and hands, and once a week over the whole body – and taking a spoonful of cod-liver oil every day. Her skin glowed a pale golden brown, with hardly a wrinkle, though she must have been at least forty-five when I first knew her. She scrubbed her teeth with a twig, and they were impeccable. Breakfast was included in the price of the room: tea and toast and honey. But whenever I was broke, which was often, she would always take pity on me, and feed me with great bowls of semolina that she cooked in a big black pot. From time to time I might get a fried egg and a strip of bacon or a sausage. She had once run a restaurant in Charing Cross Road, on the corner where Cecil Gee's stands, but it had not been a success: she had given too many free meals to down-and-out fellow countrymen, and the word had got round that she was an easy touch.

She became an essential part of my life. Without ever having any kind of sexual association, I loved her deeply, and she knew it, and returned my love. She was sister, mother and wife to me. I had had no contact at all with black people before, but the endless stream of garrulous, vivacious West Indians and West Africans who kept dropping into the kitchen at all hours of the day and night were an endless enchantment for me, and I found I was at last beginning to like people – or at least I liked black people. They bewitched me with their beauty, their elegance, their humour, their music and dancing.

I suspect some of them were having a hard time in post-war London, but they never looked sad. They made ends meet by selling things in the market – as Madame Sheba had once done, she told me – or working the black market, or peddling hash, or renting their bodies to white men and women. In all the time I stayed with Madame Sheba, there was only one other white man lodging with her, a young taxi driver she had met in unusual circumstances. At a meeting of the Black People's Liberation League at Marble Arch – whose leader was a bespectacled, scholarly man with some fingers missing – Madame Sheba had been standing in the crowd, shouting her support, when, as she told me, she began to feel something long and hard pressing against her capacious bottom.

'Now my bottom', she informed me, 'is the most sensitive portion of my anatomy, and if any man so much as looks at it, I get vibrations.'

She had turned round indignantly to reprimand the young taxi-driver for coming too close to her sacred posterior. But he had apologized nicely, and they got talking. He offered to take her home in his taxi, free of charge, and that led to his renting a room for a few weeks. But there was never anything between them.

'He is that kind of man, you know, Jimi' (as she had taken to calling me) 'who are just fascinated by big women, especially big women with big bottoms. They're harmless. All they want to do is look, and maybe touch a little. But no sir! Not this chicken!' (One of her favourite expressions.) 'If a man lays a finger on me, I hit him one in the right place with my handbag.'

Her handbag was indeed a formidable weapon, and she carried it everywhere with her. I think she kept all her savings in it. One day, when she was expecting her nephew to come and visit her from Port Elizabeth, he sent a cable saying that all the money she had sent him for the fare had been stolen.

'More likely spent on drink, horses or girls,' Madame Sheba sniffed.

But she at once opened her handbag and took out about one hundred pounds, gave them to me, and asked me to go and wire the money to her nephew's address. She trusted me completely, as she would never trust any black man, or white man either for that matter. I sent the money, and returned with the receipt, and she was so moved, she embraced me, for the first and only time, crushing my slender figure to her voluptuous bosom. I took care, when putting my arms round her waist, not to let them slip down to her bottom. Then she produced her bottle of South African sherry. She bought one every Christmas, and on special occasions we two had a sip. This was a special occasion.

When her handsome young nephew arrived from South Africa, there was a big party, with all Madame Sheba's friends invited to Schmidt's restaurant in Charlotte Street. It was a memorable evening, with everyone singing and dancing and playing musical instruments. But Madame drank very little. I only once saw her incapacitated by drink. Her nephew and his friends had decided to open a night club in Soho, not far away. Madame Sheba was consulted about the décor and the general ambience of the club, and, using some form of benevolent witchcraft, cooked up a name for it, which I have forgotten.

On the club's opening night, we were invited as special guests, and Madame Sheba asked me to be her 'beau'. We dressed ourselves up in our best finery, and Madame spent a whole hour putting on her very complicated turban behind the closed (and bolted) door of her little bedroom. When she emerged in all her splendour, she really looked like the Queen of Sheba, and I was bursting with pride as I walked through the streets of Soho with her. People kept turning round to look at us as we passed by, Madame Sheba with one dainty brown hand laid demurely on my left arm. I thought of Mrs Yashnyavalka, the fascinating masseuse in Ronald Firbank's *Valmouth*.

But when we got to the club and the festivities began, the drinks started going to our head – rum and champagne do not mix very well, I think, and that is what we were plied with, along with dishes of 'soul food' that were left uneaten as we danced the night away.

About three o'clock in the morning, when the fun was at its height, Madame suddenly collapsed, and I had to take her home in a taxi. With the help of the driver, I got her to the bottom of the stairs, then I somehow managed to hoist her up, step by step, to the top – no easy task, because I was like a wilted lily and she was nearly twenty stone. But get her up to the top of the stairs I did, then I had to drag her through the kitchen to her bedroom, which presented the most difficult problems. I did not dare undress her, and I knew I must on no account take off, or knock off, her turban. But the bed was very high – 'so the rats won't bite my bottom,' she used to say jokingly. I got her on to a chair at the side of the bed, then climbed into the bed and somehow hauled her up. She had been totally unconscious. At that moment she came to her senses, and rolled into bed, nearly crashing me to death against the wall. Then she fell asleep, and I extricated myself as gently as possible.

That was one of the big events of her life. She never tired of describing to her friends how I had brought her home and somehow put her to bed, and she would hint slyly: 'I don't know what my beau did to me while I was unconscious, I'm sure I don't. But if he did get up to some tricks, he's the first man who ever got the better of this chicken.'

And she would roll about on her kitchen chair, roaring with laughter, her eyes and teeth shining and flashing, then would suddenly put on a straight face and delicately wipe her pursed lips with her fingers in that inimitable gesture.

Sometimes we would have visits from the police at the Tottenham Court Road Police Station, just along the road. They would make inquiries about some of the people who were seen entering and leaving Madame Sheba's premises. She always indignantly defended them, and denied any involvement in the black market or in drugs. 'I don't even smoke cigarettes, man!'

she would tell the inspector, who despite himself was impressed by her size and her authoritative manner.

But sometimes one of our friends would be arrested after some white nark had given him away, and we would be called to the station to bail him out and give him a bed for the night. I sometimes had to share my narrow bed with one of these feckless, happy-go-lucky West Indians, and we would lie there close together, embracing each other for warmth and comfort, and in order to prevent ourselves from falling out to bed, sleeping in each other's arms, or lying awake smoking and talking until the first tube trains rumbled into Goodge Street Station underground, and the elevators began intoning, in that harsh, metallic recorded voice that rose right up the air shaft to my room: 'Stand clear of the gates!'

Madame Sheba used to put on a great show of hysterical indignation when the police visited us. 'Treating us like common criminals!' she would cry. 'This gentleman is a rising young poet. How could you treat me like this – I, of all people?' I adopted this saying as my personal slogan. It seemed to fit the continual contretemps of my personal life.

Madame Sheba claimed to have been brought up by white missionaries in South Africa. She also used to tell me she was an orphan educated by 'the nuns' in Port Elizabeth, and that she had been in service with aristocratic British settlers. She also claimed to have been a model – though only for hats and turbans.

'Debenham and Freedbody (*sic*) came to interview me after the manageress saw me walking down Oxford Street. They wanted me to go and model turbans in their store. Swan and Edgar, Liberty's, Bourne and Hollingsworth – they was all crazy to get me signed up. But no, sir! Not this chicken! You know what they want me to do? Model fashions for 'the fuller figure'. Me! I am not a tailor's dummy. Taking off my good clothes in front of people! Then they want me to give demonstrations how I put on my turban, at the scarf counter, where any man could walk in and touch my bottom. Asking me to take off my turban! I, of all people! No thank you, I said. The very idea! Nobody don't ever see my head, and nobody ever will, until the day I die. Not even you, angel eyes. Oh, I bless the good Lord the day he send me my Jimi!'

Sometimes she said she was Roman Catholic – 'very high class'. At other times she would sing, in a fruity contralto, extremely emotional revivalist hymns to 'my Saviour'.

My Saviour is calling me homeward today,
Homeward today, homeward today,

My Saviour is telling me Love come and pray . . .
Love come and pray, Love come and pray . . .

all in Viennese waltz tempo, in strict three/four time without *rubato*. But she also sang hymns from Moody and Sankey, and from *Hymns Ancient and Modern*, giving some of the latter a distinctly erotic or negro spiritual interpretation:

The sun is sinking fast,
The daylight dies:
Let love awake, and pay
Her evening sacrifice . . . .

But Madame also practised at times some sort of African mumbo-jumbo, what she called 'juju' or 'muti medicine' like any witchdoctor in the kraals. There were days when she closed her kitchen door and would not speak to me, when she boiled up mysterious chicken and herb concoctions in a special pot. South Africa's Suppression of Witchcraft Act demanded fines and gaol sentences for practitioners of the black arts. She used to tell me tales about little children who suddenly disappeared in the middle of the veldt, and who, when they returned after days or weeks, did not know where they had been. In Japan, my friend Akiko used to tell me similar tales about children in the snow country up north who suddenly disappeared, in sight of their parents or playmates. As a child, I had myself experienced something like that, of being rapt away by unseen forces and unable to explain to my parents where I had been. Once or twice I saw Madame taking discreet pinches of snuff, to allow her speedy communication with departed spirits. My Granny Johnson also used to take snuff, but not, I think, for that purpose: she used to say a good sneeze put her heart in order. Madame had had some training by Mrs Anna Sithole, and used to order concoctions like love potions from Louis Alter's store in Johannesburg, which specialized in selling charms by mail order – charms against lightning and fire such as are commonly found also in Japan, and sold at temples and shrines.

For a few select friends, she would perform tribal dances, rocking and stamping to 'township jive', the native street music of places like Soweto, which on her records sounded very like the early rhythm 'n' blues that the African boys were bringing into the country. Like all big people, she was a graceful dancer, though she used to shake and shiver all over. When she danced for us, she seemed to be in a world of her own; sometimes her eyes would glaze, and she would fall into a trance on the sofa, which we always kept free for such eventualities. A drop of sherry brought her round, and she would laugh uproariously at our anxious faces gathered round her.

I was the only man allowed to observe such demonstrations, and the only white person until the arrival of a large businesswoman from Reykjavik, who had somehow struck up a friendship with Madame Sheba. This Icelandic lady was a singer of Wagnerian arias and I used to accompany her on the piano for 'The Ride of the Valkyries', which used to send Madame into hysterics.

I introduced some of my friends to the charmed circle of Madame, but she did not care for all of them. She seemed jealous of my friends, as if she alone had a right to know me – a very oriental trait, for I have often found it in the Japanese. I asked David, a wonderful pianist, to play something for her, but Madame was unmoved by '*Gnomenreigen*' and Chopin's '*Berceuse*'. I remember David saying: 'She doesn't like me.' Nor did she like his wife, Angela Petter. But she took at once to Nancy, Joe Ackerley's slightly cooky sister, and to my fey friend Muriel. The poet Iris Orton was a big success, and after I left she used to have a room there.

Colin MacInnes's novels, *Absolute Beginners* and *City of Spades*, give the atmosphere of those times very well, though they were written about ten years later. In the late forties, there was still racial harmony, but throughout the fifties, tensions began to build up between blacks and whites. It never made any difference to Madame Sheba and her white friends. The black boys who came and went on their mysterious errands remained my friends for years, calling me by a variety of fond distortions of my family name – Kingcup, Kisscup, Cupcake, Cockup (my favourite), Catsup, Ketchup, Perkup and so on. I was amazed that they wanted to know the likes of me. But they accepted me as warmly and loyally as Madame Sheba did her Jimi.

She was my ideal woman, and I often wished I could marry her and take care of her, as she took care of me. In *A Trophy of Arms*,* by that divine but rather neglected poet Ruth Pitter, there is a poem called 'The Beautiful Negress', and I often wondered if she had seen Madame proceeding, 'sails fill'd, and streamers waving', through the London crowds at Petticoat Lane, where she had a stall before the war:

> Her gait detached her from the moving throng:
> Like night, advancing with long pace and slow,
> Or like unhurrying fate she seemed to go,
> By an eternal Purpose borne along.
> An unregretful elegiac Song
> Swelled in her wake; she gathered up my woe

* Published in 1936.

Into epitome, and left it so;
Still dark, but made harmonious and strong.
O solemn Beauty, when upon my way
You walked in majesty, did not the tear
Leap up to crown you with more light than day?
Did not the silent voice within the ear
Cry Fly with her to the soul's Africa,
Night, tragedy, the veiled, the end prefer?

I once made a sketch of Madame, which I have lost, but I was never able to write a poem about her, as I longed to do. Ruth Pitter's lines say something of what I wanted to express about my love for her. But I was able to write a poem about the black singers and dancers who used to come to her house as soon as they stepped off the boat from Jamaica or Cape Town or Lagos. It is 'Negro Spirituals', and appeared in *The Submerged Village*:

O, the dark hole of the thrummed guitar, electric
strings parallel with thrilling fingers, haunted mouth
drugged with the sorrow of a hidden sun! The dim
windows coin your head with cold, but you dream soft chords
of dark gold, sweet words chanted for a bitter time . . .

Calm, O languorous and mute desire for coloured,
mythical calypso shade, where in cruel heat
love's tender miracles leap naked sand, or cool
fountains, mingle deep dances in a jungle trance!
Dark is the city to your moon-tipped fingerings,
but white stars of your upturned hands in rhythmed prayer
shine on the foreign solitude. Warm in the gloom
your grieving flower lives again, and breathes its song.

She died when I was far away, in Japan, in 1968. I heard the news in a letter from Iris Orton. A light had gone out in my life.

The Poets' Other Corner

1948

The curious stroller in Hyde Park on a summer evening may find his attention drawn to a quiet little group gathered at Speaker's Corner at Marble Arch. It seems something of an oratorical backwater, set between the vociferous League for the Protection of Coloured Peoples and a kind of marriage guidance bureau run by a scornful Scotsman who keeps shouting 'Down with Women'.

For the moment, nothing seems to be happening in this quiet little group. Is it one of those interminable private arguments about 'atheism' between a Jewish refugee and a puzzled visitor forcing his opinions in a northern accent? It is certainly not one of those teenage gangs which huddle round a re-embodiment of Red Hot Momma singing 'She Wears Red Feathers' or 'Waiting for Henry Lee'. No, on closer inspection it turns out to be a poetry recital.

A plump, well-dressed middle-aged woman is standing on an orangebox reciting a Shakespeare sonnet. . . .

> Tired with all these, for restful death I cry. . . .

Her voice is refined, a little arch at times, and she can hardly be heard above the clamour of the two large groups on either side and the noise of the traffic trundling round the Marble Arch. Her round, nicely made-up face under the smart hat is serious but strangely vacant as she turns her greying head from side to side, like a professional lecturer, hands in coat pockets, enunciating crisply, from between barely opened lips severely compressed at the corners. Her mind seems to be on something else, as if she were using her makeshift platform simply in order to get a better view of the park and the passers-by. Is she in a trance, reciting on automatic pilot? Just as we are beginning to think of her as an urban Sybil writhing on a utilitarian tripod, her voice stops half way through the sonnet. She gazes a moment open-mouthed at the Cumberland Hotel, then gives a little laugh, rubs her forehead and apologizes: 'Oo, it's gone clean out of my head. Silly of me. I said it right through only last night.'

There is a faint, encouraging murmur from the rather embarrassed but sympathetic audience. Most of us don't know where to look. A fleet of lighted buses is stuck in a traffic jam in Park Lane. An elderly man takes a quick look at his watch and hurries towards the tube. A young man and his girl standing with their arms round each other smile and exchange a kiss. The lady passes over her little mishap with expert ease, and makes a little joke, to the great relief of everyone: 'Funny how you suddenly forget, isn't it?' (As if we all frequently found ourselves in a similar predicament.) 'Never mind, we can't all be elephants, can we?'

There is a little polite laughter from her admirers in the front of the small crowd. Those on the fringes have roaming eyes, seeking something, someone, keeping a watchful eye on the dim figures weaving in and out of the groups, melting into the darkness of the shrubberies.

At this point one or two of the spectators, possibly seeking a partner for the evening in some more densely packed group, begin to drift away, and the lady cries out: 'Don't go away, the night's young yet. Would any member of my audience like to step up here and give us something? Any little thing, but classical preferred. Don't be shy. We're all friends here, and we all love poetry. We get all kinds, from Shakespeare to Service. What about you, sir?'

She points to a young man in a mackintosh, very tall and beefy, whom I had already guessed to be a plain-clothes policeman. He just shifts his feet, grins, shakes his head, and moves to a more promising group. She goes on, in a plaintive, pleading voice: 'Come closer, dears. Don't be afraid, I won't bite you.'

There is a slight, irresolute forward shuffle.

'Well, now, I might as well put in a word here about our meetings. We hold them here, weather permitting of course, every Saturday and Sunday evening, from about seven to ten thirty – though we have been known to go on until midnight when the fancy takes us and the Muse descends among us. Everyone is welcome to come and listen, or better still', (in the tones of mock grandeur, with much rolling of the eyes and down-turning of the mouth) 'to render a selection from their repertoire.'

There is no laughter this time. Perhaps some of us are wondering what we could 'give' or if our memories would hold out in this distracting environment. Waving her arms invitingly, she continues: 'Now won't someone – anyone – step up here. I can't stand here all night like patience on a monument, can I? We usually have a proper stand; this orangebox is not very *safe*; I'm expecting to fall off it at any moment, so get ready to catch.' She gives a weak laugh; she has what is known as a 'fuller figure'. But no one moves back, and she pretends exasperation.

'Won't one of you come and brave the heights of poesy and get up here and give us something?'

No one offers to do so.

'Where's Peter?' the lady suddenly cries, unexpected anguish in her voice. 'Where's that man got to?'

There is a sort of splinter group of four nearby: a young woman with a ponytail hair-do, sandals and *The Faber Book of Modern Verse* is discussing primroses and the problems of communicating through verse with three young men. The lady cries jovially: 'Peter, are you trying to set up an opposition group?'

A young man in a sports jacket, blue jeans and open-necked shirt leaves the little group and comes over to ours. 'Did you want anything, Elsie?' he asks.

'I thought you might like to get up here and give us something', she replies, 'when you've finished with your intellectual friends over there. I need a break.'

The young man is diffident: he wants to be pressed, for he is one of the 'regulars' and the star of this amateur talent show.

While he is hesitating, a middle-aged man with glasses, who might be a bank clerk, pushes through the crowd and says: 'I'd like to read something if I may.' He flourishes an edition of *Omar Khayyam* bound in limp brown calf.

'We don't *read* poetry here,' proclaims Elsie scornfully. 'Reading it drives them away. In droves upon droves. They like you to do it from memory. Anyhow, we're always having old Omar – we're a bit sick of him.'

The poor man fumbles the book into his pocket and stands blushing and with hanging head as Elsie continues imperturbably:

'Doesn't anyone know *anything* else? What about you, Mac? What about dear old Rabbie Burrrns?'

A Scots working man, who has been listening to her devotedly all evening, but just waiting to be asked, climbs on the orangebox and recites 'My Father was a Farmer'. It is something he feels deeply about, he tells us shyly before he starts, for *his* father was a farmer, too. He speaks the poem briskly, with a not-too-obtrusive accent, but in so low a voice that we can only catch occasional lines.

While this recital is going on, Elsie is mingling with the crowd, urging old friends and strangers and what she calls 'my semi-regulars' to come and 'get up and give us something'. She pays no attention whatsoever to the weak-voiced Scotsman, but he does not seem to mind, and is obviously gratified by the faint sprinkling of applause when he finishes. 'Any requests?' he says hopefully. There are no requests.

A Canadian soldier comes forward and says he would like to perform 'Invictus'.

'By all means,' cries Elsie airily. 'We like *variety* here, then you appeal to every class of poetry-lover in the crowd. Get up on the box, dear.' But the soldier, who is nearly seven feet tall, refuses to do so. 'Go on, dear, get up on the box. Don't be shy. We're not proud here.'

The soldier compromises by placing one foot on the box and leaning forward with an elbow on his knee. He uses a conversational, matter-of-fact tone, as if he were telling a barrack-room story, and the poem sounds much better than it ever sounded before:

> . . . It matters not how strait the gate,
> How charged with punishments the scroll,
> I am the master of my fate:
> I am the captain of my soul.

'Lovely, lovely,' cries Elsie, as a brief round of applause greets the final line. 'I suppose you don't happen to know those immortal lines of his – Henley, wasn't it – how do they go – something about:

> I was a King in Babylon
> And you were a Christian slave. . . .

Blushing, the soldier denies all knowledge of the lines, and strides away in to the lamplit park. A prostitute accosts him but he walks straight on.

Next, a little man with a toothbrush moustache and a flashing, embarrassed smile renders 'The Road to Mandalay' with a great deal of energetic and appropriate gesture. He speaks in a loud Cockney voice that suits the subject admirably. The crowd swells as he recites, and he gets a good round of applause. Encouraged, he whispers to Elsie:

'Shall I give them "The Everlasting Mercy" by John Masefield?'

'Well, it's a bit long, isn't it?'

'It would only be selected passages, you know.'

'If you wouldn't mind waiting till later, and give someone else a chance. . . .'

Rather dashed, the little man gets down and, after a moment's thought, walks hurriedly away. He'd have had more luck with 'Cargoes'.

Peter has finally allowed himself to be persuaded, and mounts the orangebox to recite some poems, 'rather modern in manner, I'm afraid,' by Stephen Spender and Edith Sitwell – '*Dr* Edith, as we should by rights call her.' The large crowd listens patiently and appreciatively. He goes on, rather surprisingly, to 'the Lucy poems, by William Wordsworth'. These too are much appreciated. His manner of delivery is natural and clear and attractive. The lines

> Rolled round in earth's diurnal course
> With rocks and stones and trees

spoken beneath the wind-tossed plane tree in the semi-darkness of this public garden, are solemn and fitting. And all the old familiar lines come back to us renewed, with a strange shock of recognition, as if we are meeting lost friends in a totally unexpected setting:

> Strange fits of passion have I known . . .
> I travelled among unknown men . . .
> She dwelt among the untrodden ways. . . .

His memory seems inexhaustible. Was it partly because of the unusual surroundings that there should have been such an unbearably moving quality in

> But she is in her grave, and oh,
> The difference to me. . . ?

Finally, he speaks a passage from 'Prometheus Unbound', then 'When the Lamp in the Dust lies Broken', introducing them with a few well-chosen explanatory words. He says the poems plainly and without fuss; he does not, like so many professional verse speakers, try to make them sound interesting, but lets them speak for themselves. They come across with great lucidity, and the audience accepts them with enthusiasm.

Elsie once more totters on to the box, and, as if absent-mindedly, while casting round in her memory for something else, recites without stopping several poems by Housman. Then she launches out into Marvell's 'To his Coy Mistress', the poem most frequently heard at these gatherings. Her eyes, as she comes to 'desarts of vast eternity', gaze sadly down the Edgware Road. And the triumphant ending will always ring through my head with the sound of her own peculiar and fascinating voice, imbued now with some of the energetic falsity of tone of a not-very-popular gym mistress:

> Let us roll all our Strength, and all
> Our sweetness, up into one Ball:
> And tear our Pleasures with rough strife
> Thorough the Iron Gates of Life.
> Thus, though we cannot make our Sun
> Stand still, yet we will make him *run*!

One even seemed to hear the capital letters. Then, bowing to awed applause, she says: 'Well, ladies and gentlemen – 'kyou, 'kyou – I'll give you another Shakespeare sonnet, this time all about his famous dark lady, if memory holds out, that is.'

And she does give it to us. Again, it sounds surprisingly new and fresh and strangely moving. She speaks it quietly, with feeling, and with only a slight primness on 'Why then her breasts are dun'. She reaches the end without a pause, while we follow her, as she apparently racks her memory, with bated breath. There is a short hand-clap from an admirer. ''Kyou,' she says quietly, absently, giving her head a quick shake as if to disperse the fumes of the last poem, and casts her eyes on the ground. A breathless pause. Then she throws back her head and declaims a poem by Newbolt, all about India and men dying one by one without food or water. It is a decided success, and several newcomers, attracted by her ringing voice, push to the front of the crowd. Are they hecklers, mockers? She does not see them. They have just left a political meeting and a fervent anti-royalist is stabbing a finger in the direction of Buckingham Palace and shouting: 'We'll 'ang the King, we'll 'ang the Queen, we'll 'ang the Princesses, we'll 'ang the 'ole bloody Royal Family!' A policeman on the edge of the crowd interrupts him with: 'Now then – no bad language!'

The newcomers look rather bewildered at first. They look round this new audience to get the prevailing mood and see which attitude they should adopt. Some at once take up a reverent, 'thinking' pose, with hand over eyes or head inclined. Those who are looking for a rowdy anarchist meeting move away at once when they realize 'it's only poetry and stuff'. Others, with half smiles of approval and disbelief, listen with open mouth, scrutinizing the audience's faces for the right reactions to make.

At the end of the Newbolt, Elsie, flushed with success, announces: 'Well, this must be my last, I'm afraid.'

Do we detect a slight stir of relief among her admirers? The trouble with our Elsie is, she does tend to go on too long, and even an announcement of a final poem cannot always be taken seriously.

'Leave them while you're winning I always say,' Peter tells the girl with the sandals and ponytail. 'That's something Elsie doesn't understand. It's a professional thing, you know.'

If Elsie has heard this, she gives no sign: 'I don't want to miss my last bus home, like the other night.'

Always surprising, she says: 'I'd like, if I may, to give you just something different, quite a short little thing, more or less modern, really, by Wrey Gardiner, of whom you've probably never heard.'

The poem follows, a rather dim piece about a tired poet at a publisher's cocktail party, and people begin drifting away. Those who are left at the front drink in the words with touchingly uplifted faces. They remain because they think it's her last poem, and applaud it with a note of finality. But: 'Now this must really be my last,' she says, trying to keep the attention of her slipping public. 'Coo, ain't it draughty up 'ere!'

Her mock-Cockney chivvies the listeners, but they seem uneasy, not knowing quite how to respond.

'Gather round, boys, fill in these wide open spaces,' she pleads, waving her gold-braceleted arms. The remaining few shuffle a few steps nearer the orangebox. For her 'just one more little thing', Elsie begins reciting 'Go, lovely rose', by Edmund Waller. The lamplight, falling through the plane trees of summer, moves across her plain, prim face like inspiration. The traffic roars and hoots. Hysterical West Indian voices rattle off jumbles of rabid slogans. Another crowd is roaring with laughter. Far off, round the corner by the railings, the Welsh are singing 'Men of Harlech' and another group, glumly religious, is intoning

> Nearer, my God, to thee, nearer to Thee,
> E'en though it be a cross, that raiseth me-ee-ee....

And like a peaceful little island in the stormy sea of life, this small group of bent heads concentrates on the crisp, genteel voice at its centre saying 'one more little thing':

> Quit, quit for shame, this will not move,
>   This cannot take her;
> If of herself she will not love,
>   Nothing can make her:
>   The divel take her!

Is this a solution to the modern poet's problems, his growing lack of readers? Could he win back, here in the public park, that vast audience he once had, and which he has lost to a host of radio and television buffoons? The meeting has a refreshing air of spontaneity, improvisation and unforced enjoyment. There is none of the dreary stuffiness of the usual Poetry Reading; the poet in person obligingly explaining away all the mysteries of his craft before he gives us each poem.

Here, modern poetry is appreciated as well as the classics: Gascoyne is as sure of an attentive hearing as Gray. There is no dreadful 'poetry voice' to put people off. With this particular, eclectic audience in mind, there is a challenge to every poet to write poetry that is both contemporary and, however difficult, enjoyable, a poetry intended for reading aloud, not for the usual tomb of the printed page. The audience is waiting. At *this* Poets' Corner, the poets are alive.

Hell is a City

1948

My first year in London seemed like paradise after South Shields. I was making friends, writing, earning a little money, and thoroughly enjoying myself. I had made fleeting visits to London during the war, once or twice during the Blitz, to give readings of my poetry at the Progressive League, whose headquarters were in the basement of the Ethical Church in Bayswater. These monthly meetings presented live poetry and music, and the poetry was organized and introduced by a plump, bearded literary man called Alec Craig. There was a book table where one could exhibit books and magazines. One of the circulars I have retained states: 'There is no charge for admission but a collection is taken. It is particularly desired to encourage those attending the meetings to take advantage of the tea arrangements.'

The music was arranged by Ashton Burrall, and was usually of fairly high quality, with a preponderance of Viennese and German refugee singers who used to introduce their *Lieder* with long and occasionally very funny comments.

On my first visit, sometime in 1942, I think, I read my long poem 'For a Dead Gardener', and some shorter ones. It was the first time I had given a poetry reading since my university days, and I was thrilled by the warm reception I was given. Also on the bill was John Heath-Stubbs. There were always several poets at the meetings, all waiting for a chance to speak their latest poems.*

Other poets I met there during the war and immediately afterwards were George Barker, David Gascoyne, Tambimuttu, Ross Nichols, David Wright, Alex Comfort, Muriel Spark (always in a smart hat), G. S. Fraser, Norman Nicholson, Herbert Palmer, Stevie Smith, John Betjeman, Stephen

*One of these was Gloria Komai, whose Japanese father, Gonnosuke Komai, published some impressions of London life and *Dreams from China and Japan*. His *Fuji from Hampstead Heath* is a kind of guide book to Japanese culture, published by Collins in 1925. I have a copy, dedicated by the author in both Japanese and English to Nancy Price, the actress. The sepia frontispiece shows Mr Komai in formal kimono standing next to Lord Northcliffe in a Norfolk jacket, seated, cigar in hand. Gloria was a beautiful girl, and the first poet I knew who introduced Japanese sensibility into her work.

Spender and Roy Campbell. I was present on the historic occasion just after the war when Roy Campbell, accompanied by his personal bodyguard of right-wing thugs, attacked Stephen Spender while he was reading from the rostrum. I never quite understood why he did so, unless it was an attempt to assert his manliness; some said it was because Spender had advised T. S. Eliot at Faber and Faber's not to publish Campbell. It was quite an ugly punch-up, in which Spender conducted himself admirably, making no attempt to retaliate, and adopting a dignified, quietist stance. Campbell called him some nasty names while Spender just stood there, frozen with embarrassment for us all. When Campbell had been dragged away by Alec Craig and Ashton Burall, Spender went on calmly reading his poems. He taught me a valuable lesson in how to behave on such occasions, which were to come my way several times. The spite, jealousy and animosity of British poets is something that has to be experienced to be believed. The horrors of reading one's own poetry in Britain became so acute that I had to give it up altogether, with only a few tentative returns that confirmed me in my opinion that British poets are for the most part uncultivated boors and jealous ingrates. They are always putting each other down. I suppose it is because space for poetry, and for proper poetry reviews, is almost totally lacking now in Britain, so that poets have to claw and fight their way into print: it's the survival, often of the unfittest, which, together with the deadening influence of Leavis, has spelt the end of imagination and invention of modern verse.

Encouraged by my Turkish poet friends, Feyyaz Fergar and Sadi Cherkeshi,* I had frequented surrealist groups in London, notably that presided over by the Belgian poet and artist, E. L. T. Mesens, who, with Roland Penrose, edited a wonderful Surrealist magazine, *London Bulletin*, which had to cease publication in 1940. Mesens had organized the International Surrealist Exhibition in London in 1936, and a few years later became the director of The London Gallery in Cork Street. It moved to Brook Street after the war, but closed around 1949. Fergar took me to meet Mesens at the Barcelona Restaurant in Beak Street, where I seem to remember a sinister, black grand piano which Mesens told me he often made love to. He was not like an artist at all, but rather resembled a respectable businessman with surprising conversational gambits, like that other Belgian, René Magritte. Mesens is represented at the Tate by one or two rather strained, dim collages, but towards the end of the war he produced some interesting war poems in *Troisième Front*. I stayed with Sadi in a flat in Margaretta

* Who like his beautiful wife was to die of cancer, so Feyyaz told me recently.

Terrace, where George Melly also lived. Melly worked for a while in Mesens' gallery, where I met him once or twice, not realizing he was to become one of my favourite male jazz singers. After the Barcelona closed down, I sometimes went to another Spanish place, a basement in the Fulham Road, called La Fiesta, where Melly also hung out between engagements. Years later, I heard him at the London Jazz Club, where Louis Armstrong once sat in with Ken Colyer, a memorable evening indeed.

Pubs were delightful places during and after the war. I was thrilled by the 'queer' clientele at the Fitzroy, London's most notorious bohemian pub, where the Union Jacks hung down from the grimy ceiling like unmade beds. People used to throw spitballs at the ceiling, with a charming decorative effect, and the Victorian mahogany and the tinny piano completed the picture of respectable depravity.

Madame Sheba's house was just a short walk from the Fitzroy, a place much frequented by sailors and soldiers looking for a bed on weekend leaves. Saturday night and Sunday noon were the times to be seen there. The clientele was what the gay guides describe as 'mixed', but the majority of the customers in those days were men and women homosexuals, some of them excruciatingly camp and theatrical. They would 'make an entrance' as soon as the doors opened at noon on Sundays, the sun piercing the chimney-tops of Charlotte Street creating an improvised halo or spotlight and sprinkling the cut crystal flowers of the swinging doors around them as they swept in. The old piano in the corner was silent on Sundays: 'No Singing or Dancing', the notices said, as if we didn't know, for this was Sunday, British Sunday in all its dreariness, with a bedlam of church bells bouncing in Soho's cosmopolitan belfries.

The naval trophies shimmered on the wall above the Gents. The electric globes would revive and faint in cloud and sun, and the ceiling was covered with twists of coloured paper like dead bats. Stale recruiting posters from both wars still threatened and exhorted, trying to shame us into the noisy misery of another war. After an hour or so, the professional beards came in, the matelots and the girls, the lumberjacks who had seen all the latest plays, the studied army-surplus déshabillés, readers of *Time & Tide*, abreast of everything, the touching phantoms of the innocent 'twenties and the mistaken young who strayed in with capes and fringes. The Priestley types with pipe and a solid background of handmade gramophones quietly, effortlessly smiling in apparent thought, the casual provincials in their Sunday drapes, the cocky barrow-boys and swish-clothed charmers with their smart Ronson lighters: endless double-take of doubt until 'Time gentlemen – *and* you, too, ladies, please. . . .'

At the Wheatsheaf, the corner of the bar was occupied by Julian MacLaren Ross in a teddybear coat, smoking black-market Gauloises in a long cigarette holder, and looking rather like Oscar Wilde with his dark, marcelled hair and rather heavy, sallow features. I never dared speak to such an august pillar of the writing fraternity. Along Rathbone Place, the Black Horse became a gathering place for poets and painters, among them 'the two Roberts', the Scots painters Robert Colquhoun and Robert McBride, whose works seemed to me rather like linoleum in texture and composition and colour. There was also Jankel Adler, whom they both revered. But I was drawn more towards John Minton, with his strange, tortured, haunted face – which I once saw horribly battered and bruised by one of his boyfriends.

At the Black Horse, there was Keith Vaughan,* later a sad suicide, and dear old hearty Bill Belton, a wonderful, exuberant painter of spivvy boys with bulging biceps, bottoms and bumps. He had a studio in Notting Hill Gate where I often spent Sunday evenings with him and Blossom, drinking cocktails and good wine and eating delicious dinners, sometimes in the company of impoverished artists who rewarded the generosity of Bill and Blossom by stealing things or breaking up the place. Bill had foreign currency hidden in all the books in his gallery bedroom up above the main studio, for at this time travel abroad was restricted because of tight currency regulations – I think everyone was allowed only twenty-five pounds – and both Bill and Blossom had long ago spent their allowance. When I wanted to go to Paris, Blossom suggested that she would pay my return fare and hotel charges if I would let them have my allowance, then we could all enjoy a few days in Paris eating some decent food at last. I agreed, and we went. We had dinner twice *chez* Vagenande, and went to the Opéra – Flagstad in *Tristan and Isolde*. On a later occasion, Bill and I took several of his large paintings to an international painters-for-peace exhibition at the Cirque d'Hiver. The customs men could make neither head nor tail of Bill's provocative male boot-boys, but I was able to talk them into letting them through. On that occasion in Paris, we ran into Stefan Schimanski, editor of a short-lived magazine, *Kingdom Come*, and Denise Levertov, another poet from the Ethical Church recitals, who departed for fame and fortune to the USA, where she has become a leading poet. Would she have had the same opportunities, or luck, or encouragement in Britain? I doubt it.

Another regular in all the bars was Nina Hamnett, dotty, dithery, dipsomaniac, always scrounging drinks, and, however under the weather,

* A painter.

with an unconquerable natural elegance and a broad, defiant humour. In a few years' time, she would die after falling dead drunk out of her bedroom window. There was another strange woman, with straight, lank grey hair, who was known as 'the Duchess', and she, too, was always drunk, thin as a rake, slightly sinister, very sad and, like Nina, desperately courageous.

Those pub-crawlers thinking the *après-guerre* was the time of artistic revival are all dead now. All more or less forgotten. As I observed them all quietly from my bar stool, I thought how pitiful they were. On the billiard table upstairs at the Black Horse, on the way to the Gents, many a one was laid – either drunk as a lord or in sexual abandon. That billiard table could tell some tales. But downstairs in the bar, the hot sausages were the best in town.

Strange flashes of coincidence emerge from my reading: for example, in the White-Garnett letters, one dated 10 May 1942, a letter from 'Bunny' to 'Tim' is headed 'Crown Inn, Falstone, Northumberland', which is where I was working as a C.O. for the Forestry Commission on the North Tyne. I know that inn, and I may have been there that very day, enjoying the excellent brown bread Bunny describes:

> That woman at the inn here makes wonderfully good bread with a mixture of brown flour and oatmeal – the best bread I've ever eaten. The river is almost empty – the chance of catching trout is very slender.
>
> There are curlew, rock doves on the crags, wood pigeons in the birches, pheasants searching for acorn, rabbits everywhere. The first thing we saw was a mounted figure coming through the wood below the moor with a dog fetching in sheep with lambs. When we got to the farm it turned out to be Mrs Hedley, the farmer's wife. Today it is drizzling and cold. . . .

It might be the very day I describe in 'One Day in the Middle of a War'. And I knew that farm, the farmer and his wife. How strong the waves of nostalgia beat upon my memory when I read about those already-distant days in the noise and confusion of my life in London! The local names come back with a sad poetry – Kielder, Tarset, Plashetts, Sighty Crag, Peel Fell . . . Riccarton Junction!

But from Herzen's autobiography, I have retrieved an extract that speaks to me in a rather hopeless undertone:

> The past is not a proof that can be corrected but a guillotine knife; after it has once fallen there is much that does not grow together again, and not everything

can be set right. It remains as though cast in metal, exact in detail, unalterable, dark as bronze.

In a poem by Li T'ai-po, there are these wistful lines that apply to many poets, but to me especially at that period:

> Pray, may I remark, since we last parted,
>   you have become very thin;
> Of course, since then, you have undergone
>   the bitterness of writing poems.

From the same book, Florence Ayscough's biography of Tu Fu, the poet writes of his friendship with Li T'ai-po, ending with these lovely lines:

> We are both travellers on Tung Mêng Hill;
> I love my lord as younger brother loves elder brother.
>
> In autumn, exhilarated by wine, we sleep
>   under a single quilt;
> Hand in hand, we daily walk together....

In those days, one of the reasons I wrote poetry was that I thought poets were the most remarkable and beautiful people in the world, and I longed to have them as my friends, perhaps as my lovers – lying under the same quilt, and reciting each other's poems between kisses and orgasms. How incredibly naive I was.... I never found that kind of *amitié amoureuse*, nor that true poet-lover. But such impossible longings are part of youth, and their loss is part of growing up. Are they, in my case, altogether lost? I think not. I still feel within me that romantic naivety, the passion for a last possible friendship, even though I now know that such friendships belong to youth, not age. In a sense, therefore, I am glad that I have not entirely grown up; in many ways, I am still a dreaming child and a visionary adolescent, and today when I look at the faces and the behaviour of most adults around me, I count myself lucky in my loneliness. Proust says it very well in *La Prisonnière*:

> *Peut-être chez moi, et chez beaucoup, le second homme que j'étais devenu était-il simplement une face du premier, exalté et sensible du côté de soi-même, sage Mentor pour les autres ... la froideur n'était-il qu'un aspect extérieur de sa sensibilité....*

And Gore Vidal, in *Myra Breckenridge* says:

> More than ever I am convinced that the only useful form left to literature in the post-Gutenberg age is the memoir: the absolute truth, copied precisely from life, preferably at the moment it is happening....

I am Proust's 'second man', capturing life at the moment it is happening yet without rigidity, the eternal present of memory.

I was beginning to see the grimmer side of London life. While I was fascinated by the razzle-dazzle of places like a café known as 'The Lily Pond' in the Coventry Street Lyons – where I first met Quentin Crisp wearing bright Indian scarves; a true saint now, Britain's answer to Mother Teresa – I did not like the murky after-hours clubs there were such a feature of post-war Soho. With Madame Sheba to protect me, I went to the Moonglow club in Percy Street, one of the haunts of Burgess and Maclean – 'Guy and Donald' to the black barmen. There was a big West Indian club near Piccadilly where 'weed' was discreetly available, and that I was introduced to by Bill Belton. Both places appear in Colin MacInnes's *City of Spades*, and my first meeting with Colin was with Madame Sheba at the Moonglow. Not long before his death, I got to know him better, through correspondence, and I was able to tell him how much I liked his novels and his essay 'Growing Old Gayfully', for Gay Liberation Front that appeared in *Gay News*. We discussed our bisexuality: while Colin was attracted to both sexes without differentiation, my own tendency was to alternate between them, so that I would go through periods when my relationships were with women, followed by a swing to romantic friendships with men. I did not feel at all attracted to teenagers, as Colin did; if a black teenager, boy or girl, came to the house, Madame Sheba would warn me: 'Gaol bait!' But when she noticed that they had no effect upon me, she no longer troubled herself about them.

I went with Bill a few times to the Gargoyle Club: he invited me there usually after dinner at Bertorelli's or The White Tower or Schmidt's, all paid for by generous Bill and Blossom, for I could never have afforded such places. Rodrigo Moynihan, the painter, and Philip Toynbee patronized the Gargoyle, as did Burgess and Maclean, who used to have terrible fights when they were drunk. The only club I really liked was the Mandrake, in a back lane off Dean Street called Meard Street – a name as unsavoury as its reputation. I liked very much the portly, dignified and scholarly proprietor of this club, Boris Watson, who would always cash one of my rare cheques from periodicals for me. One afternoon, as I was sipping my pink gin, Boris created me an honorary member of the club, which I thought was a great distinction. He admired my poetry, and as admirers were so rare I rewarded his perspicacity by creating him an honorary member of my own select band of readers, known as 'the Elite'. Boris accepted, saying: 'Elite – now that would be a good name for a club. . . .'

Dylan Thomas and his numerous hangers-on often appeared in the

Meard Street basement, always tight and getting tighter, and making advances to any woman in sight while spouting a lot of rubbish in his ever-more-climactic poetry voice. Guy Burgess and Donald Maclean came in and the latter started fights all the time; I heard that he had bitten a chunk out of Rodrigo Moynihan's thigh.

Despite all these modest depravities, I still felt pure as a lily in my Ronald Firbank persona, though already a bit damaged. In the words of darling Mae West, 'I used to be Snow White, but I drifted.'

One of my heroes has always been Bertrand Russell. I have collected one passage from his *Autobiography* which applies to my own condition:

> Throughout my life I have longed to feel the oneness with large bodies of human beings that is experienced by members of enthusiastic crowds.... Always the sceptical intellect, when I have most wished it silent, has whispered doubts to me, has cut me off from the facile enthusiasms of others, and has transported me into a desolate solitude.... Underlying all occupations and all pleasures I have felt since early youth the pain of solitude. I have escaped it most nearly in moments of love, yet even there, on reflection, I have found that the escape depended partly upon illusion.

In my own moments of greatest solitude, the crowds of London were both a blessed cloak and a shirt of nettles. The late forties was a particularly desperate time, with police vice squads and *agents provocateurs* at every turn. Even in the apparently harmless little teashop in Wardour Street, The Tea Kettle, I saw a plain-clothes dick who had often spied upon me at Marble Arch and in the steam baths in the Edgware Road and the India Docks Road. That East End bath was where, on my very first entrance, I was accosted by one of those aggressive men who from time to time used suddenly to take a dislike to me, and I am sure he was a copper's nark, because on my further defiant visits to that 'den of vice and iniquity' there were handsome young policemen and their informers who used to smile invitingly at homosexuals and invite them to scrub their backs under the showers. I had some very narrow escapes, and now that I look back upon that dangerous period, I feel some guardian angel must have been watching over my escapades. The groping in the crowds at Marble Arch grew to such proportions that uniformed police, led by the head of the Vice Squad, began to encircle the genuine hecklers as well as the cruising 'queers'. I can remember one evening when I was at the heart of one of those promiscuous crowds of men, finding the cold eyes of the chief of the Vice Squad fixed intently upon me. I got the message, and dissolved into the night.

In fact, I got so frightened of arrest that I left London for a while, and went to live a simple country life for a few months, until things cooled down in the capital of Shelley's 'Peter Bell the Third':

> Hell is a city much like London –
> A populous and smoky city. . . .

'I'll Turn it all to Poetry!'

1948

In a sense, I was grievously disappointed that the vice squad had not arrested me. If they had done so, I could have cast triumphantly in the faces of police, magistrates and newspaper hawks my well-rehearsed Parthian shot: 'I'll turn it all to poetry!' delivered in the ringing tones of Donald Wolfit on the blasted heath. 'Is that a threat or a promise?' David had asked me once, when I had informed him and Angela of my plans. Dear David – 'always my torture', as Firbank said to Aldous Huxley, who was even more of a tease than Ronald.

But my wartime experiences should have warned me that the countryside is not for me. Like most of 'the confraternity', I am by nature an inner city man. The crowds give both protection and possibilities of brief encounters – that I always hoped would turn into permanent relationships (and some of them did).

Nevertheless, I felt that the only way to escape police persecution was to leave licentious London and disappear into the landscape. I first went to Oxford, where I stayed for a while with an old friend who had been librarian in the Felling. Dear Mona Lovell, both a friend and a Friend, had given me moral and physical support on many occasions during the war. I had had to sell my typewriter, so she typed out early stories and poems for me – paper was scarce at the time, and I still have copies of the stories she typed for me on some hideous magenta paper she had managed to unearth in Oxford. She was one of the most understanding, compassionate, intellectual and saintly women I have ever known, and I cherish her memory. Few people have ever been so good to me, in spite of bad behaviour and feckless morals and provocative ideas.

But I hated Oxford, and detested its oafish undergrads and supercilious dons. I became involved with a young man as feckless and moneyless as myself, and tried to help him when he turned out to be a deserter. As a pacifist, I was all for hiding him and keeping him out of harm's way, but we were both foolish, and were found out, causing a lot of distress and suffering to both my family and Mona's. It was a horrible, desperate, savage time in my life.

I kept returning to London for two or three days, then burying myself in the country again, pursued by some unspeakable terror that struck me as soon as I saw a London bobby. But back in London eventually, I had a haircut at the barber's in Goodge Street, who made the usual comments about my 'mop' and 'let's get this mess cleaned up', and 'I'm hacking my way through the undergrowth'. Madame Sheba was going to put me up for a few days while I looked for something more suitable than that dark, airless back room.

I have always had difficulty finding digs. My new landlady at Arnos Grove was the typical British female lodging-house tyrant, and many were the battles I had with her. She was a sharp-tongued little vixen, and an ardent Baptist. She had many rules and regulations which she strictly enforced upon her cowed lodgers. I could use the bathroom only at stated times. I was not allowed to entertain female (or male) visitors in my room. I had to come home at night no later than 9.30, after which everything was bolted and barred, and I had to appear for her horribly stodgy British meals on the dot, otherwise I got nothing to eat. I even had to clean my own shoes and put my clothes away neatly and make my own bed, supplying my own bed-linen.

With the freedom-loving habits of a born tramp, I soon fell foul of that middle-class old trout. She put another ten shillings on my rent. I refused to help her wash the dishes, and scandalized her by leaving dirty underclothes lying around my room, mixed up with drafts of poems she could not understand but thought must be just as dirty. I used to come back well past midnight, after wandering round the low dives of Soho or Bloomsbury or Chelsea. I would shin up a convenient drainpipe to a roof below my bedroom window on the second floor. My unconventional mode of entry into the locked house was discovered one night by a patrolling policeman who thought I was a cat-burglar, and the whole neighbourhood was roused from sleep by my landlady's outraged screams.

I won a little money on the dogs and horses, and moved to a small room in Finsbury Park. Although the war had ended three years before, food rationing was still strictly enforced, and officially I was allowed, for one week's ration, one egg (usually not fresh) a small loaf (mostly composed of chalk and chicken meal) two ounces of meat and equally stingy amounts of sugar, tea and butter. Such were the fruits of victory.

It was necessary to obtain food on the black market in order to survive, for meals in restaurants were also rationed, and, like most British food, largely inedible – those 'People's Restaurants' ruined many a stomach. The black market was run by picturesque near-gangster spivs who were noticeable because they were smartly though flashily dressed at a time when everyone was in old, patched and dowdy clothes.

North London – especially Finsbury Park, The Angel Islington, Camden Town, the Euston Road and Warren Street (the illegal used-car dealers' centre of operations) was one of the spivs' main territories. There, many of London's brash barrow-boys sold rare – usually 'dropped-off-a-lorry' – supplies of oranges, bananas and apples from barrows that they would push away hurriedly whenever they saw the police approaching. They also sold pairs of illicit nylons, Hershey Bars and packets of Yankee cigarettes (known as cancer-sticks), which were traded by American troops for dope ('weed'), Scotch and any kind of sex.

As black market food was so expensive, I decided that my best plan was to join the racket, through my contacts at Madame Sheba's. Thus I became acquainted with North London's seedy drinking clubs, shady caffs and dreary pubs, where deals were made under the cover of sentimental Irish labourers singing 'Danny Boy' or 'If Ye Ever Come to Ireland' with tears in their drink-reddened eyes, and West Indians, high on hemp, pounding out haunting, frenzied calypsos.

There was a wonderful atmosphere of lawlessness reminiscent of *The Beggar's Opera* and Hollywood B-movies. It was a London deeply scarred by hideous bomb-sites where pink willowherb waved its plumes of drifting white down, a city tawdry with cheap drink and cheap sex, a kind of third-rate Babylon. When I got to Tokyo in the late fifties, I found again some of that frontier fellowship of dirt and danger.

In London, I would spend all night in Soho pubs, drinking clubs and dance halls in the Tottenham Court Road, which were thronged with all the vital, lissom figures of wildly carefree blacks dancing with a gay vigour and abandon unequalled anywhere else in the world. I found a new decadent pub, The Duke of Wellington at the end of Charlotte Street, and other pubs and clubs, dubious haunts across Oxford Street: places like the Colony, Les Caves de France (where Carnera's* brother was bartender, a gentle giant of a man and an accomplished bouncer). Crossing Oxford Street from Rathbone Place was like entering alien territory.

There were visitors from Ireland and Paris – Brendan Behan, Antonin Artaud, Jean Genet (he hated London, too), Jacques Prévert and William Burroughs. Some American writers began appearing. I became friendly

* A celebrated Italian prize-fighter.

with a fellow-asthmatic, the surrealist artist Ithell Colquhoun, who created fantastic *décalcomanies* by floating sheets of paper in her bath whose water she had covered with radiant oils. She had a place in Cornwall to retreat to whenever London fog became too much for her. Occasionally William Empson would emerge from Cambridge like some Old Man of the Sea and come to London to make one of his cryptic Third Programme readings. His curious beard, which seemed to sprout from under his shirt collar, framed his bespectacled, pleasant face as in a spiky ruff, and always made me think of the popular song:

> Does Santa Claus sleep with his whiskers
> Under or over the sheet . . .?

Soho in those days was a happy place, not the sordid porno dump it has become today. I loved other parts of London, too: the cut glass, mirrors and crowded bars of the Salisbury in St Martin's Lane, the Church of St James the Less in Westminster, with its incredible profusion of Victorian decoration, the *art nouveau* of the St Gothard Café in the Fulham Road, with its Walter Crane plates and big Victorian fireplace, the florid nineteenth-century baroque style of the King and Crown public house in the Harrow Road, the Biograph Sinema (as we called it) in Victoria, and Mr Pickwick's marvellously Victorian pub, the George and Vulture, in the City. There was nothing more refreshing, on a hot summer day, than to pop into St James the Less, take off one's shoes and cool one's feet by wandering round on the glazed tile floors. And like one of Firbank's characters I often dashed into the National Gallery to tidy my hair in front of 'The Virgin of the Rocks', which makes a fine emergency mirror.

I became a connoisseur of ancient public lavatories, like the one in Holborn which had a fine gas lamp hanging in the street above the entrance, and carried the date 1897 – how Wildean! It had genuine Victorian fittings, and the roof of cast iron was supported by elegant iron columns rising from an arabesque mosaic floor. The graffiti were erotic and humorous, and wit and humour are the saving graces of such art. One of the most amusing examples of graffiti I ever saw in an English lavatory was in a small, rustic, cosy, three-stall urinal embowered in trees on the grassy bank of the River Wear just below Durham Cathedral, on whose walls some university wit had written, in flowing italic script: 'Homosexuals rejoice! Ye have a place in Nature!'

With my growing body of poems, some of them published, mounting up in my suitcase, I had ambitious plans to read them over the public-address systems at Waterloo, Paddington, Victoria and King's Cross. The stationmasters were sympathetic, but they said it might distract the passengers and cause people to miss trains or go to the wrong platform if they heard me reciting my love poems instead of the ladies with their cute elocution announcing the times to Haywards Heath or Peterborough, so with much regret the railways declined my offer (free of charge) and stuck to records of military marches between timetable titbits.

I was still desperately hard-up, and, again, with nowhere to live. In summer, I often slept out in the parks – the benches in Hyde Park were the most comfy. Or I would sleep in one of the doss houses near King's Cross, stinking public dormitories for the aged and the drunk with no other place to go to.

For a while I did various odd jobs: washing dishes in the kitchens of the Coventry Street Corner House was my most regular occupation, at ten shillings a day, with a choice of leftovers.

In my desperate efforts to find congenial work, I wrote to scores of colleges and universities and schools. But no one would have me. So I thought of doing some kind of 'creative' office work, at a good publisher's or an advertising agency.

I composed some advertisements for Shell, and sent them to what I understood to be the leading British advertising agency. I wrote witty things like: 'There's no time like the future! And at present there's no future without *Shell*!' And: 'There's no business like *slow* business. As many of us have found, to our cost, in every walk of life. But you'll get there with time to spare when you use *Shell*, the fuel of the future!' And: 'Open your eyes to facts, and Shell will tell!'

I sent these and many others to the agency, and to my surprise I received a letter asking me to attend an interview. In a state of acute nerves, I attended at the stated time, and found I was being interviewed by Paul Jennings and another person whose name I have forgotten. But I remember Paul's witty face and encouraging remarks. However, they did not feel I was 'right' for that particular post, and how right they were! In fact, as so often when I was to attend interviews for jobs, I sensed that I had been invited merely to assuage the idle curiosity of the interviewing panel, who, after dismissing me, would have a good laugh.

But a few days later, I had an extremely kind letter from Paul Jennings in which he praised one of my poems: 'The Blessed Received in Paradise', on a painting by Giovanni di Paolo, which had appeared in *Time and Tide*. I think it was Jennings who invented the slogan 'You can be sure of Shell'. I thought of him when I later got to Sendai and saw the Shell sign, but with the 'S' blown off by a typhoon. 'Yes', I thought, at that particularly difficult time of my life, 'you *can* be sure of hell.'

One day I saw an advertisement in *The Evening Standard* offering free room and board in a block of expensive mansion flats in Baker Street, not far from the tube. I wondered what the catch was: perhaps some rich lady (or gent) wanted a young gigolo? I was ready for anything. When I rang the bell of the luxury flat the door was very stealthily opened by an elderly lady wearing rather old-fashioned but high-class clothes. A thick metal chain allowed the door to open only an inch or two. When I told her I had come in answer to her small ad, she took the chain off the door and invited me into her sitting-room. The flat was of a type common in London – a 'semi-basement' – and through the windows of the sitting-room I could see above me the feet and legs of the passers-by hurrying along Baker Street.

I soon learnt why the room and the food were offered free: the old lady's basement flat, where she lived all alone, had several times been broken into by burglars who had stolen valuable jewellery and furs. The old lady told me she had grown very nervous of living alone. This rather surprised me, because she looked every inch a soldier – tall, angular, abrupt in her speech and manners, with a very grim face that never smiled. However, she told me she would feel much safer if there were a man in the house, and I felt obscurely flattered at being taken at last for a real male, especially by such a masculine-looking woman. She was unable to keep a dog, because pets were forbidden in that block of flats.

'Do you think I am a suitable person to guard your property against burglars?' I asked. 'I'm not very strong, and as a pacifist I refuse to handle arms or take any kind of violent action against a fellow human being.'

To tell the truth, I was now rather anxious to be rejected by this fearsome old lady, I thought she looked quite able to handle any intruder: just to look at her made me feel nervous. But she answered: 'I'm sure that an honest, open face like yours can be trusted. You remind me of my son who was killed in the war. And just to know that there's a man in the flat would set my mind at rest and allow me to sleep in peace. *Do* take the job, Mr Zobrowski.' (I had given her one of my pseudonymns, for no reason at all. As she found difficulty in pronouncing this Polish name, which I had taken from a brand of vodka, I told her to call me 'Zob', hoping she did not know this was French slang for prick.)

I agreed to move into my room that afternoon. There was one condition I did not like: I had to be in by six every evening, in order to bolt and bar all the doors and windows before dinner. For a night-wandering person like myself, this was a great hardship, but I privately decided that I could easily slip out of the flat, using the small window in the bathroom for an exit, as soon as the old lady retired to bed, which she told me she did every night after listening to the nine o'clock news. That would give me time to creep through the window and visit a few of the pubs before closing-time, which was at ten thirty in Bloomsbury and eleven o'clock in Soho and Piccadilly.

That first evening, after arranging a few personal possessions in my small but comfortable room – a small palm tree, and a photo of Ronald Firbank – at six o'clock I bolted and barred and locked and chained all the doors and windows according to the old lady's instructions. Then she made our dinner, which I was pleased to find was accompanied by a bottle of Riesling. She said she needed a light wine to calm her nerves and help her to sleep. I recommended an additional nightcap of a glass of Benedictine. Finally, at nine o'clock, just after the news headlines, the old lady retired to her room, and I to mine.

After waiting fifteen minutes to give her a chance to say her prayers and get into bed, I crept to the bathroom, where the small window was secured by only a small hook. I managed to squirm through the window and then I was racing along the Marylebone Road to the Black Horse in Rathbone Place. After the pubs closed, some musician friends invited me to some of the jazz clubs – the Jazz Cellar in Oxford Street and the West Indian jazz club called the Caribbean – a delightful den of iniquity just behind the Piccadilly Theatre, where I had been once or twice with Madame Sheba, and with Bill Belton.

It was two o'clock in the morning by the time I got back to the flat in Baker Street. Quietly I tiptoed down the basement steps and quietly I prized open the bathroom window. All was dark and still. Cautiously I thrust my head and shoulders through the window, and then – wham! – I received a terrific blow on the head that stunned me for a few minutes. It was the old lady who, picking up the first object that came to her hand, had whacked me over the head with a lavatory brush. When she saw it was only poor me, she was furious. She thought it had been a burglar.

'You'll leave this house first thing tomorrow morning, Mr Zob!' she hissed, her face contorted and white with rage and shock. 'Never in my born days have I met such an irresponsible, useless, drunken young man! You should be ashamed of yourself! I might have killed you!'

She might indeed, and to this day I still bear the mark where she hit me such a wallop. Next morning, I was out on the cold streets again, with not a penny in my pocket.

What *was* I to do? I decided to go to the British Museum Reading Room, which in those days was still presided over by the chill profile of fairy-like Angus Wilson, who was just beginning to attract attention with his witty short stories: his novels, those boring door-stoppers, were mercifully far in the future. At least in the BM, for which I had a ticket, I could rest, recover from my hangover, keep warm and perhaps sleep a little. I might even be able to persuade Angus Wilson to lend me a pound or two to buy some brandy and sandwiches at the Museum Tavern across the street.

But it was Angus Wilson's day off: he was not on duty at the central desk. I flipped quickly through some of the books on the open shelves; once, to my astonishment, I had found a five-pound note in one of the Spanish dictionaries. Today, I had no such luck. I was feeling bored and cross.

I wandered out into Great Russell Street, where I was greeted by a friend of mine, a London 'pavement artist' who did not work, as most did, on the pavement: he had hung some of his 'works' on the railings of the British Museum. These crude paintings were not done by my friend (a West Indian who called himself Lord Earl Duke) but were borrowed from an *atelier* in Bermondsey, a place specializing in such pictures, which were hired out to beggars for a few shillings a day. Only one or two pavement artists actually did their own paintings or pastel drawings on the pavement outside the National Gallery.

Lord Earl Duke had his usual collection of portraits of famous people – Churchill, Roosevelt, Stalin, Napoleon, Truman, Alexander the Great, Attlee and – next to a 'Man from Mars' – the homely features and bland smile of T. S. Eliot, who had recently accepted a Nobel Prize. My friend had already made about one shilling in pennies dropped into his cap by passers-by, mostly office-workers hurrying to their businesses in Holborn and Russell Square. As it was a bitterly cold morning, Lord Earl Duke asked me if I would watch his paintings while he went for a cup of tea at the ABC. When he came back, he said, he would give me sixpence for tea and a bun.

So I knelt down beside his now-empty cap under an almost Goya-like picture of the Royal Family, and, adopting a suitably humble pose, hoped for generous passers-by. During the first ten minutes, only one penny dropped into the cap. A clergyman went by, hesitated after he had passed me, then came back and handed me a leaflet inviting me to his chapel where I could have free soup at lunchtime while he extolled the glories of the

Christian religion, a religion that had done precisely nothing for me so far. I accepted the soup-ticket.

Then, to my horror, I saw approaching me the venerable figure of T. S. Eliot in person, on his way, presumably, to his office at Faber and Faber's in nearby Russell Square. I wanted to cover up his portrait but I had nothing, not even a clean handkerchief. I wanted to cover my own face, too. I did not know where to look, for I had met Eliot only three days before in his office, where, with pompous, smiling condescension, he had rejected my wondrous English verse translation of Paul Valéry's epic, *La Jeune Parque*. As he sat there in his rich, dark three-piece suit, I could have kicked him for being so blind. Or was he simply jealous of my ability as a translator? He himself had made mistakes in his wretched versions of Valéry, and the French in his poems was decidedly schoolboyish. 'Frail,' he said, smirking. 'Both you and your poetry.'

As he approached me on the pavement, I lowered my head. Fortunately I was unkempt and unshaven, so perhaps he would not recognize me. I hastily donned a pair of dark glasses, though the sun was not shining. Out of the corner of my eye, I watched the solemn approach of Eliot's big, shiny black boots, squeaking ominously, as they plodded majestically along the pavement. Soon he would see me, and soon he would see that dreadful, crude but quite recognizable portrait of himself in all his New England smugness. I was rather glad the portrait would not flatter his vanity, for it made him look like a dyspeptic preacher.

The big black boots halted in front of the picture. I kept my head down. Then I heard him speak, and it was like the voice of Milton's God: 'That is really rather a good likeness of me,' he boomed. He fished about in his purse and dropped into the cap a threepenny piece. Enough for my cup of tea! Then he proceeded on his august way, murmuring to himself, in a pleased boardroom voice: 'Not bad, not bad at all. Really rather good....'

I obtained a very boring office position as sub-editor on a trade paper, *The Advertisers' Weekly*, edited from a street running down to the Thames from Fleet Street. They also published a yearly reference book, *The Advertisers' Annual*, also known as *The Blue Book* because it had a blue cover. I was assigned to this publication, to which I devoted my talents for the next three months. I got five quid a week. The work was so dull and mechanical, and the pay so small, I did everything I could to bring a little gaiety and colour into the office. The editor of *Burke's Peerage*, published, I think, by the same firm, had an office upstairs and would sometimes come down to find out what all the laughter was about. Sometimes I would appear wearing a false nose and beard, or a clown's mask. Sometimes I would do my imitations of Dietrich, John Wayne, Bette Davis, Eartha Kitt or Winston Churchill. I slipped little joke misprints into the miles of proofs, turning objects like 'Dandy Rolls' into 'Randy Dolls'. The office manager, Robbie, was always tearing his hair at me. But the other office workers, about half a dozen young men and women, liked the diversions. 'You have to be gay to be serious,' I told them, inverting my usual motto.

My final escapade created an unprecedented uproar, in which both press and police were involved. In those days, I still smoked cigarettes. I provided some of my lighter-hearted colleagues in the office with clay pipes and bowls of soapsuds. While the manager was absent, having a quick drink before the bars in Fleet Street closed for the afternoon, we spent the time blowing soap bubbles out of our tenth-floor windows in that grim little side street. I discovered that cigarette smoke can be insufflated into soap bubbles, giving them a beautifully pearly, opalescent shimmer. We held contests to see how far we could make the soap bubbles float. Some of them drifted quite a long way, then would burst, disintegrating in a pretty puff of smoke and a shower of spit.

While we were engaged in this delightfully meaningless pastime, we were startled by the entry of two policemen, who looked like identical twins. They charged us with 'creating a disturbance in a public place', or some such nonsense. I felt the occasion had come at last for me to declaim: 'I shall turn it all to poetry!'

I looked out of the window, and saw, far below on the pavements of Fleet Street, crowds of people staring up at our drifting, shimmering smoke bubbles. Drivers of cars and taxis and buses had also stopped to gaze up into the skies, creating a monumental traffic jam. It was a period when many people claimed to see 'flying saucers' and the more sensational dailies were full of weird reports and strange photographs of 'UFOs'. The tremendous excitement down in the street was caused by people who had spotted our smoke bubbles drifting across the summer skies. They thought they were 'objects from outer space'. When the bubbles burst, leaving a trail of mysterious smoke, the spectators thought they were space-craft suddenly accelerating and vanishing from sight with supernatural swiftness.

That evening, the newspapers carried unusual headlines: 'Bubble-blowing Bard Snarls Traffic'. And: 'Flying Saucer Scare Poet's Pipe-Dream'. And: 'I'm Forever-Blowing-Bubbles Poet Sacked!' Followed by: '"He made my life a nightmare," confesses manager.' Yes, after only three months in that degrading job, I was mercifully dismissed. So was the police charge. My office colleagues wrote me a witty farewell poem.

Some say J.K. was ever so bad,
And it's certainly true to say
His camping drove the manager mad
By the end of a working day.

But mad or bad it's ever so sad
That Jimi has gone his way;
For whatever he did he was quite a lad,
And oh, he was *ever* so gay!

During my brief stint in Fleet Street, I had looked further afield for accommodation, and thought that Putney might be cheaper than the centre of town. I found a very pleasant and inexpensive bed-sitter in Werter Road, Putney, not far from the house ('The Pines') in Putney High Street where Theodore Watts Dunton had watched over Algernon Charles Swinburne. I found other literary associations in Werter Road: E. M. Forster's old aunt had lived there, and it appeared in one of Arnold Bennett's novels. Indeed, I believe I read in Margaret Drabble's fine biography of the novelist that he had lived in Werter Road.

But there, in Putney, was another literary association that was to have a profound effect upon my life and my writing career. Down by the Thames, in a flat on the top floor of the Star and Garter Mansions, named after the pub below, lived, quite unknown to me, the editor of *The Listener*, J. R. Ackerley, and his sister Nancy, with Queenie the selfish, silly, temperamental Alsatian bitch.

When I next sent a contribution to Joe at *The Listener*, giving my new address in Werter Road, I was astonished to receive an invitation to meet him at his office in Marylebone High Street.

It was the start of a new period in my life.

PART FOUR

Pre-orientations

'From gardens where we feel secure
Look up, and with a sigh endure
The tyrannies of love. . . .'

Dear Old Joe

1948–55

At my very first meeting with Joe Ackerley, which must have been some time in 1948, he said: 'I am a homosexual and I'm in love with an Alsatian bitch.' These words were addressed to me, quite loudly and clearly, across the table of a smart and crowded West End restaurant, towards the end of a superb luncheon.

I thought it best just to nod pleasantly at this unexpected information, and my silent reply seemed to satisfy him. I now think his statement must have been a kind of test: he either wanted to see if I would be shocked, or to extract a similar confession from myself. I wondered for a second or two if I should tell him the whole truth: 'I am a bisexual in love with myself,' but this thought set off a fit of giggles in me, and as Joe looked baffled at this (bafflement was one of his habitual expressions, enhanced by his horn-rims, at least whenever he was in my presence), I assured him that 'It takes all sorts to make a world, thank goodness,' and he began to laugh with me at this analysis of the absurdity of human existence. Only a little later did it occur to me that what Joe was trying to tell me was that he was perfectly aware of my own sexual ambiguity, something my androgynous appearance in those days did tend to suggest.

At that moment we became friends for life. When I remember Joe, as I do daily, it is chiefly as a person who enjoyed laughing at the same things that made me laugh and as one who could turn rather dangerous or unpleasant escapades into high camp farce. The only other persons with whom I have been able to laugh at existence in this way have been David Paul and my Japanese companion.

Joe was a marvellous mimic, especially of Wyndham Lewis, his sister, Nancy, and Richard 'Porchy' Church,* as well as of various female members of *The Listener* staff. He was a great comic, both in speech and writing, and his comic effects in both derived from a deadpan delivery. I, who am still sometimes unable to tell when someone is joking, was a useful foil for the practice of this form of wit, and I learnt a great deal from his

* A well-known traditional poet and novelist, very influential in his day in the Poetry Society.

delivery of often outrageous lines. He would endow the most scabrous details of his experiences with an exquisite looniness that used to convulse me with helpless laughter, in which, after vainly trying to keep a straight face, he would join himself, with heaving shoulders. His stories of matter-of-fact daily life often had a sudden fantastic twist, though they were always soberly recounted in that detached, mellifluous voice. And his observations about various literary figures were presented in the same way:

> 'How ghastly, dear Jim, to start one's retirement by buying a cottage in the country, only to discover, too late, that one's next-door neighbour is Dorothy Sayers or Dr Joan Evans.'
>
> 'From the poetry of Dylan Thomas I fail to extract much other than an impression of tangled knitting.'
>
> 'One of our unsigned reviews in my book pages once killed an author. It was written by that harmless nobody [a well-known historian], who has never recovered from the discovery of such power in his pen.'

That beautiful voice was one of his greatest charms, and women found it fascinating; a number of my young female Japanese students were so spellbound by it that they still talk and write to me about it, after nearly twenty-five years. There was some talk of forming a 'J. R. Ackerley Society and Study Group' in Japan, where such scholarly gatherings do much to keep English literature alive in a declining intellectual climate. But the very thought of being made the 'honorary president' of an academic caucus devoted to his own writings was enough to make him hoot with laughter. While Francis King was working as the regional director of the British Council in Kyoto – ('Such eminence!' mocked Joe) – I was approached at a party in King's palatial mansion by a timid young Japanese scholar who was hoping for some crumbs of information about Joe, as he intended to write a doctoral thesis about him. The crumbs that fell from my lips seemed to take him aback, and the thesis never appeared, to the great regret of both myself and Joe, for we were expecting to have a good giggle over it.

Michael Holroyd, in his entertaining biography of Lytton Strachey, informs us that Joe stayed at Ham Spray in 1925, along with E. M. Forster, Henry Lamb and Ralph Partridge and others. Joe told me he had liked Carrington, but found Lytton's life with her 'a strain – rather like my own life with Nancy'.

At first I thought Joe's voice was a gift he had cultivated as a radio announcer, but later I realized that it was a perfect example of a 'Cambridge accent', and, like Aldous Huxley's, of the finest quality, quite unlike the affectedly dulcet James Mason drawl of D.J. Enright and the younger Cambridge literary set. Joe once took me to dinner with Robert Harris, who was preparing to play Prospero at Stratford upon Avon, and Bobby told me that Joe would have made a good comic actor. 'With a voice like that, and his sense of timing, he could have been a matinee idol.' The prospect made Joe shake with mirth, saying: 'And I suppose my striking good looks would have nothing to do with it?' In fact, as a young man he had been strikingly handsome, with the early filmstar profile of a Leslie Howard or a Robert Donat, and even in old age he still retained a haggard, hawk-like distinction of feature.

That first meeting with Joe took place in an expensive restaurant near Broadcasting House, where Joe had invited me to lunch, as he was often to do, 'on the Corporation'.

'Do choose whatever you fancy, Jim dear,' he would tell me, 'and don't be shy – it's on the Corporation.'

Being a poverty-stricken poet who never knew where his next meal was coming from, such lunches and dinners at L'Escargot or the White Tower or Chez Victor were most wlecome, though in those days I thought it was vulgar to choose the most expensive things – something Joe soon corrected.

After *The Listener* published 'Mortally' I had kept on sending Joe poems, but he did not take another until late 1944, when he accepted two translations of poems by Jules Supervielle. Some editors seemed to like my translations more than my own poems, so I started sending out poems purporting to have been translated from French or Italian or preferably some obscurer language like Finnish or Albanian, and in this way got many of my own original poems accepted. I adopted the same policy for short stories.

Nothing more was accepted by Mr Ackerley until 1946, when he printed my version of Valéry's 'Fragment for "Narcisse"' and then three of my own poems. In 1947 he printed five; in 1948 eight. I think it was in 1948 that he first asked me to review poetry and other books for him, anonymously (which I detested), except for special numbers when I was allowed to sign my name. My first signed poetry review was of Louis MacNeice, not one of my favourite poets – *Holes in the Sky* in early May 1948. Joe had to tone it down a bit, saying: 'Jim dear, you'll do yourself a lot of harm if you persist in writing such home truths about the high priests of Faber and Faber' – crafty advice from a world-weary but still diplomatic old hand in the touchy little enclaves of insular British literary politics: advice which, perhaps unfortunately, I refused to follow.

It had never entered my head to try to make personal contact with

Ackerley or with any other editor. I just could not bring myself to insinuate my way into editorial offices soliciting book reviews and so on. I still cannot. Joe was to tell me many amusing tales about poets and other writers, whose names were well-known to me, storming his editorial offices uninvited, and about how he dealt with them. One desperate young poet, whose name I shall not reveal, threatened to shoot himself if Joe did not print his latest poem. Another had ostentatiously fingered his fly, and started to unbutton it. In both cases, Joe had repulsed attack simply by saying: 'Do put that thing away, dear boy, it doesn't look nice at the BBC.' As he later explained to me, shaking with laughter: 'Well, my dear, he wouldn't have dared do that on the open street, so why should I allow him to do it in my office? Besides, he had a dismal-looking weapon.' I am glad to say that I was not among those who forced their attentions upon Joe for the sake of getting a review or having a poem printed. Such tactics, though common in literary circles, I find despicable.

As soon as I had settled down in Werter Road I began trying to write poems again, and after about a month sent a group to J. R. Ackerley, whom I still thought of as 'Dear Sir'. Dunstan Thompson, a young American poet I much admired, and who unfortunately now seems to be totally neglected, had wisely advised me never to send just one poem to an editor – advice which had come to him straight from the august lips of John Lehmann, who had published Dunstan's work in *New Writing*. Dunstan told me: 'Always send a group, and include at least two obviously bad ones, to make the rest stand out and give idiot editors something they can see *must* be rejected. Then they usually feel they can accept one or two of the rest.' Unfortunately, when I followed this sage recommendation, some editors accepted my 'bad' ones and rejected the good ones. (Never J. R. A., to whom I usually sent only one poem at a time, hot off the typewriter!)

It was when I wrote a poem about the teaching hell at Minchenden Grammar School, 'In a London Schoolroom', that Joe at once accepted it, and added an invitation to visit him at his office and take lunch with him 'on the Corporation'.

I remember so well my first sight of Joe behind his desk, marking proofs – exactly like the photograph (who took it?) on the cover of Neville Braybrooke's splendidly produced, sensitive and almost too tactful edition of his selected letters.* I noted the bony, aristocratic face, the silky white hair, carefully brushed in charmingly period style; the tall, elegant figure, slender in worn, casual clothes; the thin, long and rather grim-looking mouth that nevertheless opened in a warm smile revealing a generous

* *The Letters of J. R. Ackerley*, edited by Neville Braybrooke, Duckworth.

assortment of big, smoke-stained, irregular teeth; and the sparkle of his hydrangea-azure eyes behind serviceable horn-rimmed spectacles. He seemed awfully old to me, yet he moved with a sprightly grace, with rather dancing steps, as I imagined Ronald Firbank must have walked, though with a more athletic stride.

On the floor by his desk was a canvas hold-all containing, to my horror, a large bloodstained parcel that might have been a severed head. This, I was to learn, was a colossal lump of horse-meat for his Alsatian bitch, Queenie – whom I was to call privately 'Queenie-Go-Home'.

He gave me a discreetly searching look as I entered, and his eyes flickered over me from head to toe, making me wonder if I had adjusted my dress before leaving: it was a sign I had learnt to recognize as homosexual interest in my person. So I brushed back, with nervous hand, my mane of blond hair, which I used as an answering signal, tilting my head back *à la* Rita Hayworth in *Lady from Shanghai*. I must have looked a proper clip.

Then he leapt up, danced towards me and shook my hand in a manner both distant and warm, cool and yet lingering, as if trying to sense through the tips of his very long and exquisite fingers what manner of man I was. His handclasp was light and intimate, like my own, which I like to compare to a recently cut French novel for suppleness. Had I gone too far with my Rita Hayworth impersonation? Slightly alarmed, I put a certain reserve into my response, and gave him, under veiled lids, my Dietrich smoulder between long, silky, bushy eyelashes, whose effect was rather mitigated by their extreme fairness, until I learned to touch them up with black-brown Cherry Blossom Boot Polish. I feel sure that he sensed and accepted at that instant that I was not 'available'. Not before lunch, anyhow, though one of my earliest mottos had been 'sekkers before brekkers'.

He asked me to sit down and wait for a few minutes until he had finished his proofs, saying something he was often to repeat to me: 'Any ass could do this tiresome job. Being literary editor of *The Listener* is something absolutely anyone could do – I come in here for an hour or so two or three times a week and it's done.' In fact, he always worked with the greatest care and attention to detail, and I was to find that he spent the greater part of his leisure time reading books for review and writing letters to prospective reviewers. His personal touch in the editing of 'the paper' was unique in the literary world, and has never been equalled.

He always carried round with him piles of typescripts that had been submitted to him – mostly poems, and these he would read in the most conscientious way, not trusting his own judgment (which was excellent) but asking his friends for their opinions, and even, on one occasion when

I was with him on the tube to Putney, submitting a poem by Auden ('Fleet Visit') to a strange young man sitting next to him and asking what he thought of it. The poem, in Auden's handwriting, was difficult to decipher, and the young man returned it with a baffled smile, getting off the train rather smartly, I thought, and standing on the platform gazing in wonder at us as we swept away waving in the style of the Queen Mother. ('Give them the smile extending,' as Firbank makes one of his characters say in *The Artificial Princess*.) 'Nice face, hadn't he?' remarked Joe. In spite of what he always insisted were his rather 'batty' methods, Joe produced a weekly of unfailing originality, with stimulating pages of art and literature that were models of their kind, and have never been surpassed for quality, variety, layout and readability. What a horrible come-down *The Listener* has suffered since he was (almost forcibly) retired!

After a few minutes he came to the end of his task, collected his proofs and handed them to a teenage office boy over whose generous endowments, clearly visible through tight-fitting clothes, Joe's eyes strayed appreciatively and affectionately. On a later similar occasion, when we knew one another better, the same boy stood waiting before the desk, pressing his thighs against the edge so that his cumbersome equipment lay like a love-offering almost underneath Joe's highly sensitive nostrils and I thought Joe was going to succumb as he stretched out his hand within an inch of the seductively presented sexual configuration – 'one could practically tell his religion,' as Quentin Crisp would have remarked – but, with a mischievous glance at me, he merely picked up a book for review that the young man had brought and laid before him on the desk. When the youth had departed, tight little bottom wagging at us, Joe turned to me and said:

'I sometimes find him very upsetting. What would happen, I often wonder, if I were to just touch his prick with the tip of my forefinger, as lightly as one would test an advocado? It could be made to look like a little accident. But on the other hand, he might go screaming to the Director General. Sometimes I think people send him to me just to provoke an unacceptable response, so that they can give me the sack. Or get my name in *The Blues of the World*, (as he called a well-known Sunday sensation-monger). 'Then we should be in a pretty pickle, shouldn't we, darling?' and he nearly shook himself out of his chair with silent laughter.

But to return to our first meeting. We dashed off to our first enchanting meal together, starting with double pink gins. As the meal progressed I was very surprised to hear him say that he knew Werter Road well because of Morgan Forster's old aunt living there. I felt it must have been manifest destiny that had drawn me to Putney in search of cheaper lodgings.

Towards the end of the meal, over coffee, after his confession of homosexuality, he smiled at me, held my hand tenderly among the wine glasses, and said, quite loudly: 'Shall we be friends?'

Those words I always love to hear! At once I replied: 'I hope so.'

'What shall I call you, dear?'

'Anything you like – Iris B. Summerforest if you wish.'

'Be serious, now!'

'My friends call me James, Jimi or Jamie.'

'What do your parents call you?'

'Jim.'

'Then I shall call you Jim. My dear Jim.'

'My dear Joe.'

My head was swimming in the most agreeable way.

Then he leaned forward across the table and kissed me lightly on the lips, a fatherly kiss. By that time, it was well after three, and there were few customers left in the restaurant: I hoped they'd noticed. In later years he was often to give me such kisses in public, sometimes in busy streets, scandalizing passing matrons and raising policemen's eyebrows. This, remember, was long before 'the permissive society' and the gutsy glamour of Gay Lib.

In a pleasant alcoholic daze, we strolled back to his office arm-in-arm. ('May I borrow your arm, dear boy – I feel rather swimmy.') Joe quickly disposed of a few more galley proofs that had just come in, then he invited me to go with him to the horse-butcher's in Soho ('*Boucherie Chevaline*' it said on the front), where he had to order more meat for Queenie. I was a vegetarian, though not a fanatical one, and the Boucherie Chevaline made me feel quite ill, but Joe was oblivious to my distress, as always when Queenie's well-being was in question. Though always courteous and kindly and considerate of others, he was sometimes curiously insensitive, and these blind spots were always the result of his constant preoccupation with the needs of Queenie, his sister Nancy, his old Aunt Bunny or Morgan Forster. I was never a jealous or possessive person, and so I could accept these lapses of attention to my presence with equanimity, though others found them impossible to bear. Queenie infuriated most of his friends, and many refused to visit him because of the fearful spectacle of her fangs and her savage barking muzzle.

After our visit to the horse-butcher's, we jumped on a bus to Putney. Joe placed the canvas hold-all with the suspiciously bloody parcel inside it on the floor between his feet, where drops of intensely red blood began to seep through. We sat upstairs at the front, where Joe kept up a flow of amusing and malicious gossip about his friends, his employers at the BBC and about the young men in the streets. When he spotted a particularly good-looking working-class boy at Green Park, who seemed to be at 'a loose end', as Joe put it with playful meaningfulness, he said: 'If I weren't with you, dear boy, I'd nip off and follow that gorgeous creature – just look at his impedimenta! The story of my life, I fear. If only I'd stuck with my own class!'

One of the main differences between us was that, being working-class myself, I was attracted to persons regardless of sex or class – 'Very liberal, our Jim is,' Joe once commented sarcastically – while Ackerley, like so many upper middle-class homosexuals, was fatally drawn towards only working-class lads and toughs. This kind of sexual fussiness in others was always a mystery to me, for I was only too thankful to obtain gratification whenever it offered itself, wherever sex reared its magnificent head, and with whatever class, age or sex. But Joe thought I was 'too comprehensive'. I thought he was 'too selective', if not downright finicky. I think he was incapable of a relationship that would be sexual, emotional and intellectual, the kind of *amitié amoureuse*, all loyalty, understanding and devotion, which was my own hopeless ideal.

'By the way,' he suddenly inquired in a very carrying voice, 'are you circumcized?'

The whole bus seemed to hang on my reply:

'No, I'm not.'

'I thought so, I can always tell.'

Joe had this fad for brutally circumcized pricks, an American characteristic that I naturally considered rather ugly. My whole life has been spent seeking uncircumcized ones, a kind of quest for the Holy Grail, and just as elusive. I don't actually mind the other kind, of course, but I much prefer my own.

'No disagreeable impediment?' he went on. 'No phimosis, I trust?'

'Oh, no,' I replied. 'I can retract the prepuce quite easily, and I always keep my foreskin and the collar of the glans scrupulously clean and tidy.'

'Splendid, splendid.'

What a conversation to have on top of a No. 14 bus, I thought. . . .

In a voice as low as psssible, I tried to bring the conversation into more literary channels:

'Did you know that Lautréamont suffered from phimosis?'

'How interesting,' he barked. I decided he was rather deaf. 'I love people who tell you things you don't know. Tell me more, Jim darling.'

'I think T.E. Lawrence must have been uncircumcized, and that his mysterious ordeal at the hands of – was it Arabs or Turks?'

'Search me, dear. . . .'

' – must have been a forcible circumcision. Very painful at that age.'

'I always *knew* Lawrence was uncircumcized. I could somehow *smell* it, just by looking at him. . . . And of course, you know, he was *that way*. . . .'

So our conversation proceeded, to the entertainment or disgust of the rest of the passengers: the first of many such zany exchanges we were to have in public.

When we got to his top-floor flat at the Star and Garter Mansions, even before he opened the front door I could hear loud, frenzied barkings from within. As I dislike dogs intensely, this alarmed me very much. As soon as Joe opened the door, a huge Alsatian, a truly magnificent beast, flung herself upon him, standing on her hind legs, forepaws on his shoulders, and managing to bark and lick Joe's face at the same time. Joe just stood there giggling helplessly: 'She's *so* passionate!' he cried, kissing her on the nose. 'Good Queenie, good girl, Queenie, good girl! Oh, Queenie, you great goose! There now, Queenie-Weenie, naughty girl – *are* you a naughty girl. . . . ?'

Here he started fondling her tits, which obviously gave them both pleasure and calmed Queenie down, though not without several ferocious growls and terrifying barks in my direction.

'*Say* something to her, dear, and she'll be all right in a minute.'

I have never known what to say to dogs, so I did what politicians are said to do when meeting for a working breakfast and the TV cameras start rolling: I recited the ABC. It had no effect on Queenie whatsoever. I was terrified out of my wits.

'Don't take any notice of the silly old girl, Jim. Oh, what a goosey-goosey gander she is! She means well, but she's so possessive – *so* flattering isn't it? Hates me to give my attention to anyone else. Let her sniff the back of your hand – you give your fingertips to a cat, the back of your hand to a dog, you know. Go on, she won't bite you, darling.'

I was not so sure. I extended, in fear and trembling, the back of my hand to Queenie, but she disdained to sniff it. Her only reaction, to Joe's delight, and feigned indignation, was to draw back her flews and bare her fangs in a savage snarl. I thought she was about to have my hand off, but, as always in a dangerous situation, I managed to remain icily calm. The deafening barks of this neurotic, jealous creature were, I thought, worth bearing for the sake of Joe's company. Indeed, I often endured the tortures of the damned and the terrors of hell, and, unlike Orpheus, I could not lull this

Cerberus to sleep with my lyre, and I had no Sibyl's sop of poppies and honey. Later, when I came to read Joe's diaries, I was amused to see that he had noted I was absolutely without fear when meeting Queenie.

We had managed to get into the kitchen with the bloody horse-meat and Queenie kept on barking and leaping around while Joe switched on the cooker and put the meat in the oven. I was perhaps over-fastidious in those days: the thought that Joe and Nancy used the oven to cook both their own food and Queenie's filled me with horror, and I resolved never to eat dinner there, though even this resolution was broken in order to enjoy the company of Joe, Nancy and Aunt Bunny.

Soon things began to calm down a bit, and we went into the sitting-room to have gin and tonics – always Gordon's gin in that dark green bottle that looks as if it ought to contain poison. There were few decorations and no knick-knacks. There was a framed photograph of some naked black sailors sleeping entwined in a pendulous hammock, and a small statue, bronze, I think, of some Grecian *éphèbe*, with his characteristically small, uncircumcized prick, much rubbed. Joe showed me a little hole just above the formally curled pubic hair where a fig leaf could be attached 'in the presence of ladies of the parish'.

'Your type, I think, isn't he?' He indicated the foreskin. 'Morgan Forster says he's always disappointed by Greek male statuary – either broken off or infantile.'

I agreed. I told him how, whenever I visited museums and saw a male nude statue, I always felt impelled to stroke its private parts, as many had obviously done before me, but that I was afraid my action might set off an electric alarm in the curator's office and I would be arrested for *attente à la pudeur*. In such a case, I said, I always had my parting shot ready: 'I'll turn it all to poetry!'

'And send it to *The Listener*!'

'Mind you, I doubt whether my editor would let it in. . . . '

Nancy and Aunt Bunny were not present on that first visit to the flat. I seem to remember that Nancy was in hospital having electric shock treatment, and Joe was desperately worried about her. I thoroughly disapproved of such treatment, and told him so, and this only intensified his agony about his beloved sister. Later, when Nancy came out of hospital and came to live with Joe, I was to fall in love with her cool, gentle loveliness. She was one of the sweetest and serenest human beings I had ever known, deeply affectionate to me, and devoted to Joe. She was intelligent, and had a surprisingly sharp wit of her own which I think Joe never really appreciated.

I saw them as a British version of Scott Fitzgerald and Zelda Sayre. They must have made a wonderful twenties' pair.

To my surprise, Joe reveals in his diary that he was jealous of my friendship with Nancy, which was very unfair, for Joe had hundreds of friends, while poor 'old Nance', as he called her, had very few. I adored Nancy, and still remember her with deep affection. We used to take Queenie out for 'walkies' or visit our favourite vegetarian restaurants together or go to the movies and hold hands during the more frightening bits. I remember going with her to see *The Snake Pit*, a brave choice for Nancy, whose own mental state was never of the steadiest. Mentally disturbed women have always been attracted to me, and I to them. I always found Nancy a lucid, relaxed and beautiful companion, and in some ways I loved her much more than I did Joe.

Dear old Aunt Bunny was sometimes at the flat, and I adored her for other reasons. She had been on the stage in her youth, I believe with Frank Benson's company,* and had obviously been a great beauty and a wit in her time. She could still entertain us, reciting speeches from Shakespeare and from Victorian melodramas she had appeared in. She was an endearing old soul, and Joe cared for her at the end of her days with great devotion, as can be seen from his letters. At the same time, Joe would say the most awful things behind their backs – 'silly old trout', was one of the names he would call Aunt Bunny after she had talked too much on too much wine; and 'Natter, natter, natter, mumble, mumble, mumble. . . .' he would say in an unkind imitation of poor Nancy's rather low, monotonous delivery of entrancing banalities. Joe had the homosexual's viperish tongue at times; I was accustomed to that kind of attack, and I know he spoke ill of me (and wrote ill of me) behind my back – the letter to Francis King about my goings-on in Sendai from which Braybrooke cautiously omitted my name (I couldn't have cared less) – is clear evidence of his occasional spitefulness in order to entertain his host in Kyoto. But I did not mind his two-sided nature, which I realized, when I got to Japan, was very oriental. And as long as things are said behind my back, and not to my face, I am grateful – one of my own oriental traits. I would forgive Joe anything.

After we had got the horse-meat into the oven and had a few more gin and tonics, Joe and Queenie and I went for a 'run' on Wimbledon Common. It was the first time I had been up there, and on that fine, sunny day in early March, walking there with my new friend, I had a sense of profound happiness. He told me of his friendship with the Ranger, and of an elderly

* A famous repertory company that performed Shakespeare in Edwardian times.

exhibitionist who sprang out of some bushes at him brandishing a 'very unsatisfactory-looking organ'. I did not believe this, for I had once encountered a flasher on Hampstead Heath who in the dusk had mistaken me for a young lady, and as he saw me looking at his appurtenances with interest, he suddenly screamed: 'Piss off! I don't show myself to the likes of you! I know what you want! Well you won't find it at this counter!' I was pursued by cries of 'Poof!'

Joe told me, as he told all his new friends, about how he had once thrown a ball for Queenie which had accidentally disturbed a rabbit, so that ever afterwards Queenie expected a rabbit to pop out whenever he threw her a ball. But dizzy dame Queenie was incapable of catching even a ball, never mind a rabbit.

We walked by a pond with some leafless birch trees round its edge – always my favourite tree, so Slav – and we stood there for a while watching the sunset gilding the pale trunks, while Queenie lay panting at our feet, for once mercifully silent. From those moments of communion with each other and with nature came my poem 'Legend', which I wrote for Joe that night, and which he published later in the month:

> Winter's pale birches bare, so bare, they seem
> the silver ghosts of light in which the eyes
> look and are lost, yet bear a melting frost
> of frailest green upon their brittle crests. . . .

I included this, with several poems Joe had published, in my second book, *The Submerged Village*, which, with his permission, I dedicated 'To J. R. Ackerley'.

I first met William Plomer, John Morris and E. M. Forster in Ackerley's flat. I think Joe had convoked them all to give me the once-over, for in those days I was even more of a curiosity than I am now. They were all reserved at first, but Forster and Morris soon loosened up. However, William remained almost completely silent, and what I remember best is his immobility. He hardly moved and never stirred from his rather uncomfortable chair. Because of that, I at once thought of him as a Buddha, and in 1959, in an essay published in Japan in *Eigoseinen*, shortly after my arrival, I described him as such. He was of medium height, broad and stocky, with a close-fitting cap of rather crinkly pale hair, a sort of pepper-and-salt mixture of faded blond and turning grey. His face was square and almost expressionless, though his eyes behind his horn-rimmed glasses were often twinkling with some kind of private joke. He was silent to an unusual degree, and this made me feel sympathetic towards him, because I am 'the silent type' myself and am not interested in carrying on conversations. His eyes in their pale lashes were a light blue-grey. He had a rather small mouth but nice teeth, which he seldom revealed, for he rarely smiled. Altogether he gave a pleasant impression of mysterious intelligence and unusual wit, and I sensed that his secret powers of observation and expression must be formidable.

I remember the simple kindliness and friendliness of all these people towards me – a poor, unknown, struggling poet. But there was in Forster something that transcended all this: his small, rather stout, homely figure and plain, open face glowed with gentle good-will and joy. I think I have never met anyone who gave me such an impression of deep, quiet happiness and inexhaustible patience and sympathy.

Despite the constant barkings of Queenie, Morgan and I had a long conversation about all kinds of things – about the great influences on his own work, Jane Austen, Samuel Butler and Matthew Arnold, about animals and food and drink, about modern poetry, about sport and clothes and the theatre. We also talked about our mothers – for Morgan was ever as devoted to his mother as I was to mine. This was a great common bond between us. Then we started talking about the nature of friendship, a subject on which he was an expert, because he had devoted friends of all kinds – from labourers and farmers and policemen to university students, Indian scholars and great composers like Benjamin Britten. Indeed, to the very end, Morgan's most devoted friend was an ex-policeman, Bob Buckingham. In the Prefatory Note to *Abinger Harvest*, tribute is paid to his policeman friend along with Ackerley, Plomer and Isherwood.

It was his utter lack of class-consciousness and conceit that attracted me to Morgan, and allowed him, the leading English man of letters, to talk to me as an equal. Our talk about friendship was quite un-solemn and unpompous. But I recall he told me that only in a true democracy could friendship between men flourish in freedom. This was an important statement. Forster, like myself, did not think very highly of democracy, which is why he called his second collection of essays *Two Cheers for Democracy*, saying: 'Two cheers are quite enough: there is no occasion to give three. Only Love, the Beloved Republic, deserves that.' To Morgan, 'Love, the Beloved Republic', was part of the Greek ideal he had inherited from Goldsworthy Lowes Dickinson, an ideal republic of loving friends far removed from the ordinary crude popular concept of homosexual relations.

On that first meeting, he made one of those spontaneous gestures that in Morgan amounted almost to genius. He had just come back from a weekend in the country, and had brought with him half a dozen fresh farm eggs. At that time, eggs were still rationed, and each person received only about one egg a month – usually a stale egg. So fresh eggs were almost as precious as gold. As he was leaving, Morgan – who at times looked rather like a fussy little brown hen himself – started to give an amusing imitation of a hen cackling after laying an egg. Then, with a smile and a hug, he presented me with one of his precious eggs, wrapped in a page of *The New Statesman*.

I was overcome not so much by the priceless gift of a fresh egg as by the symbolism of this act of perfect grace and loving friendship. With the gift of that egg, I felt Morgan had offered me not only his friendship, but a promise of poetic fertility. I did not eat the egg, but kept it carefully packed in a special little box for many years, until, in one of my numerous removals from one dismal lodging to another, it was broken. Strangely enough, the smashed egg had no bad odour, but smelt curiously sweet and wholesome. I thought the end of the world had come when that egg broke. Years later, I reminded Morgan about his gift, and he remembered our first meeting perfectly, saying: 'I remember you were wearing white socks. When you crossed your left leg on your right knee, you revealed a few inches of suntanned shin above the top of your sock.' It was this kind of detail, seen with the constantly recording eye of the born writer, that Morgan loved to remember when talking about his friends.

I was proud of my friendship with Joe Ackerley. Ours was never a sexual relationship, as he once told me his with Forster had never been. But one day when I happened to mention to David Archer* in 'The Black Horse' in Rathbone Place that I had made friends with Joe (whom he had never met), he threw back his head and gave that loud, stupid braying laugh of his, and assumed a very knowing look which filled me with the utmost detestation for him from then on. I thought of putting the evil eye on him, but as he was handicapped I let him off.

It was about this time that Joe began to warn me against certain people in the literary world, in which I was still a total innocent. He told me to be on my guard against certain BBC officials and Bloomsbury and Soho bohemians with whom, in my naivety, I had thought I might have something in common, all members of a common fellowship of art, poetry, love and all that rot. It was Joe who first revealed to me the cruelty and bitchiness of literary life in Britain.

He also warned me that if I continued to publish regularly in *The Listener*, as he wanted me to do, I would 'put myself beyond the pale' in the jealous

* The poetry publisher.

literary world, where there was so much envy of the paper's large subsidy by the BBC. This enabled it to be published at only threepence a week – half the price of other weeklies. There was some kind of journalistic vendetta going on against *The Listener*, against Joe and his regular contributors. I believe this was the reason for the long delays in publishing, reviewing and accepting as masterpieces of literary style Joe's later, perfect works. Certainly many of the poets I introduced to Joe – Iris Orton, Gloria Evans-Davies, Christopher Leech and David Paul – not to mention myself, found it difficult or impossible to get their works printed outside *The Listener,* and, after Joe's retirement, not even there. All these petty literary cabals depressed and worried Joe, not for his own sake, but on account of his friends and contributors.

A letter in *The Times* of 11 June 1969 from Richard W. Briginshaw, joint general secretary, Society of Graphical and Allied Trades, is very revealing:

> Sir, – An extraordinary position appears to be present with regard to that very useful publication of the BBC, *The Listener*. The Periodical Publishers Association is involved in what can only be described as a sharply restrictive practice with regard to their efforts against *The Listener*. There has been a continual campaign to restrict the growth of *The Listener*. The efforts have been based on a claim that the BBC, in publishing *The Listener* in its present form, provides unfair competition to private enterprise magazines. . . .
>
> . . . The Association believes it is wrong that BBC money, some £40,000 per year it is understood, should be used to support such a publication. Such an assertion seems odd from an association whose members take a goodly share of the £300m. per year spent on advertising which, in the end, comes from the public pocket.
>
> We are entitled to wonder what sort of headlines would have been used in most newspapers if a union's involvement in what might be a legitimate industrial dispute had the possible effect of the death of a periodical of the type of *The Listener*. . . .
>
> . . . One can easily visualize the headings: 'A Blow at Freedom of the Press', 'Publication Wilfully Maimed', 'Vicious Trade Union Action Hits Paper', and so on. So far as can be seen, the BBC themselves appear to be quite spineless about the matter. . . .
>
> . . . In drawing attention to the double standards of some of those engaged in this campaign against *The Listener,* I have to declare publicly on behalf of our organization, our industrial interest in this matter, with a fervent hope that we shall not be called upon to activize ourselves in a counter campaign.
>
> Yours faithfully,
> Richard W. Briginshaw

I was astonished to see from this excellent letter that even in 1969 the malicious and damaging campaigns against *The Listener* were still going on, and I was amused by the well-chosen word 'spineless', which was the word Joe himself used about his employers' failure to support him. At *The Advertisers' Weekly* I had had some experience of this kind of industrial action, when a couple of members of the Union of Journalists tried to force me to join their union on the grounds that my poems were appearing in the weeklies. I refused, because I said I did not regard myself as a journalist – though some of my more spiteful critics pretended my poems showed I was a journalist and not a poet.

'What rubbish!' Joe said when I told him this. 'If ever there was a pure poet, it is you, dear boy.'

Nevertheless, he put my case to many writers he knew, including Siegfried Sassoon, E. M. Forster, W. R. Rodgers, Janet Adam-Smith, William Plomer and John Morris. Morris became the first director of the Third Programme and published in pride of place in the anthology of best items in the programme my long radio adventure-poem on caving in the Mendips, 'The Descent into the Cave'. When it appeared in print there were screams of rage from those sad old Angry Young Men, a self-publicizing coterie whose combined attacks on me were concerted by John Wain in *The Twentieth Century*.

Joe's friends all reassured him that I was, indeed, a true poet. As for the Angry Young Men, he commented:

Have they really *read* your poetry? Have any of them really met you? If they had, they would sing a different tune.'

But such attacks were only a small part of the general hostility unleashed against me, and which was to pursue me for many years. It came to a head in the 1950s, after the publication of my poem 'A Correct Compassion' in *The Listener*, and my dismissal from my Gregory Fellowship in Poetry at Leeds University by Professor Bonamy Dobrée.

There were also periodic witch-hunts in the BBC – political, homosexual, literary and censorious. I remember that around 1953 Joe asked me if I were a Communist Party member. The very idea made me burst out laughing. To me, politics is a boring and unnecessary unpleasantness cooked up by some of the least intelligent and most ruthless human beings in existence. I believe no artist should try to express the triteness of political dogma through art of any kind. I told Joe it was ridiculous to think that I might be a Communist. I really did not know what to answer, because I had never thought about the subject or taken any interest in politics except to proclaim my conscientious freedom. One of my forebears, Thomas Kirkup, wrote the first *History of Socialism* in English, and thinking of this and of my working-class origins, I said: 'I am a pacifist first and foremost. And I suppose I am a socialist, though I have little respect for socialist politicians.'

'Why are you a socialist?'

'Though I am not a Christian, I admire certain principles of the Christian religion as a religion of peace and love. I think true socialism and true Christianity are basically related. They pursue the same social and moral ideals.'

'That's exactly what I've come to think. I was discussing it with John Morris the other night, and that was the conclusion we came to. On the other hand, if you believe that socialism and Christianity are fundamentally the same, you are not a true socialist, for a true socialist would deny the value of any religion.'

'Then I am not a socialist.'

'Then what *are* you?' he asked again.

You have to be serious to be gay, so I decided to be flippant:

'Whenever I'm asked what I am, I say I'm liberal.'

Joe gave his shoulder-shaking laugh and his broad smile (sometimes so like Max Wall in later years) and capped my remark with:

'Liberal – yes, dear Jim, in every sense of the word.'

We both collapsed into giggles at that, and had another gin and tonic. Joe never mentioned the subject of politics again. I think that like me he was appalled and bored by modern politics and despised the incompetence and bluster of our politicians. We both thought Stalin and Franco were the last words in awfulness – 'the Frightful Fathers' we called them. In 1988, in Britain at least it would have to be 'the Mortifying Mothers'. We were both simply a-political – natural anarchists with a passion for misrule.

Around 1955 there was obviously some sort of homosexual witch-hunt going on in Britain from which the BBC was not exempt. Joe indicated certain names I should beware of, including some women writers as well as men. At this time, he was in a state of highly nervous tension, and so was I. Whenever we met we would regale one another with stories of odd encounters we had with suspicious-looking gents at Turkish baths or at the Marble Arch and Piccadilly. We nearly had hysterics when I described how a plain-clothes dick, obviously an *agent provocateur,* had tried to jot down a rather 'hot' poem I had composed to be recited in the Whispering Gallery of St Paul's Cathedral – it was one of my love poems to Jesus – and how he had tried to follow me even up the vertical ladder leading right inside the cross on top of the dome, from where I wanted to drop copies of my poem on the streets of London. Shortly after that, the ladder into the cross on the dome was closed to the public, 'on security grounds'.

Joe, in his wonderful dry way, then recounted how he had been visited at a friend's London flat he was caretaking, by a mysterious Indian admirer of immense girth and height who, as soon as he entered the room, unzipped his fly and produced an enormous, unappetizing and completely flaccid penis which he slapped on the table crying: 'What do you think of that?'

'What on earth does one say in such circumstances?' Joe asked me. For once, he had been at a loss for words.

'I say, what a whopper!'

'Don't frighten the horses!'

'Put that thing away – it might go off!'

Such hilarious but disturbing encounters with strange men were frequent at this period, and I still remember vividly the constant feeling of unease, suspense, danger and total absurdity, as if we were trapped in some endless Iris Murdoch novel.

All this time I was desperately poor, and Joe did all he could to find me work, but of course I could not exist on the money I got from poems and reviewing, part of which I had to send to my father and mother. Joe often gave me ten pounds as a gift when I was short, though I knew he could not spare it, and I always paid it back.

'Honest Joe – and Honest Jim!' he laughed, shaking his screwed-up body, tightly-crossed legs and wringing hands. When he came to Japan in 1960, I was still on Queer Street, and though Morgan Forster had given him the fare to fly to see me, he was short of money. But I'd have given him every penny I possessed; I told him I had 'pots of money'. We were both overjoyed when his perfect novel, *We Think the World of You,* won a thousand quid in the W. H. Smith prize contest, and we rejoiced together with Morgan and all his other friends at the reception for the prize-giving. But the money was soon spent: he was as feckless as I was with cash.

I often brought my 'conquests' to meet Joe in Putney. Some of them were young men with literary pretensions, others were girls who wanted to get into films (Joe had some vague connections with the film world and with the actor Robert Donat) or to review 'women's interest' books, for which they considered themselves eminently suitable, being women.

'Why is it believed that women are the only ones who can review women's books, or books about women?' Joe would muse. 'What have they got that *we* haven't got, dear Jim? Three holes instead of two.' Of every one of my conquests, Joe would say when we were alone together:

'Jim, dear, he's/she's not worthy of you.' This was very refreshing to me, who thought I was not worthy of them, however caddish or bitchy they might be. The only exception to this was the gorgeous and scintillating Rena, one of my lasting passions and a devoted Juno of a woman, who is described in one of Joe's letters. She was the most glamorous and witty woman I had ever known, a tireless talker and an energetic actress, lecturer, cook and *haute couturière* (she made my first *La Bohème* smock, my first caftan, my first violet velvet cape) and she fascinated Joe and Nancy. Indeed, though she was married to a splendid, handsome, attentive husband, Roger, I believe Joe was jealous of our relationship, as he was of mine with Nancy, because after Rena's death I found some letters from Joe which tried to turn her against me. Yet she was slowly dying of cancer, and very bravely, too, as Joe begins to realize in one of the letters. But all that correspondence between Rena, Joe and myself must wait until its proper period: late sixties and early seventies and another book.

I gathered from Joe's talk that some of his own conquests had been decidedly *louche*, and his accounts of how he met these people and how they behaved in bed (and out of it) were both bitterly tragic and heroically funny. All the background to *My Dog Tulip* and *We Think the World of You* was revealed to me in those conversations. Behind it all was the dragonish breath of danger and discovery and exposure of that time; we were treading a slowly smouldering tightrope over a fatal abyss of trust and treachery, and all the while splitting our sides with laughter. Those were the pre-Wolfenden days, and we didn't think post-Wolfenden was much better, either, when it came; we were within the law but still beyond the pale.

Whenever Joe thought I was in danger, or likely to be hurt by gossip or slander, he would fly to my side. Apparently I was often the centre of excited comment by ill-wishers in the literary world and in the British Council in Japan – called 'the Brutish Council' by the sensitive Japanese. Often I myself had not the faintest idea of the peril or the nastiness hanging over me. I was the perpetual innocent for whom ignorance is bliss, like the *cocu* who is the last person to hear about his wife's infidelities. I was happy in such ignorance, and had no wish to be informed of the worst – that's me all over. But I remember well those occasions when Joe came to be with me at what he considered to be perilous or tragic moments in my heedless hedonism – in London, Slapton, Leeds, Corsham, Bath, and finally Sendai. He would have come to comfort me in my extreme misery in Malaya if he had been able. I could never believe my luck in having him with me when he might have been with people so much nicer and more interesting – Jack Sprott* or Forster or Plomer or Britten or John Morris. Whenever he invited himself (with or without Queenie) to be by my side, I felt a slight chill, as I realized something must be wrong, something that Joe and everyone else knew about – only I was in the dark. But I never asked Joe for an explanation, and he never tried to give one; I preferred to be left in the dark, however lonely and sad it might be.

BBC censorship was another cross Joe had to bear. He loved to provoke and tease the stuffy, and often succeeded in putting forward some outrageous viewpoint in *The Listener* and other papers, as we can see from his letters. I shall always remember a most outspoken letter from John Minton, whom we both admired as a man and as an artist, that Joe got into *The Listener*'s correspondence columns: it was a brave defence of homosexuality against a bigoted attack on Wilde by Marie Stopes.

However, Joe was not so successful with certain short stories and poems submitted to him. One of David Paul's brilliant poems could not be printed because of details, too explicit, about copulation. The typists at the BBC, led into outraged battle by Miss Marjorie Redman, threatened to go on strike if he published my poem 'The Convenience'.† Before sending it to the printers, Joe had asked E. M. Forster for his opinion of it, and Morgan replied saying there was absolutely nothing to object to in it; he also kindly sent me a note to tell me so. The poem went into galley proof and was corrected by me. Then I had a call from Joe about the threatened typists' strike, and he said: 'My editor (Alan Thomas) won't let it be printed. I am furious. He says it's all because men can piss standing up, and for nothing, while women have to pay a penny and sit down to it. They resent this.'

In Neville Braybrooke's excellent Introduction we find a reference to this squalid episode. He quotes Miss Redman as saying: 'Do we want to read about the smell coming out of a women's lavatory?' which proves that she either had not read the poem properly or did not understand it, because it is obviously about a men's urinal. The urinal in question used to stand outside a pub somewhere in Hampstead (Haverstock Hill, I think) but has since been pulled down. It was quite a 'respectable' urinal – not a gay cottage or randy rendezvous. It was a very charming, restful and almost rustic place, as the poem explains. It was not the first or the last time my poems were to arouse the ire of ladies and gentlemen with no knowledge of poetry or the breadth of its possibilities in choosing anti-poetical subjects from modern times. My poem 'The Dustbins' in *The Listener* brought a lot

* A sociologist friend of Ackerley.

† A full account of this contemptible typists' to-do can be found in my contribution to Richard Findlater's *Comic Cuts* (André Deutsch, 1970); indeed at the time I found the whole business comic as well as contemptible.

of complaints, yet only a few years later a person no less distinguished than Rab Butler the Lord Chancellor (who had obviously not read my poem) was demanding that poets should write about dustbins!

Fortunately, the Oxford University Press made no bones about publishing 'The Dustbins' and 'The Convenience' in my next collection, *The Descent into the Cave,* which also contained poems of coprophiliac and homosexual tone like 'The Kitchen Sink' and 'The Drain', both of which Joe had managed to wangle into *The Listener*. Joe was always pleased when I sent him this type of controversial poem. As he wrote to Stephen Spender in one of the letters in Braybrooke's collection:

> I think that people *ought* to be upset, and if I had a paper I would upset them all the time; I think that life is so important and, in its workings, so upsetting that nobody should be spared, but that it should be rammed down their throats from morning to night. And may those who cannot take it die of it. . . .

Exactly my own sentiments about literature. However, when *The Descent into the Cave* was published by OUP, Joe told me he was having difficulty in finding anyone willing to review it, even anonymously, and I feel sure that the review which eventually appeared in *The Listener* must have been written by himself, for it bears many of the marks of his distinctive style, and he did not treat me lightly or uncritically, I am glad to say. But it was the beginning of the systematic suppression of my work in the journals of the fifties and sixties, and of my discrediting to the Japanese by the British Council in Tokyo, where from time to time some puzzled scholar would come to me and tell me that so-and-so (some British pen-pusher or poet) on a flying visit to Japan had denigrated my work in the most virulent and shocking terms, and with the approval of the 'Brutish Council'.

After Joe retired from *The Listener* in November 1959, I was, to his great distress, gradually dropped from its pages. Gransden published one or two minor pieces, and Thwaite printed a poem about Japan that had been broadcast and therefore couldn't very well be refused, then that was that. Neither were any of my books ever reviewed in *The Listener* after Joe had gone. Not long after he retired from *The Listener* (and not long after my father's death), my long friendship with Joe began to deepen and flower in the most lovely and extraordinary way. In a sense, he became my second father, for he had known and deeply admired my father and mother, who felt an immediate sympathy for him. Joe took some pictures of me with my father and mother in our garden at Flemish Weavers' Cottages in Corsham, and I took some of him and Queenie – the latter a most difficult subject, as she would not stand still.

Unfellowly Fellowships

1950–6

I spent a summer at Slapton, near Northampton, because of its associations with John Clare, a poet I have always felt a deep affinity with, and John Dryden. The country folk there were kind enough, but I could not be bothered to look after the garden in front of the cottage, and it was soon a display place that people came from miles away to marvel at: the local girls would gather outside my gate and sing a song popular at the time, something about someone's heart being only a garden of weeds. But I enjoyed the company at the pub, and one memorable evening walked all the way to Northampton and back, just to see a performance by the Carl Rosa Company, which had as its stage manager a former pupil of Maurice Feild. I cannot remember the opera, only the friendliness of Maurice's former pupil to me and to the married lady I had walked there and back with – with the approval of her husband. It became the talk of the village.

I had been making desperate and unsuccessful applications for grants and awards, but I was utterly hopeless at presenting my case for financial support. Joe tried to help, but told me that one of the members of the Atlantic Award committee, Louis MacNeice, refused my application again and again because he said poets should suffer. One day I met Louis and his wife, the singer Hedli Anderson, on the steps of the National Gallery, to which they were taking their son, Daniel, as a 'treat' (Louis' word). He said he felt terribly embarrassed at being seen entering the National Gallery, I don't know why. Daniel had been one of my best students at the Downs School – a quiet, good-natured boy. On Parents' Day, Louis used to stand around moodily, looking bored to death, his George Raftish face with its disappointed beagle expression casting a gloom over everyone. In fact, I believe he was inordinately shy and self-conscious. I remember that on the occasion of a tribute to the recently-deceased Dylan Thomas one Sunday evening at the Globe Theatre, Louis had to appear on stage in evening dress and read some poems. I can still see him standing uneasily beside the footlights, with the poems in his hand; he kept putting his right hand in his jacket pocket, with studied nonchalance, then the left hand in his left-hand pocket, first one then the other, time and time again, in a kind of obsessive movement meant to reassure the audience but infecting us with unease and a tendency to giggle. In a recent review of his selected poems, I had pleased him by saying he had the timing of a professional raconteur, which is quite true. Eventually I got my Atlantic Award in Literature, a miserable sum that barely kept me alive during the summer.

I had to leave Slapton in a hurry: I had got into some scrape in Northampton, or Wolverton or Woburn, or was it Towcester – where I constantly ran into Sacheverell Sitwell – I can't remember where or what. Anyhow, the English countryside was beginning to feel even more sinister than London, and a brief visit from Joe and Queenie to Slapton gave me a hint that I must have been 'up to something' in the region.

Back in London, I went to Madame Sheba's place which I found in a turmoil; the police had just left, thank goodness. Madame allowed me to doss on the sofa in her drawing-room for a few nights. I was at my wits' end, and the entire future presented itself to my jaundiced eyes in various shades of mould.

Joe had told me in Slapton that there was some chance of my being appointed to the first Gregory Fellowship in Poetry at Leeds University. He did not hold out much hope, and I even less than he. I half-hoped it would never come to pass, and that the cup of Leeds might mercifully pass from me, because I knew what bickering and jealousy it would provoke among those who had been passed over.

The selection committee consisted of Peter Gregory, the amiable founder of this new form of patronage, Bonamy Dobrée, the Professor of English, and Herbert Read – 'that stronger reed', as Joe used to refer to him in contrast to Henry – 'that weaker reed'. I had no high hopes of any of them. Herbert Read in particular seemed to me a desiccated old stick who, on my few meetings with him in the company of Joe, who admired him, had gazed upon me with a sort of speculative condescension. With my permission, Joe had written a letter of recommendation to the committee, in which he stated that my hobbies were 'brandy and boys'. He said he would ask E. M. Forster, who liked my work and with whom I had corresponded since the war, to write me another recommendation, but I refused, because at that time I had not met Forster personally, and I felt it would be cheating to drum up support in that way. Then, in the midst of all the confusion at Madame Sheba's, I suddenly got word that I had been appointed to the Fellowship. My heart sank, then lifted again; at least I would have enough money to live on for a few years, and I could resume my weekly cheques to my father and mother. I had given them half of my

Atlantic Award, small as that was. The Leeds pittance was only about seven quid a week, but, as Bonamy Dobrée assured me on our first meeting, I should be able to augment that by my writing. I was doubtful about that. Bonamy was charming and affable and terribly *mondain*. I quite liked him, but could not know how he was to stab me in the back later on. I soon made a great friend on the English staff, the dear old poet Wilfred Rowland Childe. As I wrote in an essay for *The Yorkshire Post* about my appointment, I was a 'Resident Poet' who had arrived to find a poet already in residence. Wilfred and I both shared a passion for Firbank, and he always called me 'Ronald', to my great delight. He had known Firbank in Oxford.

My first OUP book of poems, *The Submerged Village*, appeared to the usual lukewarm reviews. I soon got into the habit of closing my eyes in pain whenever I saw a notice of my books, and of thrusting the paper away from me before I could open my eyes again. The reviews were so short and bitty, the reviewers showing off their superiority and pushing their own egos, giving snap judgments of a particularly nauseous perkiness. They were not worth reading, for by the time a book appeared and perhaps got one or two reviews, its contents were far in the past and I was already doing something new and quite different. So whatever advice reviewers might have given – and they usually didn't except that one should shut up – was completely useless.

I had first submitted my collection to Adam and Charles Black, and gradually worked through the alphabet until I got to OUP. Cecil Day-Lewis at Chatto and Windus read my manuscript, and was infinitely condescending in his rejection of it. He invited me to lunch at some ghastly club where he kept pointing out famous members like Arthur Bliss and Richard Church. I hate clubs like that, which is why I am such an unclubable person, as Day-Lewis at once detected. He made some ridiculous remarks about my poems, including one coyly simpering comment on my use of the word 'come' in the line 'Love, when will you come?' from the poem 'Pentecost'. I had, of course, intended the sexual ambiguity, but Day-Lewis pointed it out to me with a supercilious nudge, apparently assuming that I did not know the double meaning of 'come'. The thin lips in that incredibly wrinkled tortoise head gave a malicious twist as he cackled something about his firm's having had to publish a novel by one of their authors with the title *And Then You Came* – by Ann Bridge, I've just remembered – and added: '*So* embarrassing – but she's a titled lady, and how was one to mention the double meaning without immodesty and offence to womanly propriety?' I very nearly gave him a dose of my evil eye, but I took pity on him because he was such a pretentiously bad poet in later life. In fact, later, after I had been kicked out of my Fellowship at Leeds, Day-Lewis did me an exceptional favour – it could hardly be called a kindness – in recommending me to Clifford Ellis as 'Writer in Residence' at Bath Academy of Art, in Corsham Court, which turned out to be three years of purgatory. He had apparently changed his opinion of my poetry after it had been accepted by Oxford University Press. In 1948, I had submitted to Chatto my selection of translations from Supervielle's poems, and I have his letter rejecting them. A few years later, they were accepted by New Directions in New York. Day-Lewis's rather abysmal translation of Valéry's *Cimetière Marin* might have led one to expect that he would be more open to modern French verse, but in fact he was typical of most Englishmen in considering it beneath his notice.

On my arrival in Leeds, I found no one knew about my appointment, and I was hastily shoved into one of the men's halls of residence, a terrible experience from which I immediately extracted myself. I set off in search of digs, and the cheapest I could find were in the heart of the red light district, in Brunswick Place. I got a ground-floor room right next to the front door, so that I could smuggle in boyfriends without attracting the landlady's notice. She was an ex-madame and lived upstairs somewhere with a couple of elderly chorus-boys who now were reduced to doing months of panto every year – such a come-down after Cochran! They gave me the low-down on 'gay' life in Leeds, which was flourishing at that time, with several pubs and a notorious Turkish bath, as well as a few convenient conveniences – one of them just a few steps from Brunswick Place's dens of vice. In the basement beneath my room lived a peroxided barmaid who often came back at night with a customer or two. I felt I was seeing a bit of life after the monotony of Slapton.

But I soon found Leeds almost unbearably boring. The students were not interesting at all, and those who ventured to show me their 'stuff' did not inspire me with any enthusiasm for their work. Robin Skelton was the only one who showed a modicum of poetic talent; he is now, I believe, an authority on Synge. He was the only one who would venture into the red light district to visit me in my bed-sitter. I racked my brains to try to find something useful to say to those would-be poets whose writing seemed to numb my very eyes as I looked at it. I did not see any point in encouraging people who were obviously no good at all, and I told them so quite frankly. Again, my sterling honesty was not appreciated, and some of the girls began making complaints to their tutors about my lack of interest in their scribblings.

However, I managed to interest a few of the better students in poetry readings at lunchtime, and we did a few of those to curiously silent audiences. The drama society had a surplus of untalented women, so they asked me to devise a play for them. As the cast had to be all women, and pretty dreary women at that, I could only think of the parable of the wise and foolish virgins. This idea was accepted, and I wrote the play in one long afternoon with the aid of the Bible and a bottle of gin. I introduced the Voice of God – to be spoken by a woman's voice – at that time considered a frightfully scandalous idea. But how did they know God was a man and not a woman or some kind of wild animal? I demanded of my critics. The shock of my question shut them up completely. The play was put on with great difficulty, and was received very well. It has never been done again.

The first letter I got from Joe Ackerley after settling into my bed-sitter at Brunswick Place read:

Putney.

Dear Jim

I am really sorry not to have written before, because your long letter was so amusing and interesting. I sympathized v. much with all your reactions; the first impact of a provincial university must be formidable, and great personal qualities are needed to meet it in the right way. You have them, of course – tho' to define what they are is another matter; a passionate interest in other people is, I suppose, the foremost; and then a personal balance and a sense of humour. Although I don't know Leeds, I am a constant visitor to Nottingham where my friend Jack Sprott, with all his brilliant and curious intelligence, is rooted; interested in his subjects and in people (colleagues, students) individually, and entirely without personal ambition, he wd. not exchange his place, I think, for Oxford or Cambridge chairs, if offered; and after many visits and meeting all his co-profs, and going here and there with him, I begin to see what he sees and feels about the place. After ½ bottle of burgundy, I express myself clumsily.

I am awfully glad Blunden* wrote to you; it puts, for me, a quite different complexion on the appearance of your poem† in the T.L.S. I am pleased to think he got it, and hope he was appreciative and grateful. This one is 'not so bad', as they say. But I'll wait for something better. It has both felicities and feebleness – and makes only a very small report. You will do much better, and I shall have the best. And send anything; no embarrassments; I like reading, and don't mind rejecting.

I'm on a week's holiday, so not among the office books, but I will certainly

* Edmund Blunden, the First World War poet and literary biographer.
† This was 'Music at Night', reprinted in *The Submerged Village*.

send you some – and here, to start with, is poor dear Georges's latest exercise in mystification. If you are able, honestly, to say anything kind, or even useful, say it; but if not, let us not reproach the poor old moonshiner but ignore his beams. Ponge! surely he is punk. And Du Bouchet? – bosh? But what of M. Beckett? I am vaguely interested in that constipated fragmentary man – are the turds not perfectly shaped, irreproachably odoured? – I leave him, and Reverdy, et les autres, to you. 400 words wd. be generous.

Well, I am now casting glances at my bed, upon which Queenie is stretched, so the rest summarily:

(i) Paul on Pound was excellent. I was v. pleased. And will you congratulate me on Conquest on *Lake Success.*

(ii) I only want real first rate from your students, the thrilling thing; so see that you are a fine sieve as far as I am concerned.

Love

J.

'Dear Georges' is Georges Duthuit, the editor of the Paris review *transition* (with a very small 't') and who was a great friend of us both. I cannot remember if I accepted Joe's offer to review Georges' book on modern French writers, but I agreed with him about Ponge, and to a lesser extent about Du Bouchet, whom I had already translated for Neville Braybrooke's anthologies and magazines. As for Samuel Beckett, his plays rendered me almost extinct with boredom, and I have never been able to sit through a complete performance of *Waiting for Godot.* Nabokov dismissed the plays as 'wretched' and described the 'limpness' of *Molloy* and the other novels, judgements I agree with. I had introduced David Paul to Joe, and apparently he had written something very good on Pound; but I don't remember anything by Robert Conquest. I kept this letter because I show how wonderfully encouraging Joe was to young writers, even when they were not producing anything of much interest; he banked on their improvement, and was often justified in his support. In my lonely life at Leeds, it was inspiring to know there was someone like Joe to turn to.

Another of Joe's letters I have kept from this period in Leeds is dated 20/3/51, and in it he says some very pertinent things about the state of modern poetry that apply even more so to conditions today:

Dear Jim

Thank you for your interesting package this morning. I have not digested it yet, as you may suppose, but will do so after Easter. This is just to send you (for review) the third of the Hand and Flower Books. I know what I think about all this and that is I don't wish to pat poor poets on the back just because they are poor poets. I understand and sympathize with the fact that poetry is in a bad state and that I must do what I can to help it to sell; but I don't think it wd. be doing it any service to boost it indiscriminately. I have to discriminate over everything else; only the best novels and the best other books are sorted from the continual stream of pretentiousness and mediocrity that ripples through the office and (what am I getting at) I am rather disinclined to advertise, even by a mention, these Hand and Flower books if they are just (as looks to me the case) giving some minor poets an undeserved opportunity of getting into print their minor poems which no discerning publisher will take. I expect you will think this severe, but I not only have not the space to be anything but severe, I also think that it is necessary to have or set a standard of value, and that far too much, O far too much is being written.

Love

J.

I did not think this severe, and I could find nothing to praise in the Hand and Flower Press's selection of poets. Indeed, when I saw how low the standard was, I offered a selection of my own work, knowing it was so much better, but this was declined; I should have realized that what was wanted was mediocrity and pretentiousness. In spite of all he says, however, Joe did consistently give a hearing to writers he felt sorry for and who he thought had something to offer, trusting they would do better – an admirable editorial discernment shines through that letter.

The following letter is undated – and I never followed Joe's advice to keep correspondents' envelopes – but it must have been written during my stay in Leeds, because of the references to Wilfred Rowland Childe. I put it here because the tone and content are closely related to the preceding letter:

Putney.

Dear Jim

I'm awfully sorry about your earache and do hope it doesn't turn out so serious as a mastoid. Do let me know how you continue. Yes, I shall be here at the end of the month and shall look forward with great joy to seeing you.

Thanks for the reviews. I don't at all mind your reviewing Mr Childe's book – I like his poems too – but feel rather sorry that you add him to Merton. Does Merton really need to be done? True I am rather prejudiced against him, but your review, and quotes from him, don't make me feel less prejudiced. I was in two minds whether to send out the book at all. And now it rather looks as though you have simply used him as a convenient peg on which to hang Mr Childe. I *must* be firm about *not* giving space to poets and writers who aren't really good. I am sending the review back in the hopes that you may find someone better to take up Mr Childe. (I'll send you some more books).

And I like your 'Elegy' *very* much and am keeping it.

Love

J.

As Joe had sent me the book of Thomas Merton's poems for review, and I rather liked his work, for its religious feeling, I naturally linked it with Wilfred's book, in which the poems were also mainly religious. I wanted to give a little pleasure to my old friend at Leeds, who was visibly in a decline but of course this was exactly the sort of motive Joe so rightly abhorred. I think my review eventually appeared.

A letter from Joe dated 26/8/51 from Putney was in response to my sending him a copy of *The Submerged Village*, not without misgiving for the effect it might have on my future as a writer – misgivings that were to be amply justified. I later discovered that the review he mentions had been written by that minor poet and an arch-conservative, Richard Church, who adopted what I thought was a condescending tone – 'a bit schoolmasterish' indeed:

Dear Jim,

Yes, I shd. have written to you long ago. You have been often on my mind, and I was most awfully pleased to get the personal copy of your book of poems. Thank you so much. When ever you come here again you must write in it for me. It is charmingly produced – how good the O.U.P. are – such pretty binding and such good paper, and a very satisfactory strong and permanent look, seldom accorded to such 'ephemeral' stuff as poetry! I was awfully glad, and delighted to see my name in it (how odd one's name always looks in print), and delighted to hear that it is selling well. Wherever I open it, it seems to be a poem from *The Listener*.

You will find a review of it on the leading page of my Book Chronicle next Thursday. It was a difficult matter to know to whom to send it – sensitive, sincere and detached critics of poetry are not numerous – and although you may think the result a bit schoolmasterish, I hope you will not be disappointed in it. You are taken a little to task here and there, but not unfairly I am obliged to think, since I have occasionally scolded you, in my amateurish way, on similar grounds myself. I have no doubt at all about one thing, and that is that your next collection will more than fulfil the promise he speaks of.

I am all right, though I get increasingly bothered over my life and future – bored with living with my women, anxious over finances as I go on pulling out my small capital to keep them, and so on. I try to get Nancy going in some small remunerative job, but the idea only upsets her. How to free myself from her and resume my independence I know not. I did manage to get both of them off for 3 weeks to Dover – at vast expense – in July, and revelled in having the flat again entirely to myself for the first time for 2 years. Until next summer comes – if I can then afford to repeat that experience, the only way I can ever be alone is to go away myself. So I am going away next Friday for a fortnight, up to Sutherland, with Jack Sprott in his motor car. We start from Nottingham on Sat. morning, stay at Durham with Prof. Abbott on Sat. night, at Edinburgh with Edwin Muir on Sunday, then potter round the top of Scotland from John o' Groats to Cape Wrath, and coming down the west coast, cross over to the Island of Eigg to stay 2 or 3 days with Steven Runciman whose *History of the Crusades* vol. 1, which I have just read as a preparation, I recommend you too to read. I leave Queenie behind, of course, and hate doing that, but she is well and in good hands.

We both send our love to you

Joe

The only thing I enjoyed in my two years of academic life was the production of *King Lear* by wonderful old Wilson Knight, who took the lead. I was given the small part of Curran, and the mere sight of my beautiful legs in Elizabethan tights was enough to upstage all the other players, who included Frederick May from the Italian department as the Fool, Kenneth Muir excellent as Gloucester and Arnold Kettle camping himself sick as Oswald. The Cordelia was someone from the psychology department, which I thought was very significant at the first costume rehearsal, when I had to point out to her that she had put on her Elizabethan dress back to front. As soon as I put on my wonderful doublet and hose, I felt as if I had been born to wear them, and Arnold Kettle, taking a long look at my shimmering legs, nearly passed out with emotion as he complimented me upon my 'very authentic Elizabethan appearance'. However, the rest of the cast, particularly Goneril and Regan, were green with envy at the ease with which I could wear my costume as soon as I put it on. I myself was startled by how at home I felt in it, much more so than in my drab modern clothes – though I did try to enliven them with little inimitable personal touches like flowing velvet ribbons instead of horrid neckties, and second-hand silk waistcoats from the stalls in lovely Leeds market. The experience of wearing that costume – very similar to the one I had worn to the fancy-dress dance at my university – convinced me, as it had then, that reincarnation is a reality, and that I may have been a lowly pot-boy or even perhaps a university wit in the age of the Virgin Queen. I had the same *déjà vu* feeling when I put on a toga for *Julius Caesar*, a Greek soldier's costume for the final scene of *French Without Tears* and Greek robes in the chorus of some tragedy or other. The same thing happened when I put on a Spanish mantilla and a wonderful flounced flamenco costume, and when I wore traditional Japanese clothes for the first time. As Iris Orton once told me after delving into my murky past – 'You have an old soul, many times reincarnated.'

Another exciting occasion in Leeds was when the wife of the heart surgeon, Philip Allison, dashed round to my room early one morning and told me Philip was going to perform a heart operation and would be glad to welcome me to the operating theatre if I felt like it. Of course I did! Always avid for new experience, as Firbank puts it, I rushed to the General Hospital and was taken to Philip as he was getting ready for the operation. I had to put on a mask and a sweet little white cap like Popeye's. I expected to be given a seat among the medical students in the amphitheatre. But to my intense delight, Philip led me right up to the operating table, and got someone to bring me a stool to stand on, right next to his right elbow. I found myself standing on this little stool looking right down into that woman's heart and listening to Philip's comments and instructions, delivered in cool, impeccable English with a rather literary turn. The operation lasted four hours or more, and I was standing on that stool all the time. But it all passed as if in a minute, and at the end, when I heard a car starting up outside, I came to myself as if out of a deep trance; it might have been me who had been anaesthetized, not the patient, who recovered, for the operation was a great success. It was a mitral stenosis valvulotomy, now an outdated procedure. A few years later, the children of the woman who had been operated on asked me to sign a copy of my book, *A Correct Compassion*, which is also the title of the poem for their mother. Then they presented it to her and told her to read about her operation.

After the operation, I had a cup of tea with Philip and Doug the anaesthetist. Then I went back to the red light district and wrote down everything I had seen. It was not intended that I should write a poem, or indeed, anything. But gradually the prose notes I was writing began to compose themselves into a poem in quatrains, quite a long one, and fairly formal. I did not sleep that night, though I tried to. I went to bed. Then I kept jumping out of bed to add something to my memories, and by the time morning broke I had finished the first draft of the poem. I typed it out, and sent it to Joe.

His response was immediate:

Dear Jim,

I think this is a really wonderful poem – the best thing you have ever done (though all the poems in your letter showed a marked advance, I thought, and I have taken three more, proofs of which will go to you later). Now do give careful thought to this before passing it as perfect. It seems to me much improved by your improvements, excepting perhaps for the introduction, so courteously made, of the extra verse. Though I like it, I'm not sure that it *does* improve, and it gives 'sleeps on' as a line end, while you have 'beats on' as another line end in the next verse. It gets also, the poem, a little messy, I feel, in these middle stanzas after v. 6. Although I took a syllable out of your 'sphygmomanometer' after consultation with Webster's Dictionary, it is still, of course, quite a word, as also is electrocardiogram, and though you must have both of them if you insist, the rest of the verse seems to me to go to pieces beneath their weight. And then, wd. it not be tidier of you to run verse 7 into verse 8, somehow like

> The pink-mottled lung like a revolted creature heaves,
> Then, as if by extra fingers, is neatly held aside

What do you think? And is 'laid bare'.... 'yet is not revealed' okay?

Love,

J.

I wish I had kept his envelopes, to date the letter exactly. That was advice Joe gave me much later, when he was collecting his letters from Morgan Forster, and found that Morgan rarely dated them. Round the edges of another, longer letter, in the sepia ink I favoured at that time, I have scribbled some changes to meet Joe's generous suggestions:

> Meters record the blood, measure the heart, control the breath ...
> ... and still the heart lives alone...
> exists, alone
> heaves,
> Collapses;
> as if by extra fingers is neatly held aside ...

Some of these changes were incorporated into the final version. The 'extra fingers' were ordinary kitchen egg-whisks, flat in shape, that Philip used to hold the lung aside in order to get at the heart.

Joe's next letter came after he had had a holiday in Paris with Georges Duthuit, editor of *transition*:

Dear Jim,

A nice long letter and full of wonderful news. I've thought often of you – how indeed could I not with your mug on my wall (oughtn't you to have it in Leeds?), and had a real pang when I heard that you had phoned in my absence. I wish Leeds were not so far away, so that I cd. run up for a night from time to time, for when one embarks on a journey one usually finishes it, while letters, I find, are a very different matter.

I suppose we are all well here, except Nancy perhaps who seems tired and heavy and looks pale and says she does not sleep. I have taken rooms in Dover for her and Bunny for a fortnight from June 20, and much hope they will go when the time comes. It is a well-known characteristic of Nancy to fall down on things when the time comes. I shall be glad to be free of them for a spell for one thing: my Summer Bk. Number will be due by then. At the moment I am in the throes of it....

... You are quite right about Paul Dehn's poem – it was puff-pastry and heavy at that, but partly through tiredness (I do sometimes feel ready to drop) and partly through your bad influence, I am being kinder to the poets than they often deserve. Besides, if I waited for really good poems always, ripe plums, the journal would go fruitless to the press; so I have now some six galleys of what you may regard as abominable poems, of all shapes and sizes, so that the ladies of *The Listener* can always be sure of having something handy to plug up any crack and cranny without having to pester me with phone calls and telegrams when I am on holiday.

But I joke, I suppose, or perhaps your letter pulls me together a little, for now I come to your poem about the operation, which I do like very much, but which I think you ought to look at again. It is a poem which I shd. greatly like to have for *The Listener*, but which, I *think*, may meet with opposition from the Editor on the grounds that, like the Rembrandt side of beef, it is not a 'nice' subject for a work of art. I don't know, for I haven't tried it on him yet, but I surmise. In that case it ought to be perfect as it can be made, and I'm not sure that, as it stands, it is. May I therefore give it back to you with the following questions, which you may think unimportant but which I wd. like you nevertheless to consider:

V.2 I feel that the rhyming system is a little weak, that you meant to have 'concomitant of calm' but could not manage the rhyme, so took 'ease' and then 'repose', which those formidable glittering objects seem hardly to suit.

V.3 Is the instrument the 'result' of the gesture?

V.8 Like (ordinary) hands? And when I picture an egg-whisk, I think of that contraption where you turn a little handle.

V.9 'Black' again, as in verse 7?

Last verse. I confess to a slight prejudice against the word 'dreaming' in the sense in which you use it. It makes me think of schoolgirls, and it's unscientific.

Finally, I feel a little defrauded when you at last laid the heart bare, and thought that if Rimbaud (who was in my mind as I read you) had written the poem there would have been some profound and moving verse at that point, between 9 and 10. In any case it's a wonderfully good poem, and if you set aside all my remarks as trivial and return it unchanged I will do my best to publish it....

In part of the letter about Paris, which I have omitted, Joe mentions going to the Salon de Mai* with Georges, so that helps to date it. Both the letters I quote (and there were many more) show clearly Joe's passionate interest in the contributions sent to the journal, and how eager he was to help struggling poets both financially and poetically. Certainly I adopted many of his suggestions, and together we were able to create the poem in its final form. It was published a few weeks later in *The Listener* and created the expected storms of protest, but Philip loved it – I had of course consulted him during the early drafts – and on the morning it appeared Smith's in Leeds sold out their stock of *The Listener* before eleven. Some medical students who were friendly with me – I much preferred them to the dull Eng. Lit. lot – were afraid that the poem might be taken as self-advertisement by Philip Allison, and that he might be hauled over the coals by the Medical Council, but of course Philip pooh-poohed the whole notion, and in fact no one in the medical world made any objection. Indeed, I had many letters from doctors and surgeons praising the poem. But my real delight was when *The Nursing Times* asked to reprint it, for I have always loved having my poems in unlikely places. It was the first time they had ever published a poem. I also had poems in *The Leeds Fireclay Company Journal*, *The Evening Standard* and *The South Shields Gazette and Shipping Telegraph*.

Philip wrote to me in a letter dated 18 May 1951:

> Dear James,
>
> I am amazed at the way you entered completely into the atmosphere of our operation. It was good to have you there and it is good to experience it all through your eyes and feelings.
>
> It would be presumptuous for me to congratulate you on your poem. I can only say that it affected me deeply. You have hit off strings the vibration of which I can recognize so clearly,
>
> It was most kind of you to send me the poem – I feel I have 'pinched' a bit of your immortality....
>
> Yours
>
> Philip

With Philip and his wife (who was reading for a degree in English at Leeds) and their children I made several excursions to Wensleydale to see Fred and Muriel and Sonia, for Philip was quite a good amateur painter, and loved to go out painting with Fred. I was often in Wensleydale while I was in Leeds, and wrote a number of poems (unpublished) about that wonderful part of northern England.

Philip died in March 1974, while I had my Fellowship at Sheffield, so

* An annual art show in Paris.

with a friend I drove to the Service of Thanksgiving at Kettlewell Parish Church, where his wife had asked me to read my poem as part of the service. It was a moving occasion for all of us.

A CORRECT COMPASSION

To Mr Philip Allison, after watching him perform a Mitral Stenosis Valvulotomy in the General Infirmary at Leeds.

CLEANLY, sir, you went to the core of the matter.
Using the purest kind of wit, a balance of belief and art,
You with a curious nervous elegance laid bare
The root of life, and put your finger on its beating heart.

The glistening theatre swarms with eyes, and hands, and eyes.
On green-clothed tables, ranks of instruments transmit a sterile
  gleam.
The masks are on, and no unnecessary smile betrays
A certain tension, true concomitant of calm.

Here we communicate by looks, though words,
Too, are used, as in continuous historic present
You describe our observations and your deeds.
All gesture is reduced to its result, an instrument.

She who does not know she is a patient lies
Within a tent of green, and sleeps without a sound
Beneath the lamps, and the reflectors that devise
Illuminations probing the profoundest wound.

A calligraphic master, improvising, you invent
The first incision, and no poet's hesitation
Before his snow-blank page mars your intent:
The flowing stroke is drawn like an uncalculated inspiration.

A garland of flowers unfurls across the painted flesh.
With quick precision the arterial forceps click.
Yellow threads are knotted with a simple flourish.
Transfused, the blood preserves its rose, though it is sick.

Meters record the blood, measure heart-beats, control the breath.
Hieratic gesture: scalpel bares a creamy rib; with pincer knives
The bone quietly is clipped, and lifted out. Beneath,
The pink, black-mottled lung like a revolted creature heaves,

Collapses; as if by extra fingers is neatly held aside
By two ordinary egg-beaters, kitchen tools that curve
Like extraordinary hands. Heart, laid bare, silently beats. It can
  hide

No longer yet is not revealed. – 'A local anaesthetic in the cardiac nerve.'

Now, in firm hands that quiver with a careful strength,
Your knife feels through the heart's transparent skin; at first,
Inside the pericardium, slit down half its length,
The heart, black-veined, swells like a fruit about to burst,

But goes on beating, love's poignant image bleeding at the dart
Of a more grievous passion, as a bird, dreaming of flight, sleeps on
Within its leafy cage. – 'It generally upsets the heart
A bit, though not unduly, when I make the first injection.'

Still, still the patient sleeps, and still the speaking heart is dumb.
The watchers breathe an air far sweeter, rarer than the room's.
The cold walls listen. Each in his own blood hears the drum
She hears, tented in green, unfathomable calms.

'I make a purse-string suture here, with a reserve
Suture, which I must make first, and deeper,
As a safeguard, should the other burst. In the cardiac nerve
I inject again a local anaesthetic. Could we have fresh towels to cover

All these adventitious ones? Now can you all see.
When I put my finger inside the valve, there may be a lot
Of blood, and it may come with quite a bang. But I let it flow,
In case there are any clots, to give the heart a good clean-out.

Now can you give me every bit of light you've got.'
We stand on the benches, peering over his shoulder.
The lamp's intensest rays are concentrated on an inmost heart.
Someone coughs. 'If you have to cough, you will do it outside this theatre.' – 'Yes, sir.'

'How's she breathing, Doug? Do you feel quite happy?' – 'Yes, fairly
Happy.' – 'Now. I am putting my finger in the opening of the valve.
I can only get the tip of my finger in. – It's gradually
Giving way. – I'm inside. – No clots. – I can feel the valve

Breathing freely now around my finger, and the heart working.
Not too much blood. It opened very nicely.
I should say that anatomically speaking
This is a perfect case. – Anatomically.

For of course, anatomy is not physiology.'
We find we breathe again, and hear the surgeon hum.
Outside, in the street, a car starts up. The heart regularly
Thunders. – 'I do not stitch up the pericardium.

It is not necessary.' – For this is imagination's other place,
Where only necessary things are done, with the supreme and grave
Dexterity that ignores technique; with proper grace
Informing a correct compassion, that performs its love, and makes
  it live.

Leeds, Brunswick Place, May 1951
(*A Correct Compassion and Other Poems, OUP, 1952*)

The 'mug' that Joe refers to in that letter is the portrait of me painted by Maurice Feild at the Downs School. During my interminable moves, I had left it with Joe for safekeeping, and he hung it over the mantelpiece of his study at the Star and Garter Mansions, where it became slightly smoked. Joe grew to like the painting very much, and was reluctant to let it go when I asked some friends to collect it, have it cleaned, and send it to me in Nagoya.

In Leeds, I became friendly with the Professor of Painting, Maurice de Sausmarez, his wife and daughter, who was then about six and a very formidable young lady I thought; I was always intimidated by the precocious daughters of artists and writers. Maurice de Sausmarez also did a portrait of me, which I am told now hangs in the office of the Chancellor of the University. In it, I am holding a sea shell to my ear, and looking wonderfully decadent and affected, but some people mistook the sea shell for a half-eaten sandwich until the symbolism was explained to them. Another artist at Leeds was the sculptor Reg Butler, who did his prize-winning 'Unknown Prisoner' there. I did not care at all for his work. There is one of his lumpy nudes – female of course – in the entrance to the British Council Library in Kyoto, which I sometimes tiptoe past. There was also Martin Froy, for whom I wrote a poem. He later joined me on the staff at Bath Academy – a fine painter and a great teacher.

One of the interesting events during my stay in Leeds was the arrival of the Russian writer Boris Polevoy, author of *We are Soviet People* and a prolific novelist in the social-realist style, whose *Story of a Real Man* is his best-known work. He came to give a lecture on Soviet writers, and afterwards held a question-and-answer session with university members. It was a time when I became involved in the Authors' World Peace Appeal.

A fine editor, W. L. Andrews of *The Yorkshire Post*, headed the list of supporters, who included some of my friends – Alex Comfort, Elizabeth Goudge, Anna Kavan, Naomi Mitchison, Herbert Read, Alexander Reid, Paul Rotha, Siegfried Sassoon, Dylan Thomas and Sylvia Townsend Warner, as well as leading literary figures of the time like Cecil Day-Lewis, Christopher Fry, Rupert Croft Cooke, Edmund Blunden, Vera Brittain, Jack Lindsay, Sean O'Casey, Dr Edith Sitwell and Ruby M. Ayres. I had been invited to make a friendly visit to the Soviet Union by Ilya Ehrenburg, together with A. E. Coppard and others. So I was anxious to meet a real Russian author and find out something about the circumstances writers lived in there. I was particularly interested in finding out what controls were put upon writers, whether poetic and dramatic self-expression were censored, whether writers were allowed to write antisocial and experimental works, how they got their works published and what the attitude was towards Jewish and homosexual writers. I attended the conference with Wilfred Rowland Childe, who was firmly anti-Russian, and our friend from the Spanish and Portuguese Department, Agostin de Irizar, a good, sweet, gentle scholar who was a refugee from Salazar and Franco.

I cannot remember much about Polevoy's lecture, except that I was left with the impression that he was just another bureaucrat extolling the greatness of the USSR. Questioning was very heated, and I only managed to get one question in, about freedom of expression and experimentation in the novel and in poetry. Polevoy's replies were all very evasive. He avoided Wilfred's questionings about the treatment of poets like Mandelstam, Akhmatova and Tsvetaeva, which made other questioners indignant. On the whole, I received a bad impression of the sort of life writers enjoyed under Stalin. Polevoy's writing was a glorification of the Russian heroic fighter and worker, and he was obviously a Communist Party committee man, the sort who turns thumbs down on any writer of originality. He died about thirty years later, crowned with conventional distinctions like the Order of Lenin (twice) and was made a Hero of Socialist Labour. His equivalent under Gorbachev is Yevtushenko. I decided not to accept Ilya Ehrenburg's invitation.

While I was in Leeds, and for several years afterwards, I was invited to read and lecture at the summer school of drama run by Hull University College. The first school was held at Hickleton Hall, near Doncaster, formerly Lord Halifax's residence, and now part of St Hilda's Priory. The nuns who looked after us were so impressive in their quiet kindness and their unostentatious devotion to good works, and to our creaturely comforts. The leader of the school was the vital and energetic producer, Ida Teather, and in charge of stage design and costume was a wonderful woman who became a great friend (as did Ida), Stella Mary Pearce, who was the wife of Eric Newton.* Stella had worked on designs for many early poetic dramas, including Eliot's *The Rock* and *Murder in the Cathedral*. She was, and still is, a fount of brilliant ideas and witty scholarship. I loved every moment of those courses, where I was supposed to be a lecturer encouraging students to write plays – not very successfully, I am afraid; in fact I was just another student, for I learnt something new every day from Ida and Stella. Another strong influence was the director of movement, a fine, athletic dancer from the Laban School of Movement, Warren Lamb. Stella and Warren were to work with me on three of the dramatic works that emerged from my studies with them: *The Triumph of Harmony: A Masque*, which I was commissioned to write by the Girls' Friendly Society and was performed at the Albert Hall; *Candle in the Heavens*, a verse play about St Hilda and the Synod of Whitby; and *Upon This Rock*, a dramatic chronicle of Peterborough Cathedral, where it was produced by the TV director, Christian Simpson. It was a memorable production, in which I played St Chad hanging his cloak on a sunbeam, and there was splendid music and choral singing by a young composer, Roy Teed. But by the time the final dress rehearsal came, it seemed as if the play would never be ready. One of my happiest memories of that final rehearsal is of the Dean's plump calves in his gaiters as he knelt in prayer, pleading with his God for mercy. His prayers must have been effective, for the production was a tremendous success, and the text was published by the OUP. There was another amusing incident, when the Dean came to me on opening night, obviously in a state of great distress, and informed me that the Duchess of Gloucester, who was attending one of the performances with her sons, would be meeting the cast, but had expressed a wish not to meet me. The poor Dean seemed to think this was a terrible calamity for me, but I assured him it did not matter in the least. I had no wish at all to meet the Duchess, and indeed was relieved at not having to do so.

Among the guest performers at our summer schools were the fine actor Richard Ainley, son of the great Henry, with a voice to match his father's, and the exquisite Rosalinde Fuller, who with Richard and a pianist gave a wonderful presentation of Thomas Hardy's poetry. I can still hear Ros reciting, in that inimitable, mischievous, musical voice 'A Tramp Woman's Tragedy'. She also gave us an unforgettable dramatization of stories by the Austrian Arthur Schnitzler, author of *La Ronde*, so popular as a film. Ros wanted me to write a play about Rimbaud for her, in which she intended

* The well-known art critic and author who wrote regularly for Joe Ackerley.

to play the poet: I devised an opening scene with Arthur pissing as high as he could – we did not get much further than that. Joe was horrified at the idea of a *woman* playing Rimbaud, but Ros would have done it very well, for she had the poet's spirit, and his boyish figure. Now she is dead, it has been revealed that when she was starting her career, in New York, she had as her lover Scott Fitzgerald. She would have made an adorable Zelda.*

At a performance of my *Candle in the Heavens*, we were honoured by the presence of Michael Ramsey, then Archbishop of York, a magnificent cleric who always reminded me of what Dr Johnson may have been like. I was sitting next to him in the front row, with Muriel Metcalfe on his other side. It was an outdoor performance, and I was convulsed with laughter when one of the monks in the cast sat down on the ground, revealing under his rather short robe a pair of white Y-fronts. If the Archbishop noticed that, he did not let on, but later in the play when I was laughing at my own jokes, he turned to me and said: 'It's the first time I've heard a playwright laughing at his own jokes,' with a charming, quizzical smile. Muriel instantly leapt to my defence: 'And why shouldn't he?' she inquired hotly, reducing the 'Arch', as we called him affectionately, to confused silence.

This episode reminded me of an earlier occasion when Joe and I had met the novelist P.H. Newby – who was also a BBC producer; he produced my radio poems 'The Descent into the Cave' and 'The Observatory', as well as a talk I gave about the poet's life on the occasion of the Queen's coronation. The BBC had gathered a host of 'the Queen's contemporaries' to deliver talks about their occupations, and I had cheated and got into the group by giving my age as much younger than it really is – something I love to do, just to confuse things and add a touch of fantasy to reference books. (In fact, as I regard the war years as a non-existent period in my life, I feel justified in deducting five or six years from my real age; sometimes I tell people I am much older than I really am, in order to enjoy their astonished 'But how *young* you look!'.)

My talk for Newby did not satisfy me, and I had to rewrite the whole damned thing for him. One of his complaints was that I seemed to think 'the world owed me a living'. Joe was present when he said that, and at once defended me: 'And why shouldn't the world owe him a living? Does it not owe *you*, and me, and all of us a living? What should we become if

* I feel sure that the delightful drawings made by Edward Shenton for the first appearance of Scott Fitzgerald's *Tender is the Night* in *Scribner's Magazine* used Rosalinde as the model for figures of the heroine. Ros wrote a 'Memoir' of her liaison, which has never been published.

it didn't? Jim deserves everything he can get.' Newby retired crestfallen. But I still had to rewrite my speech.

My friend from the Portuguese department, Agostin de Irizar, introduced me to modern Spanish and Portuguese writers, and to the poets in particular. Through him, I began my lifelong passion for the works of the heteronymic hero of modern Portuguese poetry, Fernando Pessoa. Agostin was to be instrumental in getting me an appointment at the University of Salamanca some years later.

After two years at Leeds, I had become accustomed to the place, and had made some friends in the magic gay world outside the university, including, according to one letter from Joe, a pastrycook. There was lots of ballet and opera at the Grand Theatre, and magnificent concerts of classical music. One of my best friends was the extraordinary painter Jacob Kramer, with whom I spent many a happy, bibulous lunchtime and evening in the pubs around City Hall, accompanied often by the art critic of *The Yorkshire Post*, W.R. Oliver, and his amusing wife, who often invited us to their home for supper after the pubs closed. On one of these occasions, I remember taking all my clothes off and dancing around their drawing-room in the nude, something Jacob never forgot. He did a nude drawing of me waving a pearl-handled revolver and an ostrich-feather fan, but I don't know what has become of it. I hope that, too, is in the office of the Chancellor of Leeds University. There was a humorous poet named Scriven who often met us in the pubs, and Leonard Clark was another companion, who greatly disapproved of our antics and of my not-very-flattering poems about Leeds and Temple Newsham. Leonard was an Inspector of Schools, poor soul. Jacob was at that time in declining health, which he did nothing to help to cure by incessant smoking and drinking. Often I had to escort him back to his digs, where he lived with a devoted landlady. Sometimes I wondered if I should still be able to drink with him next morning; I thought he must expire in his sleep. But he was always there at opening time, as cheerful and Russianly feckless as ever, ready to start on a new binge. There is something of the Baltic Slav in my own make-up, and I think this is why we got on so well together. I was looking at a record sleeve of a re-issue of some old recordings by Caruso, decorated by a self-caricature made by Caruso himself, and it looks very much like Jacob, with his big nose and aggressive cleft chin and twinkling eyes, a really roguish and irresistible smile and even the sort of old-fashioned trilby Jacob used to wear wherever he went. But the best portrait of Jacob, one that has conferred upon him an immortality his painting never quite succeeded in bringing him, is the

Epstein bust, which is in the Tate Gallery. I often pop in to see it, and felt sad recently when I could not find it on display. But I have a photograph of it, signed by Jacob; I can still see his big, red, swollen fingers clutching the pen very awkwardly. At the end, he was hardly able to hold a paintbrush. He was my greatest friend and defender in Leeds – 'Fight the hypocrites! Fight the pedants! Fight the philistines!' he used to shout as we staggered towards his lodgings after the pubs closed. He was a passionate artist in everything he did, and a noble creature, a magnificent animal, and I am proud that he loved me.

I needed defenders like Jacob. Resident poets were such a novelty in Britain, I aroused a lot of resentment among the academic staff and among my fellow writers. When Lawrence Gowing took up the post of Professor in the Department of Fine Art at King's College, Newcastle upon Tyne, he invited me to visit him there soon after I got to Leeds. One of his letters says: 'I feel full of forebodings about your appointment at Leeds. I have no doubt that what Universities (secretly) want most with us is to stop us writing or painting. . . .'

I began to feel this was true in Leeds. Some of the students were nice enough, and I had my friends, Wilfred and Agostin, with whom I often took tea and walnut cake at Fuller's. They came to visit me in Brunswick Place from time to time, and Wilfred invited me to lunch at his home in Harrogate. But the rest of the English department seemed curiously distant, as if they placed no reliance upon my reality, and some of the students were unkind and frankly hostile. When my poem about the heart operation was first published, however, I did receive a compliment from Kenneth Muir, who told me that if I never wrote anything else, that poem would have justified my stay in Leeds. I did not quite know what to make of this; it rather sounded as if he thought I had not written anything else but that poem, and would never again write anything to equal it, an attitude that was to become so common among the ignorant – academics who like to be able to express a cut-and-dried opinion and people who were too mentally lazy to see the poem as an exception among my work – that I began to refuse to allow it to be printed in anthologies like Kenneth Allott's Penguin *Contemporary Verse,* for which I offered him poems I thought were more representative of my poetry. There had been many letters from strangers about my poem, one of the most curious an epistle in verse form from the actor George Baker, who sent me a large, signed glossy studio portrait of his manly, handsome countenance. I wrote to thank him for it –

... a face,
On glossy paper printed, chemically achieved.
Posed, lit, photographed technically. The trace
of character removed by brush re-touching. ...
... I saw the knife with you, and with you caught
My breath, I saw a strange physician mending hearts
And for a moment, I was civilized, at peace.
I saw the smile upon this face of love ...

– but we never met, I'm sorry to say. I was beginning again to doubt people, to suspect their motives, to shy away from company except for a few close friends. My childhood unnatural quietness and paralyzing shyness, which I thought I had begun to overcome, were engulfing me again, and at times I could not face the street, I could not bear the sight of other people's faces. Neither could I bear my own face, my own company, very long. I found a reproduction of Cranach's 'Portrait of a Prince of Savoy', from the National Gallery of Art in Washington, and was struck by its resemblance to the photograph taken of me at the age of three – the same eyes, nose, determined mouth, firm chin, and even a suggestion of the fist I had made of my right hand, as if expecting to have to do battle with life. The picture moved me so much I carried it everywhere with me while I was in Leeds, as if it were protecting me, preserving what I feared was a disintegrating identity. But the Prince's hair is shoulder-length, a pale golden-auburn, and on his head is a tilted wreath of myosotis; no one had laid a wreath on *my* head. Or was ever likely to.

All the time, I was obsessed by faces and appearances, and most of them seemed menacing, sinister, destructive. Sometimes, when I was sitting with Jacob in the little pub in front of City Hall, he would give me a little nudge when certain men entered the bar and give a quick, searching look around them, lingering on our faces rather too long. 'Plain-clothes dicks,' Jacob would whisper, not moving his lips. Once when I was at the counter ordering another round of drinks, one of these men standing next to me at the bar looked at his companion and muttered: 'This one?' His companion saw that I had heard, and merely shook his head, giving the man a warning look. I remember I was wearing a workman's white-spotted red handkerchief round my throat, with an open-necked turquoise blue shirt, and of course my hair was very long and fair. Perhaps I had touched up my eyelashes a little with Cherry Blossom Boot Polish, and dusted my cheeks with the butterfly wings of *papier poudré,* in my favourite tint, 'Rachel'. I must have looked rather unusual in those days, those unliberal, unliberated times. Today, I see such images as I then presented everywhere around me, and no one takes the slightest notice. Well, I was before my time. The police were a constant source of unease and even terror, yet at the same time I went on putting myself in dangerous and compromising situations, as if in defiance of that fear. The fleeting, illicit sexual contacts I made were often terrifying, but they relieved briefly my panic loneliness, my feeling that the world around me was totally unreal. It was about that time I began to think again that I might well be a secret visitor from space, an unwilling emissary from some undiscovered planet, but I had forgotten the purpose of my mission, and the mystic code of communication, and now I could not get back, I was doomed to live on surrounded by aliens. Would they one day find out my duplicity, destroy that ambidextrous solitude that was my only protection from arrest and imprisonment?

The steam baths that those elderly chorus boys had introduced me to, and that my doctor, Grantie, had fleetingly mentioned with a knowing look that was both encouragement and warning, were for me a place of unending fascination. They were old-fashioned, utilitarian, rather grim, yet in the steam room were seductive males, lonely creatures like myself longing for a touch, a caress, a fraternal embrace. I spent many afternoons and evenings there. Our clothes were hung in open cubicles, and one afternoon, after I had been a long time in the steam room, I found that my address-book had been removed from my jacket. On another occasion, I entered the steam room and when I got used to the dimness I recognized on one of the benches a senior police officer from the Leeds vice squad, a not very attractive figure carefully draped in a towel, and pretending not to take much notice of the furtive fumblings that were going on. I betrayed no fear, but sat for a few moments, casually draped, looking at nothing in particular, before indolently rising and leaving the steam room. The officer did not follow me; he had his eye on someone else, and I was powerless to give any warning. Regretfully, I dried myself and dressed in a leisurely manner, then strolled back to my red light district. But I had learnt a lesson: I never went back there again.

However, I did not let the memory of that brief encounter with authority worry me too much; there were too many other worries, very real ones. I had almost reached the end of my second year at Leeds, and there was no talk of renewing my contract. Then I had a call from Bonamy Dobrée, inviting me to dinner at his flat. He had always been very correct with me, unobtrusively well-disposed, or so I thought. He had given me signed copies of his many critical works on Rochester and English prose style, and his translation of Alain Fournier's *Le Grand Meaulnes*, which I did not prefer to the original, as some sycophants had told him they did.

When I accepted his invitation to dinner, I expected that he would discuss my next year at Leeds. He was alone in the flat, and had prepared dinner himself. To my horror, the main dish was some revolting mess like brains. I could hardly touch it.

We had started off with dry sherry, then we had two bottles of excellent red wine, and finally generous doses of brandy, which I had taken a dislike to, despite Joe's indications to the selection committee. We took seats on the sofa.

Bonamy began to talk to me about how pleased he had been with my performance as Britain's first resident writer, praising the poems I had written, and then complimenting me on my elegant and graceful and attractive appearance – which made me think he was coming on rather strong, and wonder what he was getting at. I was impatient to hear him confirm my appointment for a third year, which was the minimum that had been agreed. Instead, he flung his arms around me and begged me to go to bed with him. I was touched by this tribute, which I found astonishing and pathetic, as well as slightly comic. As gently as I could, I withdrew from Bonamy's impassioned embrace, and told him I could not accede to his request. Poor Bonamy seemed utterly deflated and so sad, but I told him not to worry, I bore him no feelings of ill-will.

We had a final drink, and said goodbye on amicable terms. I walked back to Brunswick Place in a state of puzzled panic. I had never suspected Bonamy of being a covert homosexual, but when I mentioned the episode, in strictest confidence, to Joe and Wilfred, they said they were surprised I had not known.

A few days after that, I was informed that my Fellowship was at an end. I was out on the streets again, and on the run.

As before, my panic distress drove me out of the city and back into the country. I spent a week or so with my parents on Tyneside. My father had retired from a lifetime of hard, poorly-paid and only intermittent work, and was now preparing to enjoy some years in the sun. They were both anxious to get away from South Shields; they had finally realized they had had enough of a place I had run away from years before. I promised to look out for a cottage for them somewhere in the south.

I replied to a small ad, and found myself in a pleasant room at Merlin Haven, in Wotton-under-Edge, a charming country town in beautiful countryside. I was alarmed to find that the formidable Dr Joan Evans, the sort of woman Joe had warned me against, lived almost next door. But fortunately I never met her, and I do not suppose she knew of my existence.

Merlin Haven is not far from Stinchcombe, the village where Piers Court stands, the manor house in which Waugh and his family lived for about twenty years after his second marriage in 1937. During the last fifteen years or so of his life, Waugh was renowned for his choleric disposition and for his hatred of casual visitors. Indeed he had several times treated reporters, photographers and BBC staff who came to interview him with physical violence. There was even a rumour in the neighbourhood that if Waugh saw an unexpected or unwelcome visitor arriving he would take an ancient blunderbuss and fire a volley of shot at the unfortunate intruder from an upper window. Everywhere on Waugh's estate there were notices saying 'Keep Out!' or 'No Admittance Except on Business!' or 'Trespassers will be Prosecuted!' There was even a notice in French which read: '*Entrée interdite aux promeneurs!*'

One May morning I was out collecting some wild flowers from a hedge in a narrow country lane when I suddenly heard a terrifying voice shouting at me: 'What the bloody hell d'you think you're doing? That's my hedge!' I turned round and was horrified to see that the owner of the voice was no other than the master in person, Evelyn Waugh himself. He was standing there on that warm summer morning, red-faced, stout, perspiring, dressed in stiff, expensive country tweeds, looking every inch the traditional British squire who has caught a boy pinching apples from his orchard. I noted with dismay that he was also carrying a thick walking-stick, which he raised threateningly in the air as he advanced upon me. I was struck dumb with terror as he glared at me in fury and barked: 'Do you not know, sir, that you are trespassing upon private property – my property?' I felt my knees turn to water, but with my usual presence of mind at difficult moments I remembered some lines by Wordsworth which seemed to fit the situation, so in self-defence, holding up my little posy of wild flowers by way of explanation, I stammered out: 'Sir, I am but

'a fingering slave,
One that would peep and botanize
Upon his mother's grave.'

These odd lines from 'A Poet's Epitaph' caused an extraordinary change in Waugh. His face lost its congested redness, and he lowered his stick (to my great relief) and gave me a smile of singular sweetness. 'I see you are a man of letters,' he commented brusquely, and then went on, with increasing amiability: 'It's nearly lunch time. Come and have a sherry.' His essential kindness and great charm of manner were qualities in the man that I shall never forget. Once one got to know him, no one could be nicer. He was the sort of person of whom we say in England that 'his bark is worse than his bite.'

I enjoyed my two or three months resting in the country after the horrors of Leeds. There was a fine old pub, The Ram, where I drank pint after pint of rough cider, absolutely delicious. On one occasion, I was so overcome by its potency that I had to crawl back to Merlin Haven on my hands and knees. I found a small cottage there for my parents, and soon they had taken up residence there and were enjoying leisurely days in the country.

While they were there, I was invited to become Writer in Residence at Bath Academy of Art, a newly-created post. The director and his wife at Corsham Court, Clifford and Rosemary Ellis, were friendly and enthusiastic teachers and artists, with an extraordinarily wide range of interests. They had a small daughter, Charlotte, who, like Maurice de Sausmarez' daughter, I found very intimidating and unpredictable, though now we have become good friends. Clifford and Rosemary had gathered around them some of the finest modern artists, and working with them in that exciting atmosphere was one of the most wonderful experiences in my life. Among the painters were two from Cornwall who are now no more, but whom I found especially sympathetic: Peter Lanyon and Bryan Wynter. Other artists I liked were Terry Frost, Anthony Fry, Jack Smith and the sculptors Lynn Chadwick and Kenneth Armstrong. The last-named taught me a very valuable lesson. We were both sitting together at lunch in the dining-room, surrounded by lively students and argumentative artists laughing with Clifford and Rosemary. The dessert was an excellent plum pie, and as I ate my portion I arranged the plum stones very neatly along the rim of my plate. Kenneth suddenly noticed this, leaned over, and with his spoon roughly disturbed the prim arrangement I had created, saying: 'You're too tight, James, come on, relax, let yourself go!' I saw at once how well he had identified my dilemma. He had put his artist's finger precisely on my problem, that feeling of constriction and menace (a relic of my emphysema?) that had made my life so unhappy and dangerous in Leeds. My heart at that moment was very full. That Kenneth should have bothered to help me at all was something wonderful, but he had done it in such a casual, natural way that I felt indescribably grateful to him. But I could say nothing; I just smiled my comprehension of his act. Then we helped ourselves to generous second helpings of the plum pie and started to eat them. I noticed that Kenneth treated his plate and spoon as if they were an artist's materials or implements, and he spooned up his dessert as if he were mixing paint or clay or plaster. I was so fascinated by this procedure that I ate my helping without really noticing what I was doing. Then I was brought back to reality by a shout of laughter from Kenneth. He was pointing at my plate, where I had again arranged my plum stones in a tight circle! But now I knew what to do. Under Kenneth's approving gaze, I took my spoon and broke the stiff little pattern, and swirled the stones around in the rich red juice and the luscious cream, making new, abstract patterns that delighted my eye. It was a beginning. From that moment on, I began to untie all the knots within myself, and to enjoy life and poetry in a new way. I abandoned the rather too formal poetry I had been forcing myself to write – quite the opposite of my early surrealist work – and started to use words in a more plastic way, as an artist would handle whatever materials came to hand, and my poetry took on new life and promise, as did my life. I don't think Kenneth ever realized how much he had done for me.

Lord Methuen, the owner of Corsham Court, himself a fine painter who had been a friend of Sickert when that artist lived in Bath, had restored the old weavers' cottages on the main street just next to the entrance to the Court. When one of these was advertised to let, I took it and brought my parents there to live with me.

For a time, we were very happy. I was working well in my new style, and enjoying my teaching of drama and literature to mostly appreciative students and staff. In the spacious attic at the top of the house I wrote the first volume of my autobiography, *The Only Child*, and then the second volume, *Sorrows, Passions and Alarms*. My two poems in the *Penguin Book of Contemporary Verse*, 'House in Summer' and 'Tea in a Space Ship', were written there, and the former is a portrait of our house in Corsham.

But again, gradually, insidiously, something was going wrong. What could it be? I remembered with a sudden chill a rather disturbing incident that had occurred when I had first arrived in Flemish Buildings, and was awaiting the arrival of my parents. The gas had not yet been connected, and I used an electric kettle to make my tea. Then only a day after my arrival an official of the gas company arrived to check the meter and accused me of having somehow used the gas without paying for it, though I could not understand how on earth that could have happened. I told him that it was impossible for me to use the gas, as I had no gas stove or cooker at that time. But he insisted that I had been stealing the company's gas. It was very puzzling. He left the house to make a report to the company, and the next thing I knew there was a young local policeman at the door to investigate my 'theft' of the gas. I invited him in to look round the house, where there was still almost no furniture. I asked him if he would like a drink, which he refused; but he accepted a cigarette, and stood in our downstairs sitting-room with his back to the fireplace, looking intently at me as I explained how impossible it was for me to have used the gas. He had not bothered to remove his cap, I suddenly noticed, and this lack of elementary courtesy chilled me. But he must have accepted my explanations, because there was no more trouble. The gas men came and connected the gas, and one of them, a kind young man, when I explained what had happened, said that the whole thing was completely silly, and that the company inspector ought to apologize to me for making such unfounded accusations; the loss of gas had resulted simply from a slight leak somewhere, which he soon discovered and put right. Of course, I received no apology, either from the gas company or from the police.

I had thought I had put this incident out of my mind, but it began to return again and again as I pondered the vague sense of unease I had, and that seemed to be affecting my mother and father, too. My father, who occasionally had gone for a pint at the local pub across the street, stopped going there, and my mother had no friends except for a strange lady in a cottage on the other side of the street, who had lived in Egypt and who often came in to talk to us, for she was living alone, too, and had no friends.

Lord and Lady Methuen, in their ancestral abode at Corsham Court, were always very kind to me. Several times Lady Methuen sent round a note inviting me to dinner at the Court – 'We don't dress' was the ambiguous afterthought, at which I rather took offence, but only very mildly, wondering if she thought that the likes of me would not possess a dinner jacket. (I didn't, until I had to go to Malaya by ship.) The dinners were delightful, and there were often well-known guests. The triple-cube drawing-room was magnificent, full of fine old furniture and pictures.

The Methuens must have been aware of the troubles we were going through in their village, because Lady Methuen politely suggested that my mother might like to come and visit her. I could not see my dear mother doing that: it was hardly the sort of thing she was accustomed to. And why had Lady Methuen not invited my father also? Why did she not invite all three of us to dinner? These thoughts raced through my mind, and I found myself answering: 'Why don't you come and see her?' To which Lady Methuen replied:

'I don't go to people, people come to me.'

I was so taken aback by this arrogance that I declined all further invitations. Lord Methuen, too, liked to demonstrate his authority. We had hardly got settled into the weavers' cottage in Flemish Buildings than His Lordship came knocking at the front door, asking to be allowed to take his visitor, who was James Pope-Hennessy, someone whose books I liked very much, around this restored showpiece. So we let them in and I showed them round. My parents suffered the greatest embarrassment by this unannounced visit. 'I wish he'd let me do the beds before he came,' worried my mother. But the occasion was a very special one for me; I at once recognized James Pope-Hennessy as the young man who had picked me up outside Lyons in Coventry Street on New Year's Eve during the war, and who had given me thirty bob to go and find an hotel room. I wonder if he recognized me? He gave my book on Malaya a good review. His gruesome murder some years later made me very sad. I had liked him so much, and I felt I had so much to offer him. He could have been the 'ideal friend' I was always seeking.

But it seems that those who go seeking ideal friends end up with a dagger in the back.

When Joe came to stay with Queenie, I realized something must be wrong, and that it was something connected with my obvious homosexuality. Was it creating talk in the village? I felt sick at heart. One day, my father, obviously in a highly emotional state, suddenly said to me, in my mother's presence: 'Don't worry, Jim. It's all a lot of nonsense.' When Joe came to stay with us, he asked me how my parents felt about my homosexuality, and I repeated what my father had said. But what was the 'worry' he spoke about? Yes, I did feel a vague unease, but nothing worse than what I had often felt in Leeds, London and on Tyneside. A curious feeling of being suspended in a void, and of being about to drop into some black and endless abyss of horror and despair. Joe approved of what my father had said, and as always they got along very well together. We went to the pub, and there I noticed for the first time an old man, one of the locals, in a cap and raincoat, who seemed to be staring knowingly at Joe and me. I felt a flash of hatred for his impudence. But it was not just the village people who were against us; some of the so-called intellectuals in the Bath Academy of Art were, too, and some of the students made no secret of their growing hostility. I could stand it no longer, and resigned.

Clifford and Rosemary tried to persuade me to stay on, but I could not bear the thought of the hurt the situation was causing my poor father and mother, and I insisted on resigning. I know that Clifford was sorry to see me go, and indeed a couple of years later, after my return from Spain, he invited me back to Bath Academy of Art. I was terribly hard-up, so I accepted, but only for a short series of lectures and lessons to the local school children, in the teaching practice course for the art students.

I wanted to leave Corsham at once, but where were we to go? I hunted for some acceptable country accommodation all over the south of England, but in vain: nothing was suitable. Then I got the chance of a new job: to teach for the Swedish Ministry of Education for one year, travelling all over Sweden and teaching all levels of students, from small children to air force cadets, from high school students to university graduates.

My parents urged me to accept, and I left them alone in that sinister place. I knew my mother wanted to leave at once, just as much as I did. Her excuse was that she found the stone floors too damp. But I knew that was just a kind effort to conceal the truth from me. My father, too, was under great strain, his face pale and drawn and unhappy. It broke my heart. But I left for Sweden, and when I came back before the end of my contract, we found a house in Bath, and moved there just before I left to take up my next appointment, in Spain, at the University of Salamanca. It was while I was in Salamanca in the winter of 1957 that my father died of a heart attack. It was apparently brought on by shovelling snow from our front path. But I knew, and my mother knew, that he had died of despair, of a broken heart, because of the son he had brought into the world. As he lay dying, he told my mother: 'Mary, you've been a good wife. Take care of Jim.'

My last sight of him was on the stairs, on the landing at home, where I shook his hand in goodbye as I left for Spain after our last Christmas together. Through all our tribulations and disagreements, my love for him had never faltered. I kissed his cold brow as he lay in his coffin in our front room. And I wrote a poem for him that comes at the end of *The Prodigal Son*.

However, my father, who admired Dickens and adored *The Pickwick Papers,* would not want me to end this book on such a sad, tragic note. So I shall add an episode – from the period prior to 1956, when this book ends – which is both comical and stupid.

The Oxford Poetry Society had invited me to give a reading of my work, and as I needed the small fee, I accepted. They put me up at the Mitre, and invited me to take dinner with them before my reading. I had grown sick of public readings, and I was in a state of considerable nerves when I went in to dinner with the undergrads. All the future angry young men were seated at the table, including John Wain and Kingsley Amis. The latter was sitting almost opposite me. I think it was Christopher Levison sitting next to me. To cover my nervousness, I started chattering on the most ridiculous themes, informing my neighbour, with hoots of shrill laughter, for example, that I had been to France where I had caught the dancing mania that devastated the Middle Ages by eating ergot in rye bread, or some such nonsense. I added that one symptom of the derangement was that I could not bear the sight of the colour red, or of pointed shoes. All this was greeted by my neighbour with looks of polite disbelief. John Wain sat at the end of the table looking sardonic and contemptuous, as usual.

Then I heard Kingsley Amis pipe up, in a loud stage-whisper addressed to the entire company: 'He's queer as a coot, and doesn't care who knows it.' There was what I hope was an embarrassed silence, and I went on talking with even greater frivolity.

I should have got up and left the table and shaken the dust of Oxford from my feet. But I calmly went on eating, as if I had heard nothing. I was wondering how, after that display of bad manners, I was going to be able to face my audience. It was not so much that both statements by Amis were incorrect – how could he possibly know the truth, when he had only just met me? – but that a guest should have been treated so ignominiously. However, the dinner ended without further ado, and I prepared for my reading.

The hall was packed, and there were even people standing at the back. I felt surprised but gratified by this large turn-out for a largely unknown poet. I had been requested to read from *The Submerged Village* and from *A Correct Compassion*, and to be sure to end my recital with the title poem from the latter volume. In my diary for 1952, the 4 November entry reads: 'G. M. MacBeth – New College, 6 p.m. Reading Oxford University Union at 8.15.' So I guess that good old George, a fellow farceur if ever there was one, was responsible for the ludicrous events that were to follow.

All went well at first. The audience was attentive, and seemed appreciative. Then I took a deep breath, and started to read 'A Correct Compassion', a poem which it was always torture for me to read. After the first two or three verses, in the midst of the anatomical details, a young man in the front row fainted and had to be carried out. I went on reading. Then another youth fainted and was carried out. I believe there was even a third fatality, but I was so intent on getting through my long poem, I almost lost consciousness of my surroundings. I got to the end of the poem without a mistake, and there was a round of applause. I took a deep breath, thankful that the evening's ordeal was over. I had hardly noticed the fainting youths. But such was my belief in the poem that I felt no surprise at seeing people faint during my reading of it.

The next morning, I was doing some research in the Bodleian when a gentleman of vaguely clerical aspect came up to me and congratulated me on my reading; he had been in the audience the night before. 'What did you think of those people fainting?' he asked. I shrugged and smiled, not knowing how to express my modest satisfaction at this proof of the power of the word. 'I nearly fainted myself,' I replied, and we laughed.

It gradually dawned upon me that the faintings were a hoax, meant to deflate and humiliate. I suppose it must have been one of the very first 'happenings'. I have always looked back on the occasion with a mixture of amusement and repulsion. After that, I gave two or three other readings at Oxford, at one of which I was gratuitously insulted by that Christian boor, C. S. Lewis, always jealous of the success of poets, for he was a failure at poetry himself. He displayed towards his nervous guest a singularly un-Christian lack of charity. But then, from Christians charity is the last thing one expects. I remember he called Louis MacNeice 'an astonishingly ugly person' because John Betjeman (whom he also hated) had praised his poetry. I gave C. S. Lewis a good flash of the old evil eye, and he was in trouble ever afterwards.

It had now become apparent to me that I was not welcome in Britain, and I decided to leave in search of a more congenial home in some other land. My quest for that ideal place took me all over the world, but I have finally settled in Japan, and after living here almost continuously since 1959, I do not contemplate another move. I have at last found a country where the people like me, and where I feel at home as I never did in terrifying Britain. For ever since childhood, the British have terrified me. But that is all over now. Though I have had some problems in Japan, which I shall deal with in detail in my next volume, I have never felt threatened here.

In closing, let me recall something I heard from Elias Canetti round about 1945, when I was staying with Angela Petter in her flat in Hampstead Square. Canetti was living on the top floor with the unusual novelist Anna Sebastian, who fascinated me. In 1935, Canetti's *Auto da Fé* had been published, and Veronica Wedgwood, with Canetti's help, was making an English version. (I had already read it in German.) Anna Sebastian's novel, *Let Thy Moon Arise,* dedicated to Canetti, I thought a most remarkable work. It was published in 1944. I was impressed by Canetti, too, by his silences and composure as much as by what he said. He, like Joe, like my Japanese mentor Atsuo Kobayashi, like Jacob Kramer, was a father figure to me. I tried to make some suggestions about the translation of German words and expressions, but I do not know if he or Veronica Wedgwood accepted them. I only met him a few times, but when, years later, I read of his curious relationship with Dr Sonne at the Café Museum in Vienna I realized that I felt the same about Canetti as he did about that mysterious genius. Canetti told me: 'One should not be a slave to writing, and writing should not be one's slave either. One should simply go on writing.'

I am not sure if those were his exact words, but they give the essence of what he told me. I have always followed his advice, and still 'simply go on writing'.

Epilogue

Journey to a Microsecond

In those days of my youth, everything was poetic, everything a subject for my verse, and everything I saw and did turned naturally into poetry. It was not that I consciously willed each moment of the day to be a poem; the poem of the moment came offering itself to me, so openly, candidly, like a friendly cat or dog, like a trusting child, or a lover with only one idea in mind.

So who was I to refuse such instant gifts? Sometimes the way certain men and women approached me – total strangers wanting immediate intimacy – reminded me of the way a poem would come and go directly to the point of experience, just as today some poor old sex maniac puts his withered hand straight on my agreeable prick, and I let him have his way, not out of pity, but because I want him as I want the moment, with shameless urgency.

Sometimes the days seemed almost too full. There was so much to see, to feel, to write about. I remember just one of those days, about thirty years ago, which began its store of riches with a poem I wrote as soon as I got out of bed that morning, at dawn:

> We know that death grows nearer every night and day,
> and that each second is a life we spend
> with careless prodigality: we all cast recklessly away
> these hours and seasons that we think will never end
> because we dare not measure their relentless tread,
> or dream, in winter memorizing shafts of sun,
> that dawns of summertime may be for ever fled,
> and that we shall not finish what we have begun.
>
> Yet we shall finish everything, and be
> accomplished by the stilling of our songs:
> our fumbling words shall make of silence more than we
> could ever say . . . the inexpressible where poetry belongs.
> – Still we believe that death will wait, not come
> upon a certin time, whose hour is neither late

nor soon. Then let us gladly meditate upon the sum
of all our days, and go with wonder to our death's unalterable date.

Martial music, Sousa's 'Washington Post', was being played over the amplifiers of the public address system that morning at Waterloo Station. The music is a fatuous and dashing march, all glittering brass, whose brashness hid the secret tread of soldiers' boots marching to their death in endless wars. It was the march my pioneering uncle brought to England, recorded on a waxen cylinder, out of the New World, to be the wonder of the gay and dancing girlhood of my mother Mary.

The time is nine o'clock. And on this first day of February that is suddenly, after the long winter, warm and sunny, windy with clouds, and every now and then a fine dust of airy rain, I walk across Waterloo Bridge and into Waterloo Station, trying not to keep in step with Sousa beneath the snow-dirtied dome of the high glass roof, thinking of her, my mother, with love and happiness among the shouts, the talk, the jets of steam and the echoing footfalls of the office workers proceeding with rolled umbrellas, bowlers, briefcases, handbags, newspapers, books from the suburban circulating library, all in business suitings and good dark coats, box-pleated serge skirts; or in the casual smartness of shabby raincoats, trotting on high, hard heels, in sensible shoes towards a dream of business, to the morning cups of coffee at the office, the good-mornings, pleasant hellos, nice days, the private gossip, shop-talk, back-chat, the little lusts and flirts, cheap lunches, snacks, the busy fight for food, or love, or petty power.

The march abruptly stops, but they go marching on, in a kind of vacuum, safe, and yet unsure, protected by a vulnerable, mute, provincial defiance, a background of the river, Surrey, tennis, bridge, and spruce little villas, neighbourly semis. In the sudden hush, the thousands of rushing feet sound like a sea, a withdrawing tide on acres of shingle. The announcer's scrambled tones proclaim, with garbled clarity: 'Uh-the next uh-train for uh-Teddington will leave at uh-nine uh-twenty from p-uh-latform uh-two, uh-stopping at uh-Vauxhall, Clapham Junction, Earlsfield, uh-Wimbledon, R-r-r-raynes uh-Park, Malden, uh-Norbiton, uh-Kingston, Hampton Wick and-uh-Teddington.'

With a rough cluck, the voice clicks off and the band fades in again. . . .

My grassgreen ticket punched by a shaft of sun, I enter the empty train, that waits, whining and faintly throbbing, while the packed green Southern Electrics glide alongside, slide to a standstill, crammed with creatures that burst the coaches open at innumerable seams and disgorge from swinging doors.

Upon the fawn upholstery, with mute excitement I dispose myself ... the little triumph of 'getting a compartment to yourself' ... oh, memory of summer holidays beside a northern sea! ... pales now beside the even greater triumph of having to myself a carriage, an entire train.

I sing with happiness, and, spreading a discarded *Daily Telegraph*, put up my feet upon the worn moquette; but then, impulsively jumping to my feet again, I stride possessively about, slam windows down, do breathing exercises, handstands, jive, and generally raise the dust inside this tomb within a tomb.

But an impending fellow passenger goes by with disapproving stare – he does not care for my inviting wave, intended to discourage. My mouth is full of sweets, and I have taken off my shoes, and placed my stockinged feet out of the window, where the sun's delicious filtered freshness sparkles inventively upon the blonded down, my tanned ankles above my wrinkled socks.

In such a way I must compose myself to face reality, the journey to the shrine of science where I must behave, be good, remembering the lab at school that made me shake with fear. Today I must control myself, be attentive to the things I understand only by intuition, and prepare to steel myself against the further horrors and excitements of the day that is to come. Sousa dies away under the train's motor and the guard's thrilling whistle. Ooh! we're off!

With electric promptness, the whole caboodle lumbers off, all clattering and creaking, clumsily rocking over racketing points, bouncing and sliding and fitfully riding, rumbling and tumbling and cleverly stumbling, now ambling, now speedily scrambling and shambling, on with a rattle of windows and a battle of wheels out of the giant and sunstruck porches of metal and sheds of glass, and bang into the clash of open air, into sun I plunge, into heat and dust and haste and dazzle, the whizzing web of glittering rails that flash and fork and veer and vanish one into the other – out into the world that lies apart and active, like the faded photographs in this compartment (sepia, taken in the twenties) of the Henley Regatta, the Thames at Hampton Wick, and Teddington Lock.

There on the left – (I am riding with my back to the engine now, in case, I suppose, of accidents) – there the river muddles and sparkles under the Houses of Parliament, blocks and hives of offices and flats, the dome of the Tate, the flash of its white steps and before I know where I am the train is in dimness again, in the drab succession of station amenities ... Gentlemen, Ladies, Guinness is, Waiting, Booking, Guinness is, Porters, Guinness is

Good for, Gentlemen Ladies, Way Out! Way Out! – Vauxhall! Vauxhall! Vauxhall! Vauxhall!

A brief stop, the noise of a single slammed door, and a sinister, far-off whistle as non-stop trains, jam-full, sweep through to Town.

On past the Battersea Power Station's classic calm, romanticized by wisps of wind-ripped smoke from the four lofty chimneys; blocks and blocks of flats, all windows, balconies, birdcages, window-boxes, casement curtains, fluttering swags of sheets and bloomers and shirts and drawers and nighties all the way to Clapham Junction, one vast commotion, the station announcer's language shockingly clear, next to my ear: 'Stopping all stations! Stopping all stations!'

The defenceless backs of houses, privvies and privacy in full public view, low in their dark little gardens and allotments and backyards where the cold overnight washing damply and limply droops in the lingering morning-early brick-walled dankness, hanging in wait for the dusted sun to riddle and dry pillowcases and handtowels.

We swoop now through thickly cabled banks of grey cement, a ripple of wooden railings silently rattled by a non-existent running stick in the hands of my boyhood: on and flying along beside and over the laid-out cemetery, checkered with slabs of white and squares of green, not very tidy either, a freshly dug grave, there, with the ghosts of yesterday's mourners ... the sagging flowers, drooping wreaths, a fluttering black-bordered card with demented condolences sincere in back-tilted handwriting, and footprints in the clay of the trampled earth that leads into shabby Earlsfield, Earlsfield, Earlsfield....

Out high over local High Streets, passing the caged day-nursery black with perambulators, baby-booming. And here is an olive green stream bearing bergs of dead white detergent foam like slaughtered swans, drifting, drifting....

On into fields and a rigid ditch that catches a crack of sun, the factory, factories, factory-stacks, houses in rows and mock-Tudor pubs as we smoothly proceed to gentility, semi-detached, and the back-to-back gardens, gardens; we dip, and the Town train crashes past higher and higher, all papers and heads, faces, hats in electrified dullness, smugness, a blurring of first class and third, a merging of holders of season and weekly passes. Oh, that elderly steam locomotive is simple and slow and sedate with its jumble of goods-trucks and rolling-stock vans, the bespectacled guard on the verge of retirement with his back-garden rose buttonhole smiles at his lowered window, a flag intensely green agreeable as shamrocks waves in his reliable hand as on sun-spun rails that dizzily dash and divide, into elegant Wimbledon dimness we sunnily glide . . . pause . . . then out past the squash and badminton club . . . O, for a girl with a long-handled racket! . . . out into roofs that are wet here with dew, slates that are razor-bright over respectable roads, a tall chimney waltzes away on a background of common, parkland and woods to the bank and the shops and the white-fronted Rialto . . . Raynes Park! Raynes Park! the station announcers all bark, then a gabble of names and a slamming of doors as we fly into flickering trees, past the seed manufactory, flowerbeds bare and the cute model golf course . . . 'Golf courses laid out anywhere, anywhere, Golf' the noticeboard promises.

Gardens and fields with a red tennis court for the long summer evenings set like a bloodbath in acres and acres of goalposted, tree-sheltered sports grounds belonging to Works. Into Malden, the very-near rural with shrubs on the platform, the cream-painted steps of the signalbox urgently steep, down through a cutting and under a railway bridge where trains flurry over, a coal depot mountain of coal, coke and clinkers, the back-garden glasshouses flashing to level and lower-class allotments.

There, look, is a children's playground in the municipal green of a local park, the swings hang empty, and the slide gleams like a waterfall shined by the friction and luminous speed of a million backsides, all now shining the common bench of school, while I, lucky Jim, on a whim of the bright anarchic sun, whirl on my whole-day holiday run!

Everything's new! I'm seeing things like old converted air-raid shelters in backdoor plots where the men are gone and only the women of all the mornings gossip and gaze. Through a standing train's filthy windows, the washing is fluttering high on the propped-up clothes-pegged line; there are birds dipping the upshot telegraph wires flailed and slashed by implacable poles, and a mad dog, black and white, is flinging itself on the wire mesh at the garden's bottom, and barking loud, but I cannot hear in the rushing train that slowly slowing, stopping just outside Norbiton, brings me face to face with a pudgy baby snugly seated in a smart new pram. It looks at me. I put out my tongue at it . . . Ugh! . . . and pull a ferocious face . . . Boo! It stares in amazement a moment, then it begins to collapse its face, and a silent howl stretches its angry mouth like a tragic mask. I throw it a sweet, and a woman, drying her hands on a butcher's apron, dashes out of the dishwashing, bed-making, bread-baking house, but before the baby can tell her what is the matter, hurrah! the train is off and away, leaving behind us a small perplexity. 'Norbiton! Norbiton!' the announcer absurdly shouts, and his voice seems conscious of its absurdity. If you say 'Norbiton' often enough it becomes meaningless, as he has long since discovered.

Its nonsensical sound lingers in my mind all the way to Kingston, where women with baskets enter my carriage, my compartment. Kingston-upon-Thames, where the river is high, and the station is cool and calm under its sunny glass, past the gasometers, woodyards, coal-washing plants and loaded barges, over the bridge to Hampton Wick bedraggled in a fringe of houseboats, and the train suddenly runs high in the trees, in the treetops of gardens, a glimpse of an orange-red brick Victorian terrace, then gasworks, gasworks again and again, only just restrained by their elegant metal corsets, and old, comfortable-looking detached houses 'standing in own spacious grounds' as the estate agents say. Yes, definitely now we are in a neighbourhood known as better class – 'The river gives it distinction, of course, with its wonderful bridges,' one lady informs another, but looking warily at me, as if she could not be listening to what she was saying. 'And Kingston, after all, is such a good shopping centre ... yes, such convenient shops.... Lovely, lovely ...'

I leave the ladies to their chatter, and descend at Teddington. I'm there at last! Teddington! Teddington! Teddington!

Why have I come here? I hardly know, because I do not like to think about what is going to happen. So, for a moment, I think of other things, but find myself regarding everything with a sense of occasion, with that revolting clarity, so persuasive in delirious dreamings, that clinging memory that is said to accompany our final, drowning view of life.

Is this my final view of life? Not exactly, though in a way it is, as each second is the whole of time, that final second, and this life is the only one that we shall know unless we find illumination in the earth, or in ourselves, a Zenergy of meditation. We all go now towards a last illumination, the final flash of knowledge.

But Teddington is not Damascus. Teddington is nice, despite the dangerously leaning double-decker buses and the dinky villas. This was where Nöel Coward spent a precious, precocious theatrical childhood – suburbia produces some curious throwbacks. Throwbacks to what? From where? What secrets lie behind these dark brick mossy walls that sometimes bulge across a worn, uneven pavement, weed-hung, wind-sown extensions of melancholy privacies they would exclude us from – the long-neglected paths and gardens of another age's country leisure. Here are a pleasant few late Victorian, bow-windowed streets, the paper blinds half-lowered, as if in half-mourning, the white lace curtains tightly drawn on glimpses of dark brown chiffoniers, mahogany stands for aspidistras, and dimly papered walls where hang green-spotted, shallow pools of mirror glass. An air of lost importance, of being somewhere, but nowhere in particular, yet nice, and a trifle off, embracing the 27 bus terminus in Adelaide Road, filling-stations, sweetshops and the Clarendon Hotel. And somehow, in the trembling air, the hint of the bright-light river-waters running somewhere beyond the slated roofs, the mittened chimneypots, the railway bridge.

Down a straight, neat little street I go, passing the Children's Riding School, the stables where the patient horses stand and sniff and follow me with their so-gentle, dark and liquid eyes as I tiptoe past the high wooden fence, making a long neck to look, and whisper my name and business to them. They do not seem quite to understand, but that does not matter. In a way that I cannot understand myself, we understand each other. They are my last contact with the outer world, and so they are very precious to me; for beyond these elegant wrought-iron gates I see before me, I do not know exactly what to expect. Oh, there will be people, certainly, and I can even see some now, walking at liberty among the square brick buildings, whose modern windows give on mysteries.

But they are beings who look – though it is wrong to think so – not like ordinary people. Beside them, I feel guilty, lost, afraid and vague. These, I feel, are superior beings who have everything in order. They, surely, are able to plan ahead, their lives well-organized, austere and good. They must be able to fill in forms with impeccable adroitness: they do their Income Tax as others do the Pools, and their contributions to National Health Insurance, holiday funds, house purchase, pensions and the like are scrupulously paid. They are the norm that is desirable and good. My own haphazard helplessness is like a burden now. I do not fit, as these do, into a new society, a brave new world. I feel my guilt is great. Again, they are, one supposes, scientists, and I am not a scientist. The gulf is wide. Shall we be able to understand each other? Shall we communicate in common words, with a communion as intelligible as the swift, instinctive knowledge that the horses had of me, and I of the horses? Scientists, I feel, must be a race apart, and not as close to me as the animals we so mistakenly call 'dumb'. But though they speak another tongue, we, the others, the outsiders, must learn to master it, and speak to them.

And here with gratitude I remember others whom one might truly call scientists – those who have a knowledge peculiar to themselves – the great surgeon expressive as an actor, the astronomer gentle as a child, the acrobat of my schooldays, with his stream of circus chat and imprecations. The flamenco gypsy dancer's male, abrupt and voluble *zapateado*. The northern miners, the pit lads with their donkeys, the shipyard workers, and the beggars, expert in chosen vocabularies.

All these I understood, though often what they said was strange. I want to understand the scientists, the new gods of the terrible techniques that kill or save us. But though I know that those beyond the gates will speak the English of my ancestors, they will be using words that I shall not have learnt, and whose half-glimpsed significance I grapple blindly after, in a daze of half-forgotten Greek and half-remembered Latin. Yet the gift of tongues is in us all, if we will use it. There is no language barrier; only the barrier of will, and prejudice, the only one that separates, antagonizes. 'There's none as deaf as those who will not hear.' But I want to hear, and understand. There is an intelligence within the heart and in our common flesh, an irregular but ordered syntax. These shall be interpreters, translators of our understanding in an idiom we all must share.

I pass the gates, out of the sun, into the shadows of 'Enquiries', where a temporary pass is issued – a mortal slip of perishable stuff that I must treasure like my own identity. I am that person it declares itself to stand for, and mustn't forget it.

It is ten o'clock. My punctuality is royal. I am alive on time.

The grounds are as agreeable as a Teddington villa's – lawns and flower-beds; a bare-patched wilderness of grasses that in summer is a putting green. All lie dead today, and mute beneath the deep, insistant throbbing of the air around the immaculate Compressor Plant.

But here, in a sheltered bay by an office block, Iris Stylosa prematurely stains its grassy plaits with purple in a sun that curls last summer's brown and papery blades. There is a small cemented stream, its waters miraculously simple, ever-changing; a bridge, and shrubbery, and trees around the building that houses the meticulous atomic clock, a miniature solar system in a ring of quartz ... though even this appears to gain in summertime, and lose in winter. 'We are fairly sure that it does not, in fact, behave in this way, and the inference is that it is the unit of time that is changing.' A dizzy thought – 'And though our atomic clock is a welcome piece of constructive science, it will not entirely replace the earth as a standard that will still control the six pips and the time signals.' – It will not entirely replace the earth – thank God for that.

A chestnut here, outside the Royal Residence of Bushy House, that Charles II, as tradition has it, well and truly planted, now is an ancient, black and sprawling, lightning-palsied hulk, still inexplicably alive, and noble.

There is everywhere a casual, yet busy air – the noticeboards are alive with notices of lectures, sociable activities and clubs – the Christian Union, the Savings Group, the Film Society, the Old-Time Dancing, Camera Club, the Amateur Dramatic Circle, who present another sparkling West End success.

Under an acid sun, white-coated workers flash bleak spectacles in air as blue as waterworks, and walk briskly, their faces brightened by the upcast brightness of technical reports, upon the well-kept gravel paths, or, deviating seriously, stroll upon the little lawns.

A uniformed guardian from the gatehouse, pleasantly chatting, now conducts me to my assignation with a microsecond . . . to the High Voltage Laboratory, a tall and sunny theatre, in whose chill enormous thunderstorms are generated. 'Are they going to do a few big bangs for you?' the kind custodian inquires. 'I'm afraid so,' is my reluctant answer. For I who as a boy was struck by lightning on the way to a forbidden rendezvous – with Mae West in black and white – still feel appalled by memories of shock, by what my vague and unscientific mind describes as 'anything electric'.

They are nice to me inside . . . a handful of youthful operators and assistants, and one in charge who has the contemplative, abstracted air of a poet or a dreamer, who speaks with authority, yet in a gentle, distant voice, as if the constant storms around his head had made him realize the value of quietness.

In an obscure corner, hidden by forests of apparatus, someone is sending electric currents through small carborundum disks, exploding them with gay science, practised precision. 'These disks,' he explains, 'are being semi-conductor tested. We've picked some duds, specially for you, because we want you to see them really bust. Here's one – look, we turn the fractured side away from you – you get quite a lot of splinters flying about, you know, in this kind of test.'

I watch with wary eyes: a sharp crack, a spark of light, and the test is over. 'Nothing very fierce,' they say. They talk of cathode-ray oscillographs and voltages with the charming assumption that I understand, and curiously enough this makes me understand. Their good will smashes the language barrier.

At the other end of the colossal hall there stands the contraption that really does the trick: the Surge Generator, 'which produces voltage surges having a peak value of two million volts'. Four tall towers of giant insulators are branched with aluminium rods and spheres – 'We call those spark-gaps.' The towers are chocolate brown, banded with sky blue rings, the inter-stage gaps. 'Why this particular colour scheme?' – 'Well, the brown is the colour of the natural glaze, and that particular shade of blue is ... well, I believe we thought it would go nicely with the chocolate brown.' The reply is very reassuring; there is an aesthetic here among the mathematical formulae and scientific calculations.

In another corner, two gigantic aluminium spheres hover one above the other, with a hand's breadth between them. 'These are the sphere-gaps,' I am told. 'Oh. Yes.' – 'For measuring voltages,' the explanation adds, and I reply: 'I see.' And I *do* see, though not, perhaps, what they do.

High in the roof, two glassy tubes of gleaming insulators seem to point towards the awful gap between them.

'You see, it became necessary to investigate the phenomena that occur when the voltage applied to electrical equipment exceeds the safe limit.'

'I see.'

'Breakdown depends not only on voltage, but also on the distance across which the voltage exists, and the time for which it is maintained.'

'Yes?'

'High voltages are safe only if they exist across sufficiently large distances, and the High Voltage Laboratory was specially constructed to provide exceptionally high voltages across big distances, both accurately controllable. . . .'

So that is how the lightning is created, and the thunder made.

'In this way, a great deal of work is done for manufactories of transformers and cables who need to know how their products will behave in service when subjected to voltage surges, as when lightning strikes overhead lines.'

'Oh, yes, the effect of lightning. . . .'

'The various manifestations of breakdown – puncture, flashover and associated phenomena like corona discharges – are investigated.'

I screw my eyes, and seem to see already a flash that blinds me, hear a detonation so immediate that I am stunned and blinded equally at once.

'We'll do a few big bangs for you, if you like. . . .'

'I would like, very much. . . .'

The operator ascends to the control room. The workers leave the laboratory, and, from behind a glass partition, prepare to watch, while I am left alone inside the place, behind a safety-railing, feeling ridiculously small, vulnerable, and remote.

There is a humming noise. Somebody shouts. 'We're just warming up!' The noise grows louder. My hands, I find, are tightly clenched, so I unclench them. But in a moment they are, I notice, clenched again, and I keep them clenched, irrationally clenched.

I stand, waiting, enshrined in my winter overcoat, both chilled and fevered, hoping, yet not hoping, for it to be over and done with. . . . The sunlight glitters on the metals and the tiles, upon the glassy rods between which, in a brilliant microsecond, two million volts will pass, and I standing beneath them. This is what it must feel like to be waiting for execution in the electric chair.

I press my back against the wall. The noise increases to a howl. I remember a definition: 'Noise is sound unwanted by the recipient.'

Teeth, now, as well as hands are clenched against I know not what convulsive agony of shock. The noise rises to a scream. I look up, at once am blind with absolute light, then see again, the penalty for seeing is then a resounding crack of thunder that rolls away around the blasted hall.

At school, in the physics lessons I so much hated and feared, I was taught, I think, that thunder is the noise of heated air expanding suddenly. Again and yet again the vision is accorded me, till I begin to see, battered by whip-crack storms, the track of energy that thrills my spine; my hands. My fingers chill and tingle. They're growing louder! Flash and flash and flash! I see myself a prophet on the summit of a mountain, holding the lightnings in either hand, or Lear upon the blasted heath. The vision ceases, and I behold instead an experiment in science. Vision and experiment are one.

I have had my moment of illumination, as after long meditation, years of Zen, the microsecond revelation of eternity. My stiff legs tremble as I walk outside, shake hands, and give my thanks to science and her priests.

Outside, where there are trees and grass and wind and sun and the unaffected birds, I turn away. This is what I came for, and it is done. Shattered and renewed, restored to life, and listening half to my guide's consoling chatter, half to my own interior commotion, I proceed to view the reverberation chambers, the high-speed wind-tunnels and the ship-testing canals.

I look and listen, listen, look and look. All day I wander, from laboratory to laboratory, seeing nothing but that supernatural and real blaze whose after-image lingers in my brain, my eyes scorched irretrievably with caustic sight. I blink in the sun whose light, I feel with gratitude and disappointment, is too small, a winter gentleness of afternoon after the tropic furnaces of morning. But I have seen! I have seen! Illumination enfolds me in waves of ecstatic energy and thrills of panic.

At dusk, I go towards the gates again, establish my identity – am I still the same person as when I entered? – and walk out freely into the unseeing world, into the clear-dark sunset air of winter, passing the homely, scented stables, under heavenly fires, impending stars, into the long reversal of my outward journey, whose destination was that microsecond flash – back to the terminus that was my new beginning, where, with evening sentiment, an old-time waltz is playing my mother's favourite: 'Nights of Gladness'.

This, too, is part of the vision, as the music moves to 'Gold and Silver', and I go back into the long reversal of my life, my birth that speeds regretfully, in painful ignorance, towards a certain close, the final flash of dying, the ultimate illumination of the dark.

But have I really understood? What is that dated death whose microsecond no one knows?

Index

Abbott, Professor Claude, 216
Absolute Beginners (MacInnes), 155
Ackerley, Joe, 71, 72, 95, 226, 227, 231; as *Listener* literary editor, 4, 83–5, 120, 184, 189–92, 200–202, 206–7, 215, 219–20; encouragement of and friendship with Kirkup, 84–5, 120, 184, 187–98, 200–207, 208, 209, 236; first meeting with, 187, 189, 190–6; sexuality, 187, 191, 192, 193, 194, 196, 203–4, 205; wit and mimicry, 187–8; voice, 188–9; jealousy, 197, 205; as father-figure, 207, 239; correspondence with, 212–16, 217–20; on modern poetry, 213–14
Ackerley, Nancy, 155, 184, 187, 188, 196–7, 205, 215, 219
Adam-Smith, Janet, 202
Adelphi, The, 49, 83, 96
Adler, Jankel, 168
Advertisers' Annual, The, 182
Advertisers' Weekly, The, 182–4, 202
Aida, Yuji, 129
Ainley, Richard, 225
Akhmatova, Anna, 224
Alexander, Rolf, 79
Allison, Kathleen, 220, 221
Allison, Professor Philip, 217, 218, 220–23
Allott, Kenneth, 228
Amherst College, Massachusetts, 106
Amis, Kingsley, 237, 238
Amitiés particulières, Les (Peyrefitte), 25
And Then You Came (Bridge), 210
Anderson, Hedli, 208
Andrews, W. L., 224
Angell, Norman, 16, 48
Anglo-German Circle, 52
Apparitions (Ashton ballet), 77
Appleby, 93
Archer, David, 200
Armstrong, Kenneth, 233–4
Armstrong, Louis, 167
Artaud, Antonin, 176
Artificial Princess, The (Firbank), 192
Aryan Path, The, 49
Asahi Evening News, 132
Asahi Shimbun, 131
Ashton, Frederick, 76, 77
Atlantic Award in Literature, 208, 209, 210
Auden, W. H., 26, 82, 111, 115, 119, 192
Augustine, St, 72
Authors' World Peace Appeal, 223–4
Auto da Fé (Canetti), 239
Ayres, Ruby M., 224

Baden-Powell, Lord, 53
Baker, George, 228
Balanchine, George, 77
Balfe, Michael, 81
Ballet Imperial (Balanchine), 77
Ballet Joos, 79
Banting, John, 91
Barbette, 31
Barbusse, Henri, 48
Barker, George, 165
Basel, 39
Bath Academy of Art, 55, 211, 223, 233, 234, 236
Batley, James, 117–18
Baudelaire, Charles, 18, 35
Bayliss, John, 85
'Beautiful Negress, The' (Pitter), 155–6
Beauvoir, Simone de, 35
Beckett, Samuel, 213
Behan, Brendan, 176
Béjart, Maurice, 79
Bell, Madeleine, 11–12
Belton, Bill, 168, 171, 180
Belton, Blossom, 168, 171

Benda, Julien, 3, 4
Bennett, Arnold, 184
Bentley, Eric, 9
Berg, Alban, 79
Bernhardt, Sarah, 28
Betjeman, John, 165, 239
Between Two Worlds (Murry), 96
Biel, 19
Blishen, Edward, 48
Bliss, Arthur, 210
Blunden, Edmund, 212, 224
Bradshaw, Harry, 11
Braybrooke, Neville, 190, 197, 206, 213
Breguet, Jacques, 22
Breguet, Louis, 22
Breton, André, 13
Brevier, Ein (Grabbe), 9–10
Bridge, Ann, 210
Briginshaw, Richard W., 201
British Broadcasting Corporation, 8, 70, 189, 200–202, 226; witch-hunts in, 202–3; censorship, 206
British Council, 188, 205, 207
Britishness of the British, The (ed. Toshihiko), 130
Brittain, Vera, 224
Britten, Benjamin, 26, 199, 206
Buckingham, Bob, 199
Bund Deutscher Mädel, 52
Burgess, Guy, 77, 171, 172
Burra, Edward, 90
Burrall, Ashton, 165, 166
Burroughs, William, 176
Butler, R. A., 207
Butler, Reg, 223

Callas, Maria, 80
Campaign for Nuclear Disarmament, 110
Campbell, Roy, 82, 166
Canetti, Elias, 239
Carl Rosa Opera Company, 80, 208
Carrington, Dora, 188
Castle Bolton, 90, 92
Céline, Louis-Ferdinand, 48
Chadwick, Lynn, 233
Chamberlain, Neville, 22, 26, 40
Chapiet, Mary, 11
Chatterton (Vigny), 4
Chatterton, Ruth, 81
Chatto and Windus, 210, 211
Chekhov, Anton, 92
Cherkeshi, Sadi, 11, 18, 82, 166
Childe, Wilfred Rowland, 210, 214, 224, 228, 231
Chur, 38, 39
Church, Richard, 187, 210, 215
Churchill, Winston, 40, 56, 130
Cimetière Marin, Le (Valéry), 211
City Center Joffrey Ballet, 79
City of Spades (MacInnes), 155, 171
Clare, John, 208
Clark, Leonard, 227
Classic German Theatre (Bentley), 9
Cliburn, 94–5, 107
Cocteau, Jean, 5, 31, 35
Collins, Cecil, 90
Colquhoun, Ithell, 177
Colquhoun, Robert, 168
Colwall, 115–19, 120
Colyer, Ken, 167
Comédie Française, 28
Comfort, Alex, 83, 166, 224
Comic Cuts (Findlater), 206n
Compton-Burnett, Ivy, 11
Condorcet, Marquis de, 3
Conquest, Robert, 213
Constant Wife, The (Maugham), 81
Contemporary Verse (ed. Allott), 228, 234
Coppard, A. E., 224
Corsham, 55, 207, 211, 233–7
Cortot, Alfred, 28
Craig, Alec, 165, 166
Cranach, Lucas, 229
Crevel, René, 35
Crime and Punishment (Dostoevsky), 92
Crisp, Quentin, 171, 192
Croft-Cooke, Rupert, 224

Dante Alighieri, 9
Darkness in Summer (Kaiko), 35
Darley, George, 13
Day-Lewis, Cecil, 82, 210–11, 224
De Sausmarez, Kate, 223
De Sausmarez, Maurice, 223
Debussy, Claude, 28
Dehn, Paul, 219
Desbordes-Valmore, Marcelline, 22
Descartes, René, 3
Desnos, Robert, 71
Deutsch-Englischer Kreis, 52

Dick, Kay, 70
Dickinson, Goldsworthy Lowes, 199
Dint, 82
Dobrée, Professor Bonamy, 202, 209, 210, 230–1
Dominique (Fromentin), 4
Don Carlos (Schiller), 9
Donat, Robert, 204
Dostoevsky, Feodor, 92
Douai, 20, 22, 28–9; Ecole Normale d'Instituteurs, 10, 11, 22–6, 29, 31–4
Douglas, Keith, 82
Downs School, Colwall, 115–19, 208, 223
D'Oyly Carte Company, 81
Dryden, John, 208
'Duke, Lord Earl', 181
Durham, 177
Durham University, 18, 20; Armstrong College, 3–12, 37; French Society, 5, 10, 11, 15, 37; degree from, 3, 8, 45
Dürrenmatt, Friedrich, 72n
Dussane, Béatrix, 28
Duthuit, Georges, 213, 218, 220
Dyall, Franklin, 81
Dyall, Valentine, 81

East Witton, 85, 87, 88–90, 92, 93
Ehrenburg, Ilya, 224
Eigoseinen, 198
Einstein, Albert, 110
Eliot, T. S., 56, 83, 85n, 166, 181, 182, 225
Ellis, Charlotte, 233
Ellis, Clifford, 211, 233, 236
Ellis, Rosemary, 233, 236
Eluard, Paul, 5, 11
Emmet, Dorothy, 12
Empson, William, 177
Enfants du paradis, Les (film), 82
English Festival of Spoken Poetry (1954), 78
Epstein, Jacob, 92
Evans, Dr Joan, 188, 231
Evans-Davies, Gloria, 201
Evening Standard, 220

Faber and Faber, 56, 166, 189
Façade (Walton), 76
Faith called Pacifism, The (Plowman), 17, 49, 50–51, 56
Falstone, 169
Farjeon, Annabel, 76
Fausset, Hugh Ianson, 85, 99
Faux Monnayeurs, Les (Gide), 35
Feild, Maurice, 116, 117, 118, 119, 208, 223
Fergar, Feyyaz, 11, 82, 166
Feu, Le (Barbusse), 48
Findlater, Richard, 206n
Firbank, Ronald, 11, 15, 152, 174, 191, 192, 210, 217
Fisher, H. A. L., 57
Fitzgerald, Scott, 226
Flaubert, Gustave, 35
Fléchier, Valentin, 3
Fleming, Ian, 96–9
Fokine, Michel, 37
Fontane, Theodor, 9
Fonteyn, Margot, 76, 77, 78
Forestry Commission, 59–68, 85, 87, 88–90, 169
Forster, E. M., 188, 196, 198, 202, 204, 206, 209, 218; and friendship, 199–200
Four Quartets (Eliot), 83
Franca, Celia, 76
Franco, General, 18
Franklin, Benjamin, 16
Fraser, G. S., 165
Fromentin, Eugène, 4
'From Childhood's Hour' (Poe), 69
Front Populaire, 27
Frost, Terry, 233
Froy, Martin, 223
Fry, Anthony, 233
Fry, Christopher, 224
Fuji from Hampstead Heath (Komai), 165
Fulcrum, 82
Fuller, Rosalinde, 225–6
Fyvel, T. R., 86

Gardiner, Wrey, 83, 85, 163
Gascoyne, David, 13, 164, 166
Gastinel, Professor Pierre, 27
Gay News, 171
Gayan, Pierre, 28
Genet, Jean, 35, 176
George, Stefan, 9
Gide, André, 5, 31, 35
Gidley, James, 93
Girdlestone, Professor Cuthbert M., 9, 18, 27, 29, 32–3, 37; persecution of Kirkup, 3, 4–8, 10–11, 12, 20; Kirkup's desire to murder, 3, 5, 7

Girls' Friendly Society, 225
'Go, lovely rose' (Suckling), 163
Gods go A-Begging, The (Ashton ballet), 76
Goethe, Johann Wolfgang von, 9, 38
Golden Heresy, The (Plowman), 49
Goudge, Elizabeth, 224
Gowing, Lawrence, 228
Grabbe, Dietrich Christian, 9–10
Graecen, Robert, 83
Grammaire, La (Labiche), 28
Grand Meaulnes, Le (Alain-Fournier), 230
Grapelli, Stéphane, 25
Great Illusion, The (Angell), 48
Green Table, The (Joos ballet), 79
Gregory, Peter, 209; Fellowship, 202, 209–10, 211–12, 230–31
Grey Walls Press, 83, 85
Grigson, Geoffrey, 100
Grillparzer, Franz, 9
Gryszpan, Herschel, 33, 34
Guer, Professor Guerlin de, 27

Hamilton, Willie, 88
Hamlet (Helpmann ballet), 76, 91
Hamnett, Nina, 168
Hand and Flower Press, 213–14
Harris, Robert, 189
Harrison, Eric, 36
Hauptmann, Gerhart, 9
Heath-Stubbs, John, 165
Hebbel, Friedrich, 9
Heine, Heinrich, 9
Helpmann, Robert, 76, 77, 91
Hepworth, Barbara, 85, 100
Herring, Robert, 83
Herzen, Alexander, 169
Hesse, Hermann, 9
Hewitt, Jack, 76
Heytesbury House, 72
Hickleton Hall, 224
Hiroshima, 109, 110
History of Socialism (T. Kirkup), 203
Hitler, Adolf, 51, 53
Hitler Youth, 52, 53
Holes in the Sky (MacNeice), 189
Holroyd, Michael, 188
Howard, Andrée, 76
Hoyland, Geoffrey, 115n, 119
Hull University College summer schools, 224–6
Huxley, Aldous, 174, 188
Huysmans, J. K., 35

Iden, Rosalind, 81
Indications, 85, 97
Infante de Castille (Montherlant), 21
Inglesby, Mona, 79
'Insensibility' (Owen), 73–4
International Ballet, 79
International Surrealist Exhibition (1936), 166
Irizar, Agostin de, 224, 227, 228
Irving, Washington, 69n
Isherwood, Christopher, 26, 199

Jackson, George, 90
Jennings, Paul, 178
Jervaulx Abbey, 89–90
Jeune Parque, La (Valéry), 144, 182
Joos, Kurt, 79

Kafka, Franz, 9
Kaiko, Takeshi, 35
Kavan, Anna, 224
Kennedy, Ludovic, 77, 78
Kenzaburo, Oe, 35
Kerr, Rose, 52
Kettle, Arnold, 216
Kettlewell, 221
Kikkawa, Professor Jun'ichi, 133
King, Francis, 85, 188, 197
King Lear, 216
Kingdom Come, 168
Kipling, Rudyard, 56
Kirkup, James: childhood, xiii–xxi, 135–7; 'apartness' and loneliness, xiv, xv, xviii, xx, 13, 69–72, 170, 230; androgynous appearance, xiv, xv, 55, 187, 190; asthma and emphysema, xiv, 11, 86, 96, 100, 105, 106, 233; exhibitionism and tomfoolery, xv–xix; 'gift of tongues', xviii; gift of laughter, xviii–xix; multiple personality, xix–xxi; as *farceur*, xix, 4, 10, 18; pacifism, xix, 6, 15–17, 18, 26, 33, 39, 40, 48–58, 72–4, 95, 105, 110–11, 115, 203; longing for ideal friend, xxi, 71, 170, 236; university life, 3–12, 15, 18, 37; study of French and German, 3–5, 7, 8–10; disappointing degree, 8, 45; self-destructive nature,

10–11; pre-war year in France, 11, 19, 20–35; writing of surrealist poetry, 11, 12, 13, 82, 84, 85; constraints of home life, 15, 17, 18–19, 145; pretended flippancy and decadence, 18, 19; bisexuality, 19, 21, 30, 33, 34, 54, 55, 86, 95, 96, 105, 106, 171, 193, 194, 204–5, 241; 'evil eye', 23, 57, 87, 239; academic life in France, 23–5, 27, 29, 31–2; and growing political tension, 26–7, 31, 33–5, 38, 53; musical, operatic and theatrical occasions, 28, 36, 76–82; amateur hustling and encounters, 30, 33, 34, 86, 99–100, 172, 174, 230; literary enthusiasms, 35; and existentialism, 35; summer vacation teaching in Switzerland, 37, 38; return home on outbreak of war, 39–41; registered as conscientious objector, 48, 53, 55–7, 75; rift with father over pacifism, 53–5; later reconciliation, 55, 75, 110, 111; land work, 57, 59–68, 85, 87, 88–96, 99, 101–4, 107–10; literary activity, 59, 82–6, 117; solitude, 69–72, 172, 230; 'invisibility', 70; gradual recognition as writer, 83–5; 'on the run', 90, 95; artist friends, 90–92, 100, 118, 168, 227–8, 233; as tutor in West Country, 100; ill-health, 105–6; peacetime teaching posts, 115–20, 145; failure as teacher, 118–20, 144; release from National Service, 120–21; indigent life, 121–3, 178, 181; applications for grants and awards, 123, 208, 209; furore over conciliatory attitude to Japanese, 124–32; and British attitude to Japanese, 132–3; poor employment prospects, 144–5; translation efforts, 144; 'escape' to London, 145 *et seq.*; lodgings and landladies, 146–56, 175, 179–80, 211; literary life, 165–6, 168–9, 189 *et seq.*; animosity of British poets, 166, 239; pub and club life, 167–9, 171, 176; brief country spells, 174, 208–9, 231–3; and black market, 176; search for employment, 178; as deputy for pavement artist, 181–2; as sub-editor on trade paper, 182–4; bubble-blowing episode, 183; as reviewer and poet, 189, 190, 204, 206–7, 210–11, 214–15, 219–23, 228; in Ackerley circle, 198–200, 204, 209; and bitchiness of literary and academic life, 200–202, 203, 205, 207, 209; feeling of unease and hostility, 202, 204, 205–6, 207, 229–30, 234–5, 236; attitude to politics, 202–3; return to academic life, 202, 209–10, 211–12, 228, 230–31, 233, 234, 236; belief in reincarnation, 216; present at heart operation, 217–18, 219–23; and summer schools of drama, 224–6; return of childhood shyness, 229; new enjoyment of life and poetry, 234; teaching in Sweden and Spain, 237; settlement in Japan, 239;

WRITINGS:

'Blessed Received in Paradise, The', 178
Candle in the Heavens, 225, 226
'Convenience, The', 206
'Correct Compassion, A', 202, 217–18, 219–23, 238
Cosmic Shape, The, 92
Creation, The, 92, 117
'Croquis', 82
Descent into the Cave, The, 202, 207
'Drain, The', 207
Drowned Sailor, The, 82, 85, 90, 100
'Dustbins, The', 206, 207
'For a Dead Gardener', 165
'Hornpipe', 82
'House in Summer', 234
'In a London Schoolroom', 190
'Kitchen Sink, The', 207
'Legend', 82, 198
'Mortally', 85, 189
'Music at Night', 106, 212n
'Negro Spirituals', 156
'Not Cricket', 129
'One Day in the Middle of a War', 59–68, 169
Only Child, The, 70, 234
Paper Windows: Poems from Japan, 129n
Prodigal Son, The, 237
Refusal to Conform: Last & First Poems, 84, 90
Search for Love, The, 144
'Ship, The', 121
Sorrows, Passions and Alarms, 92, 234
'Sound of Fountains, The', 23
'Still Life', 86
Submerged Village, The, 106, 120, 121,

WRITINGS—*contd.*
156, 198, 210, 212n, 215
'Tea in a Space Ship', 234
'Ten Pure Sonnets', 90
These Horned Islands, 99
'They've Got Me', 84
Triumph of Harmony, The: A Masque, 225
Upon This Rock, 225
'Variations on a Theme', 83
'Wild Wilbur', 100
Kirkup, James Harold (father), 37, 85, 105, 204, 207; and son's childhood, xiii, xiv, xvii, 15–17, 136; son's growing away from, 15, 17, 54; war service, 15–16, 50; and son's pacifism, 15–16, 17, 53–4, 55, 75; awareness of son's sexual preferences, 19, 54; and son's disappointing degree, 45; acceptance of son's sexuality, 55, 236; opposition to 'artistic' interests, 76, 80; reconciled to son's pacifism, 110, 111, 115; distress over conciliatory view of Japanese, 125, 126, 128, 132; worry over son's career, 144, 145; generous offer, 145; retirement, 231, 233, 234–7; distress over villagers' hostility, 236–7; death, 237
Kirkup, Mary (mother), 37, 46, 53, 85, 105, 204, 207; and son's childhood, xiii, xiv, xvi, xvii, 136; and son's disappointing degree, 45; acceptance of son's pacifism and sexuality, 55, 75, 110, 115; sympathy over love of music, 76, 80; distress over hostile publicity, 125, 126, 128, 132; worry over son's career, 144, 145; life in country, 231, 233, 234–7; and village hostility, 236–7
Kirkup, Thomas, 203
Kleist, Heinrich von, 9
Knight, G. Wilson, 81, 216
Kobayashi, Atsuo, 239
Komai, Gloria, 165n
Komai, Gonnosuke, 165n
Kondoh, Tetsuji, 124, 125, 126, 128, 130, 131–2
Kramer, Jakob, 92, 227–8, 229, 239
Kraus, Karl, 19
Kyoto, 130, 133, 188, 223

La Fayette, Madame de, 4
Labiche, Eugène, 28
Lamb, Henry, 188
Lamb, Warren, 225
Lambert, Constant, 78, 91
Langham, 96
Lannes, Roger, 31
Lansbury, Angela, 95
Lansbury, George, 95
Lansbury Gate Farm, Clavering, 95–6, 98, 99
Lanyon, Peter, 233
Last Puritan, The (Santayana), 13
Lautréamont, Comte de, 194
Lawrence, D. H., 8
Lawrence, T. E., 194
Lawson, Fred, 91–2, 220
Le Piquet, 31
Leavis, F. R., 166
Leech, Christopher, 201
Leeder, Sigurd, 79
Leeds, 36, 217, 220, 227–8, 229–30; General Infirmary heart operation, 217–18, 221–3
Leeds Fireclay Company Journal, 220
Leeds University, 81, 216, 223–4, 227, 228; Gregory Fellowship, 202, 209–10, 211–12, 230–31
Lehmann, John, 82
Leopardi, Giacomo, 9
Lessing, G. E., 9
Let Thy Moon Arise (Sebastian), 239
Levertov, Denise, 168
Levison, Christopher, 237
Lewis, C. S., 239
Lewis, Wyndham, 187
Leyburn, 90, 92, 93
Li T'ai-po, 170
Life and Letters Today, 76, 83
Lille, 20, 27–8, 29, 30–1, 34
Lindsay, Jack, 224
Listener, The, 82–4, 184, 191–2, 206; Kirkup's contributions to, 4, 85, 120, 121, 189, 202, 207, 219, 220; vendetta against, 200–202
'Lodge, The' (Batley), 117–18
London Bulletin, 166
'Loneliness Persona' (Sakutaro), 71
Lorenzaccio (Musset), 27
Lotus Press, 117
Lovell, Mona, 174

Ludwig, Otto, 9
Lyra (ed. Comfort and Graecen), 83

MacBeth, George, 238
McBride, Robert, 168
Macgregor, D. H., 8
Macgregor, Lilias, 9
MacInnes, Colin, 155, 171
Maclean, Donald, 171, 172
MacNeice, Daniel, 208
MacNeice, Louis, 82, 189, 208, 239
Magritte, René, 166
Makoto, Tamaki, 187
Manchester Guardian, 26
Mandelstam, Osip, 224
Mann, Thomas, 9
Marais, Jean, 31
Marvell, Andrew, 161
Massachusetts Institute of Technology, 70
Massine, Léonide, 36
Maugham, Somerset, 35, 81
Maupassant, Guy de, 35
May, Frederick, 216
Medea (Pasolini film), 80
Melly, George, 167
Mémoires d'une jeune fille rangée (Beauvoir), 35
Mennie, Professor Duncan, 3, 9, 37, 38
Merlin Haven, 231, 232, 233
Merry Christmas, Mr Laurence (Van der Post), 128
Merton, Thomas, 214, 215
Mesens, E. L. T., 166
Metcalfe, Muriel, 91, 117, 220, 226
Methuen, Paul Methuen, Lord, 234, 235
Methuen, Lady, 235
Meyer, Konrad Ferdinand, 9
Michaux, Henri, 13, 117
Michelangelo, 9
Miller, James E. Jr, 85n
Minchenden Grammar School, Southgate, 119–20, 145, 190
Minton, John, 168, 206
Miracle in the Gorbals (Helpmann ballet), 76
Misanthrope, Le (Molière), 4
Mitchison, Naomi, 224
Molière, 4, 28
Montale, Eugenio, 9
Montherlant, Henri de, 5, 21
Moore, Henry, 90, 91
Morris, John, 198, 202, 203, 206
Morton, William, 124–7, 128, 133
Moynihan, Rodrigo, 171, 172
Muir, Edwin, 216
Muir, Kenneth, 216, 228
Mur, Le (Sartre), 35
Murdoch, Iris, 146
Murry, John Middleton, 49, 83, 96
Music Ho! (Lambert), 79
Musil, Robert, 9
Musset, Alfred de, 27
Mussolini, Benito, 53
My Dog Tulip (Ackerley), 205
My Host the World (Santayana), 13
Myra Breckenridge (Vidal), 170

Nabokov, Vladimir, 213
Nagasaki, 110
Nagoya University, 130, 223
Nakasone, Yasuhiro, 133
Nash, Paul, 90
Nausée, La (Sartre), 35
New Directions, 211
New Writing, 190
Newby, P. H., 226
Newcastle *Journal*, 124, 128
Newcastle upon Tyne, 3, 8, 15, 37, 55; wartime, 75–9, 86; theatre and opera 15, 28, 76–82
Newman, Sydney, 12, 37
Newton, Eric, 117, 225
Nichols, Ross, 165
Nicholson, Norman, 165
Nicolson, Ben, 100
Nielsen, Carl, 37
Nietzsche, Friedrich, 7
Nourritures terrestres, Les (Gide), 35
Nursing Times, 220

O'Casey, Sean, 224
Oliver, W. R., 227
Oomi Town, 131
Opening Day (Gascoyne), 13
Orton, Harold, 11
Orton, Iris, 155, 156, 201, 217
Orwell, George, 86
Oshima, Nagisa, 129
Owen, Wilfred, 72–4
Oxford, 174
Oxford Poetry Society, 237–9

Oxford University Press, 90, 207, 210, 211, 215

Paganini Rhapsody (Rachmaninoff), 36
Palmer, Herbert, 165
Paludes (Gide), 35
Paris, 40–41, 168
Partridge, Ralph, 188
Pasolini, Paolo, 80
Paul, David, 11, 12, 45, 99, 155, 174, 187, 201, 206, 213
Paul, Helena, 99
'Paul, Tancred', 82
Peace Pledge Union, 16
Pearce, Stella Mary, 225
Penrose, Roland, 166
Pessoa, Fernando, 227
Peter, Professor John, 85n
Peterborough Cathedral, 225
Petrarch, 9
Petter, Angela, 99, 155, 174, 239
Peyrefitte, Roger, 25
Pitter, Ruth, 155–6
Platitude, 82
Plomer, William, 83, 85, 99, 198–9, 202, 206
Plowman, Max, 16, 17, 26, 48–51, 56, 95
Plowman, Tim, 17
Poe, Edgar Allan, 18, 69n
Poetry London, 83
Poetry Quarterly, 83, 85
Polevoy, Boris, 223, 224
Polish Ballet, 79
Ponge, Francis, 213
Ponteland, 107, 109
Pope-Hennessy, James, 71, 99 ('well-dressed young gentleman'), 235–6
Portrait of a Planet (Dürrenmatt), 72n
Potts, Matthew, 101, 102, 103, 104
Poudre aux yeux, La (Labiche), 28
Pound, Ezra, 82, 213
Praze Downs, 100
Prévert, Jacques, 176
Price, Nancy, 165n
Prince of Homburg, The (Kleist), 9
Princess de Clèves, La (La Fayette), 4
Prisoner of the British (Aida), 129
Prisonnière, La (Proust), 170
Progressive League, 165–6
Prospect Theatre Company, 72n
Proust, Marcel, 5, 35, 170
Pryce-Jones, Alan, 117
Puccini, Giacomo, 80
Putney, 184, 192, 193, 195–7, 204

Rachmaninoff, Sergei, 36
Racine, Jean, 29, 37
Radiguet, Raymond, 31
Raine, Kathleen, 85
Rameau, Jean Philippe, 6–7
Ramsey, Michael, Archbishop of York, 226
Read, Herbert, 209, 224
Red Shoes, The (film), 77, 78
Redman, Marjorie, 206
Reed, Henry, 209
Reid, Alexander, 224
Reid, Louis Arnaud, 12
Renan, Ernest, 3
Rendezvous, Les (Ashton ballet), 76
Renwick, Professor William L., 3, 11
Ribbentrop, Joachim von, 52
Richardson, Judge, 6, 55–7
Richet, Professor Charles, 22
Richmond (Yorks), 92
Right to Live, The (Plowman), 49
Rilke, Rainer Maria, 9, 13, 55, 57
Rimbaud, Arthur, 35, 219, 225
Robinson, Miss (French and German teacher), 28, 51, 52–3, 95, 116
Rodgers, W. R., 202
Rosenthal, Michael, 53n
Ross, Julian MacLaren, 168
Rossi, Tino, 25
Rotha, Paul, 224
Rousseau, Jean-Jacques, 3
Runciman, Steven, 216
Russell, Bertrand, 12, 110, 172

Sachs, Hans, 9
Sakutaro, Hagiwara, 70–71
Salamanca, University of, 227, 237
Santayana, George, 13
Sartre, Jean-Paul, 35
Sassoon, Siegfried, 72, 202, 224
Schiller, J. C. F. von, 9
Schimanski, Stefan, 168
Schnitzler, Arthur, 225
Schubert, Franz, 71
Schwarzkopf, Elisabeth, 80

Scriven, R. C., 227
Searle, Ronald, 133
Sebastian, Anna, 239
Sedaine, Michel, 3
Sendai, 99, 178, 197
Shawe-Taylor, Desmond, 79
Shearer, Moira, 76, 77–8
'Sheba, Madame', 146–56, 171, 175, 180, 209
Shenton, Edward, 226
Sheppard, Rev. Dick, 16
Si le grain ne meurt (Gide), 35
Simenon, Georges, 35
Simpson, Christopher, 225
Sinclair, Dr Grant, 105–6, 230
Sitwell, Edith, 161, 224
Sitwell, Sacheverell, 209
Skelton, Robin, 117, 211
Slapton (Northants), 208, 209
Slobodskaya, Oda, 79–80
Smith, Jack, 233
Smith, Stevie, 165
Snow, C. P., 70
Society of Friends, 16–17, 57–8
Soupault, Philippe, 11, 13
South Shields, 37, 45, 105, 106, 109–10, 123, 144–5, 231; childhood in, xiii–xxi, 135–7; wartime, 45–8, 75, 86–7, 100; post-war, 134, 137; fairground, 138–43
South Shields Gazette and Shipping Telegraph, 123–6, 127, 220
Spark, Muriel, 165
Spender, Stephen, 82, 161, 166, 207
Spider's Banquet, The (Howard ballet), 76
Sprott, Jack, 206, 212, 216
Staples (publishers), 70
Stefano, Giuseppe di, 80
Stinchcombe, 232
Stone, Frederick, 79
Stone and Flower (Raine), 85
Stopes, Marie, 206
Storm, Theodor, 9
Story of a Real Man (Polevoy), 223
Strachey, Lytton, 188
Strasburg, 19, 20
Student Christian Movement, 109
Supervielle, Jules, 5, 11, 117, 211
Sutherland, Joan, 80
Swedish Ministry of Education, 237
Sylphides, Les (Fokine ballet), 77
Sylvia (Darley), 13
Symons, Julian, 83

Tambimuttu, 83, 165
Teather, Ida, 224, 225
Teed, Roy, 225
Tender is the Night (Fitzgerald), 226n
Thirsk, 93
Thomas, Alan, 206
Thomas, Dylan, 171, 188, 208, 224
Thomas, John Ormond, 85
Thompson, Duncan, 82, 190
Thompson, Mervyn, 52
Thwaite, Anthony, 207
Time and Tide, 178
Times Literary Supplement, 85, 212
'To his Coy Mistress' (Marvell), 161
'Today I Went Walking with a Friend' (Desnos), 71
Tokyo, 80; British Council in, 188, 205, 207; Japan Women's University, 73; Yasukuni Shrine, 131
Tolstoy, Leo, 92
Tomlinson, Madame, 9
Toplady, Augustus, 146
Toshihiko, Professor Kawasaki, 130
Toynbee, Philip, 171
Trahison des clercs, La (Benda), 3, 4
transition, 213, 218
Tribune, 85, 86
Troisième Front (Mesene), 166
Trophy of Arms, A (Pitter), 155
Tsvetaeva, Marina, 224
Tu Fu, 170
Turgenev, Ivan, 92
Twentieth Century, The, 202
Twentieth Century Verse, 83
Two Cheers for Democracy (Forster), 199

Under the Net (Murdoch), 146
Ungaretti, Giuseppe, 9
Unser Lager: Our Camp, 51–2, 53

Vaduz, 38
Valéry, Paul, 5, 11, 144, 182, 189, 211
Vallette, Jean, 8
Valmouth (Firbank), 152
Van der Post, Laurens, 128
Vaughan, Keith, 168
Verdenal, Jean, 86n

Verdi, Giuseppe, 80
Verlaine, Paul, 35
Vidal, Gore, 170
Vienna, 19
Vigny, Alfred de, 4
Villon, François, 27, 35
Voleur d'Enfants, Le (Supervielle), 117
Voyage au bout de la nuit (Céline), 48

Wadsworth, Edward, 90
Wahlverwandschaften, Die (Goethe), 38
Wain, John, 202, 237, 238
Waiting for Godot (Beckett), 213
Waller, Edmund, 163
Walser, Robert, 9, 19
Waltenberg, Alex, 126–7
'Wanderer to the Moon, The', 71–2
War Agricultural Executive Committee, 93, 107
War Resisters' International, 16, 95
Warner, Sylvia Townsend, 224
Waste Land, The (Eliot), 83, 85n
Watson, Boris, 171
Waugh, Evelyn, 232
We are Soviet People (Polevoy), 223
We Think the World of You (Ackerley), 204, 205
Wedgwood, Veronica, 239
Whistler, Rex, 91
Whitman, Walt, 99
Wilde, Oscar, 33, 81, 206
Wilson, Angus, 181
Wissant, 20–22
Wittgenstein, Ludwig J.J., 105
Wolfit, Donald, 81
Woolf, Virginia, 145
Worcester, 116
Wordsworth, William, 51, 161, 232
Wotton-under-Edge, 231
Wright, David, 82, 165
Wynter, Bryan, 233

Yevtushenko, Yevgeny, 224
Yorkshire Post, 210

Zayde (La Fayette), 4
Zomosa, Maximiliano, 79
'Zoroastre' (Rameau), 6
Zullig, Hans, 79
Zürich, 38